The Conspiracy of Pontiac

THE CONSPIRACY OF PONTIAC

AND THE INDIAN WAR AFTER THE CONQUEST OF CANADA

From the Spring of 1763 to the Death of Pontiac

By Francis Parkman

Volume II

University of Nebraska Press
Lincoln and London

Manufactured in the United States of America

The paper in this book meets the minimum requirements of American National Standard for Information Sciences—Permanence of Paper for Printed Library Materials, ANSI Z39.48–1984

First Bison Book printing: 1994
Most recent printing indicated by the last digit below:
10 9 8 7 6 5 4 3 2 1

Library of Congress Cataloging-in-Publication Data
Parkman, Francis, 1823–1893.
The conspiracy of Pontiac and the Indian war after the conquest of Canada: From the spring of 1763 to the death of Pontiac / by Francis Parkman.—Bison Book edition.
p. cm.
"Originally published in 1851. This is a reprint of the revised 1870 edition published by Little, Brown, and Company, Boston"—CIP galley.
ISBN 0-8032-8737-2 (pbk.) Vol. 2
1. Pontiac's Conspiracy, 1763–1765. I. Title.
E83.76.P2793 1994
973.2′7—dc20
94-20956 CIP

Originally published in 1851. This is a reprint of the revised ninth edition, with additions, published by Little, Brown, and Company, Boston, in 1870.

CONTENTS OF VOL II.

CHAPTER XVIII.

1763.

FRONTIER FORTS AND SETTLEMENTS.

CHAPTER XIX.

1763.

THE WAR ON THE BORDERS.

CHAPTER XX.

1763.

THE BATTLE OF BUSHY RUN.

CHAPTER XXI.

1763.

THE IROQUOIS. — AMBUSCADE OF THE DEVIL'S HOLE.

CHAPTER XXII.

1763.

DESOLATION OF THE FRONTIERS.

CHAPTER XXIII.

1763.

THE INDIANS RAISE THE SIEGE OF DETROIT.

CHAPTER XXIV.

1763.

THE PAXTON MEN.

CHAPTER XXV.

1764.

THE RIOTERS MARCH ON PHILADELPHIA.

CHAPTER XXVI.

1764.

BRADSTREET'S ARMY ON THE LAKES.

CHAPTER XXVII.

1764.

BOUQUET FORCES THE DELAWARES AND SHAWANOES TO SUE FOR PEACE.

CHAPTER XXVIII.

1764.

THE ILLINOIS.

CHAPTER XXIX.

1763–1765.

PONTIAC RALLIES THE WESTERN TRIBES.

CHAPTER XXX.

1765.

RUIN OF THE INDIAN CAUSE.

CHAPTER XXXI.

1766–1769

DEATH OF PONTIAC.

APPENDIX.

A. — THE IROQUOIS. — EXTENT OF THEIR CONQUESTS. — POLICY PURSUED TOWARDS THEM BY THE FRENCH AND THE ENGLISH. — MEASURES OF SIR WILLIAM JOHNSON.

THE

CONSPIRACY OF PONTIAC.

CHAPTER XVIII.

1763.

FRONTIER FORTS AND SETTLEMENTS.

We have followed the war to its farthest confines, and watched it in its remotest operations; not because there is any thing especially worthy to be chronicled in the capture of a backwoods fort, and the slaughter of a few soldiers, but because these acts exhibit some of the characteristic traits of the actors. It was along the line of the British frontier that the war raged with its most destructive violence. To destroy the garrisons, and then turn upon the settlements, had been the original plan of the Indians; and while Pontiac was pushing the siege of Detroit, and the smaller interior posts were treacherously assailed, the tempest was gathering which was soon to burst along the whole frontier.

In 1763, the British settlements did not extend beyond the Alleghanies. In the province of New York, they reached no farther than the German Flats, on the Mohawk. In Pennsylvania, the town of Bedford might be regarded as the extreme verge of the frontier, while the settlements of Virginia extended to a corresponding distance. Through the adjacent wilderness ran various lines of military posts, to make good the communication from point to point. One of the most important among these passed through the country of the Six Nations, and guarded the route between the northern colonies and Lake Ontario. This communication was formed by the Hudson, the Mohawk, Wood Creek, the Oneida Lake, and the River Oswego. It was defended by Forts Stanwix, Brewerton, Oswego, and two or three smaller posts. Near the western extremity of Lake Ontario stood Fort Niagara, at the mouth of the river whence it derived its name. It was a strong and extensive work, guarding the access to the whole interior country, both by way of the Oswego communication just mentioned, and by that of Canada and the St. Lawrence. From Fort Niagara the route lay by a portage beside the great falls to Presqu' Isle, on Lake Erie, where the town of Erie now stands. Thence the traveller could pass, by a short overland passage, to Fort Le Bœuf, on a branch of the Alleghany; thence, by water, to Venango; and thence, down the Alleghany, to Fort Pitt. This last-mentioned post stood on the present site of Pittsburg — the point of land formed by the confluence of the Alleghany and the Monongahela. Its position was as captivating to the eye of an artist as it was commanding in a military point of view. On the left, the Monon gahela descended through a woody valley of sin gular beauty; on the right, flowed the Alleghany, beneath steep and lofty banks; and both united, in front, to form the broad Ohio, which, flanked by picturesque hills and declivities, began at this point its progress towards the Mississippi. The place already had its historic associations, though, as yet, their roughness was unmellowed by the lapse of time. It was here that the French had erected Fort du Quesne. Within a few miles, Braddock encountered his disastrous overthrow; and on the hill behind the fort, Grant's Highlanders and Lewis's Virginians had been surrounded and captured, though not without a stout resistance on the part of the latter.

Fort Pitt was built by General Stanwix, in the year 1759, upon the ruins of Fort du Quesne, destroyed by General Forbes. It was a strong fortification, with ramparts of earth, faced with brick on the side looking down the Ohio. Its walls have long since been levelled to the ground, and over their ruins have risen warehouses, and forges with countless chimneys, rolling up their black volumes of smoke. Where once the bark canoe lay on the strand, a throng of steamers now lie moored along the crowded levee.

Fort Pitt stood far aloof in the forest, and one might journey eastward full two hundred miles, before the English settlements began to thicken. Behind it lay a broken and woody tract; then succeeded the great barrier of the Alleghanies, traversing the country in successive ridges; and beyond these lay vast woods, extending to the

Susquehanna. Eastward of this river, cabins of settlers became more numerous, until, in the neighborhood of Lancaster, the country assumed an appearance of prosperity and cultivation. Two roads led from Fort Pitt to the settlements, one of which was cut by General Braddock in his disastrous march across the mountains, from Cumberland, in the year 1755. The other, which was the more frequented, passed by Carlisle and Bedford, and was made by General Forbes, in 1758. Leaving the fort by this latter route, the traveller would find himself, after a journey of fifty-six miles, at the little post of Ligonier, whence he would soon reach Fort Bedford, about a hundred miles from Fort Pitt. It was nestled among mountains, and surrounded by clearings and log cabins. Passing several small posts and settlements, he would arrive at Carlisle, nearly a hundred miles farther east, a place resembling Bedford in its general aspect, although of greater extent. After leaving Fort Bedford, numerous houses of settlers were scattered here and there among the valleys, on each side of the road from Fort Pitt, so that the number of families beyond the Susquehanna amounted to several hundreds, thinly distributed over a great space.[1] From Carlisle to Harris's Ferry, now Harrisburg, on the Susquehanna, was but a short distance; and from thence, the road led directly into the heart of the settlements. The frontiers of Virginia bore a general resemblance to those of Pennsylvania. It

[1] There was a cluster of log houses even around Fort Ligonier, and a trader named Byerly had a station at Bushy Run.

is not necessary at present to indicate minutely the position of their scattered settlements, and the small posts intended to protect them.[1] Along these borders all had remained quiet, and nothing occurred to excite alarm or uneasiness. Captain Simeon Ecuyer, a brave Swiss officer, who commanded at Fort Pitt, had indeed received warnings of danger. On the fourth of May, he wrote to Colonel Bouquet at Philadelphia: "Major Gladwyn writes to tell me that I am surrounded by rascals. He complains a great deal of the Delawares and Shawanoes. It is this *canaille* who stir up the rest to mischief." At length, on the twenty-seventh, at about dusk in the evening, a party of Indians was seen descending the banks of the Alleghany, with laden pack-horses. They built fires, and encamped on the shore till daybreak, when they all crossed over to the fort, bringing with them a great quantity of valuable furs. These they sold to the traders, demanding, in exchange, bullets, hatchets, and gunpowder; but their conduct was so peculiar as to excite the just suspicion that they came either as spies or with some other insidious design.[2] Hardly were they gone, when tidings came in that Colonel Clapham, with several persons, both men and women, had been murdered and scalped near the fort; and it was soon after discovered that the inhabitants of an Indian town, a few miles up the

[1] The authorities for the foregoing topographical sketch are drawn from the Pennsylvania *Historical Collections*, and the *Olden Time*, an excellent antiquarian work, published at Pittsburg; together with various maps, plans, and contemporary papers.

[2] Gordon, *Hist. Pa.* 622. MS. Letter — *Ecuyer to Bouquet*, 29 May, 1763.

Alleghany, had totally abandoned their cabins, as if bent on some plan of mischief. On the next day, two soldiers were shot within a mile of the fort. An express was hastily sent to Venango, to warn the little garrison of danger; but he returned almost immediately, having been twice fired at, and severely wounded.[1] A trader named Calhoun now came in from the Indian village of Tuscaroras, with intelligence of a yet more startling kind. At eleven o'clock on the night of the twenty-seventh, a chief named Shingas, with several of the principal warriors in the place, had come to Calhoun's cabin, and earnestly begged him to depart, declaring that they did not wish to see him killed before their eyes. The Ottawas and Ojibwas, they said, had taken up the hatchet, and captured Detroit, Sandusky, and

[1] MS. Letter — *Bouquet to Amherst*, June 5.

Extract from a letter — *Fort Pitt, May* 31 (*Penn. Gaz.* No. 1798).

"We have most melancholy Accounts here — The Indians have broke out in several Places, and murdered Colonel Clapham and his Family; also two of our Soldiers at the Saw-mill, near the Fort, and two Scalps are taken from each man. An Indian has brought a War-Belt to Tuscarora, and says Detroit is invested; and that St. Dusky is cut off, and Ensign Pawley made Prisoner — Levy's Goods are stopt at Tuscarora by the Indians — Last Night Eleven men were attacked at Beaver Creek, eight or nine of whom, it is said, were killed — And Twenty-five of Macrae's and Alison's Horses, loaded with Skins, are all taken."

Extract from a MS. Letter — *Ecuyer to Bouquet.*

"Fort Pitt, 29th May, 1763.

"Just as I had finished my Letter, Three men came in from Clapham's, with the Melancholy News, that Yesterday, at three O'clock in the Afternoon, the Indians Murdered Clapham, and Every Body in his House: These three men were out at work, & Escaped through the Woods. I Immediately Armed them, and sent them to Assist our People at Bushy Run. The Indians have told Byerly (at Bushy Run) to Leave his Place in Four Days, or he and his Family would all be murdered: I am Uneasy for the little Posts — As for this, I will answer for it."

The above is a contemporary translation. The original, which is before me, is in French, like all Ecuyer's letters to Bouquet.

all the forts of the interior. The Delawares and Shawanoes of the Ohio were following their example, and were murdering all the traders among them. Calhoun and the thirteen men in his employ lost no time in taking their departure. The Indians forced them to leave their guns behind, promising that they would give them three warriors to guide them in safety to Fort Pitt; but the whole proved a piece of characteristic dissimulation and treachery. The three guides led them into an ambuscade at the mouth of Beaver Creek. A volley of balls showered upon them; eleven were killed on the spot, and Calhoun and two others alone made their escape.[1] "I see," writes Ecuyer to his colonel, "that the affair is general. I tremble for our outposts. I believe, from what I hear, that I am surrounded by Indians. I neglect nothing to give them a good reception; and I expect to be attacked to-morrow morning. Please God I may be. I am passably well prepared. Everybody is at work, and I do not sleep; but I tremble lest my messenger should be cut off."

The intelligence concerning the fate of the traders in the Indian villages proved but too true. They were slaughtered everywhere, without mercy, and often under circumstances of the foulest barbarity. A boy named M'Cullough, captured during the French war, and at this time a prisoner among the Indians, relates, in his published narrative, that he, with a party of Indian children, went out, one evening, to gaze with awe and wonder at

[1] *Copy of intelligence brought to Fort Pitt by Mr. Calhoun,* MS.

the body of a trader, which lay by the side of the path, mangled with tomahawks, and stuck full of arrows.[1] It was stated in the journals of the day, that more than a hundred traders fell victims, and that the property taken from them, or seized at the capture of the interior posts, amounted to an incredible sum.[2]

[1] M'Cullough gives the following account of the murder of another of the traders named Green: —

"About sunrise, *Mussoughwhese* (an Indian, my adopted brother's nephew, known by the name of Ben Dickson, among the white people), came to our house; he had a pistol and a large scalping-knife, concealed under his blanket, belted round his body. He informed *Kettoohhalend* (for that was my adopted brother's name), that he came to kill Tom Green; but *Kettoohhalend* endeavoured to persuade him off it. They walked out together, and Green followed them, endeavouring, as I suppose, to discover the cause of the alarm the night before; in a short time they returned to the house, and immediately went out again. Green asked me to bring him his horse, as we heard the bell a short distance off; he then went after the Indians again, and I went for the horse. As I was returning, I observed them coming out of a house about two hundred yards from ours; *Kettoohhalend* was foremost, Green in the middle; I took but slight notice of them, until I heard the report of a pistol; I cast my eyes towards them, and observed the smoke, and saw Green standing on the side of the path, with his hands across his breast; I thought it had been him that shot; he stood a few minutes, then fell on his face across the path. I instantly got off the horse, and held him by the bridle, — *Kettoohhalend* sunk his pipe tomahawk into his skull; *Mussoughwhese* stabbed him under the armpit with his scalping-knife; he had shot him between the shoulders with his pistol. The squaws gathered about him and stripped him naked, trailed him down the bank, and plunged him into the creek; there was a freshet in the creek at the time, which carried him off. *Mussoughwhese* then came to me (where I was holding the horse, as I had not moved from the spot where I was when Green was shot), with the bloody knife in his hand; he told me that he was coming to kill me next; he reached out his hand and took hold of the bridle, telling me that that was his horse; I was glad to parley with him on the terms, and delivered the horse to him. All the Indians in the town immediately collected together, and started off to the Salt Licks, where the rest of the traders were, and murdered the whole of them, and divided their goods amongst them, and likewise their horses."

[2] *Gent. Mag.* XXXIII. 413. The loss is here stated at the greatly exaggerated amount of £500,000.

The Moravian Loskiel relates that in the villages of the Hurons or Wyandots, meaning probably those of Sandusky, the traders were so numerous that the Indians were afraid to attack them openly, and had recourse to the following stratagem: They told their unsuspecting victims that the surrounding tribes had risen in arms, and were soon coming that way, bent on killing every Englishman they could find. The Wyandots averred that they would gladly protect their friends, the white men; but that it would be impossible to do so, unless the latter would consent, for the sake of appearances, to become their prisoners. In this case, they said, the hostile Indians would refrain from injuring them, and they should be set at liberty as soon as the danger was past. The traders fell into the snare. They gave up their arms, and, the better to carry out the deception, even consented to be bound; but no sooner was this accomplished, than their treacherous counsellors murdered them all in cold blood.[1]

A curious incident, relating to this period, is given by the missionary Heckewelder. Strange as the story may appear, it is in strict accordance with Indian character and usage, and perhaps need not be rejected as wholly void of truth. The name of the person, to whom it relates, several times occurs in the manuscript journals and correspondence of officers in the Indian country. A trader named Chapman was made prisoner by the Indians near Detroit. For some time, he was protected by

[1] Loskiel, 99.

the humane interference of a Frenchman; but at length his captors resolved to burn him alive. He was tied to the stake, and the fire was kindled. As the heat grew intolerable, one of the Indians handed to him a bowl filled with broth. The wretched man, scorching with fiery thirst, eagerly snatched the vessel, and applied it to his lips; but the liquid was purposely made scalding hot. With a sudden burst of rage, he flung back the bowl and its contents into the face of the Indian. "He is mad! he is mad!" shouted the crowd; and though, the moment before, they had been keenly anticipating the delight of seeing him burn, they hastily put out the fire, released him from the stake, and set him at liberty.[1] Such is the superstitious respect which the Indians entertain for every form of insanity.

While the alarming incidents just mentioned were occurring at Fort Pitt, the garrison of Fort Ligonier received yet more unequivocal tokens of hostility; for one morning a volley of bullets was sent among them, with no other effect, however, than killing a few horses. In the vicinity of Fort Bedford, several men were killed; on which the inhabitants were mustered and organized, and the garrison kept constantly on the alert. A few of the best woodsmen were formed into a company, dressed and painted like Indians. A party of the enemy suddenly appeared, whooping and brandishing their tomahawks, at the skirts of the forest; on which these counterfeit savages dashed upon

[1] Heckewelder, *Hist. Ind. Nat.* 250.

them at full gallop, routing them in an instant, and driving them far through the woods.[1]

At Fort Pitt every preparation was made for an attack. The houses and cabins outside the rampart were levelled to the ground, and every morning, at an hour before dawn, the drum beat, and the troops were ordered to their alarm posts.[2] The garrison consisted of three hundred and thirty soldiers, traders, and backwoodsmen; and there were also in the fort about one hundred women, and a still greater number of children, most of them belonging to the families of settlers who were preparing to build their cabins in the neighborhood.[3] "We are so crowded in the fort," writes Ecuyer to Colonel Bouquet, "that I fear disease; for, in spite of every care, I cannot keep the place as clean as I should like. Besides, the small-pox is among us; and I have therefore caused a hospital to be built under the drawbridge, out of range of musket-shot. . . I am determined to hold my post, spare my men,

[1] *Pennsylvania Gazette,* No. 1799. I shall frequently refer to the columns of this journal, which are filled with letters, and extracts from letters, written at different parts of the frontier, and containing very minute and authentic details of the events which daily occurred.

[2] Extract from a Letter — *Fort Pitt,* June 16, 1763 (*Penn. Gaz.* No. 1801).

"We have Alarms from, and Skirmishes with, the Indians every Day; but they have done us little Harm as yet. Yesterday I was out with a Party of Men, when we were fired upon, and one of the Serjeants was killed; but we beat off the Indians, and brought the Man in with his Scalp on. Last Night the Bullock Guard was fired upon, when one Cow was killed. We are obliged to be on Duty Night and Day. The Indians have cut off above 100 of our Traders in the Woods, besides all our little Posts. We have Plenty of Provisions; and the Fort is in such a good Posture of Defence, that, with God's Assistance, we can defend it against 1000 Indians."

[3] MS. Letter — *Ecuyer to Bouquet,* June 5. *Ibid.* June 26

and never expose them without necessity. This, I think, is what you require of me."[1] The desultory outrages with which the war began, and which only served to put the garrison on their guard, prove that among the neighboring Indians there was no chief of sufficient power to curb their wayward temper, and force them to conform to any preconcerted plan. The authors of the mischief were unruly young warriors, fevered with eagerness to win the first scalp, and setting at defiance the authority of their elders. These petty annoyances, far from abating, continued for many successive days, and kept the garrison in a state of restless alarm. It was dangerous to venture outside the walls, and a few who attempted it were shot and scalped by lurking Indians. "They have the impudence," writes an officer, "to fire all night at our sentinels;" nor were these attacks confined to the night, for even during the day no man willingly exposed his head above the rampart. The surrounding woods were known to be full of prowling Indians, whose number seemed daily increasing, though as yet they had made no attempt at a general attack. At length, on the afternoon of the twenty-second of June, a party of them appeared at the farthest extremity of the cleared lands behind the fort, driving off the horses which were grazing there, and killing the cattle. No sooner was this accomplished than a general fire was opened upon the fort from every side at once, though at so great a distance that only two men

[1] MS. Letter — *Ecuyer to Bouquet,* June 16 (Translation).

were killed. The garrison replied by a discharge of howitzers, the shells of which, bursting in the midst of the Indians, greatly amazed and disconcerted them. As it grew dark, their fire slackened, though, throughout the night, the flash of guns was seen at frequent intervals, followed by the whooping of the invisible assailants.

At nine o'clock on the following morning, several Indians approached the fort with the utmost confidence, and took their stand at the outer edge of the ditch, where one of them, a Delaware, named the Turtle's Heart, addressed the garrison as follows: —

"My Brothers, we that stand here are your friends; but we have bad news to tell you. Six great nations of Indians have taken up the hatchet, and cut off all the English garrisons, excepting yours. They are now on their way to destroy you also.

"My Brothers, we are your friends, and we wish to save your lives. What we desire you to do is this: You must leave this fort, with all your women and children, and go down to the English settlements, where you will be safe. There are many bad Indians already here; but we will protect you from them. You must go at once, because if you wait till the six great nations arrive here, you will all be killed, and we can do nothing to protect you."

To this proposal, by which the Indians hoped to gain a safe and easy possession of the fort, Captain Ecuyer made the following reply. The vein of humor perceptible in it may serve to indicate that he was under no great apprehension for the safety of his garrison: —

"My Brothers, we are very grateful for your kindness, though we are convinced that you must be mistaken in what you have told us about the forts being captured. As for ourselves, we have plenty of provisions, and are able to keep the fort against all the nations of Indians that may dare to attack it. We are very well off in this place, and we mean to stay here.

"My Brothers, as you have shown yourselves such true friends, we feel bound in gratitude to inform you that an army of six thousand English will shortly arrive here, and that another army of three thousand is gone up the lakes, to punish the Ottawas and Ojibwas. A third has gone to the frontiers of Virginia, where they will be joined by your enemies, the Cherokees and Catawbas, who are coming here to destroy you. Therefore take pity on your women and children, and get out of the way as soon as possible. We have told you this in confidence, out of our great solicitude lest any of you should be hurt; and we hope that you will not tell the other Indians, lest they should escape from our vengeance."[1]

This politic invention of the three armies had an excellent effect, and so startled the Indians, that, on the next day, most of them withdrew from the neighborhood, and went to meet a great body of

[1] MS. *Report of Alexander M'Kee, deputy agent for Indian affairs at Fort Pitt.*

warriors, who were advancing from the westward to attack the fort. On the afternoon of the twenty-sixth, a soldier named Gray, belonging to the garrison of Presqu' Isle, came in with the report that, more than a week before, that little post had been furiously attacked by upwards of two hundred Indians from Detroit, that they had assailed it for three days, repeatedly setting it on fire, and had at length undermined it so completely, that the garrison was forced to capitulate, on condition of being allowed to retire in safety to Fort Pitt. No sooner, however, had they left their shelter, than the Indians fell upon them, and, as Gray declared, butchered them all, except himself and one other man, who darted into the woods, and escaped amid the confusion, hearing behind them, as they fled, the screams of their murdered comrades. This account proved erroneous, as the garrison were carried by their captors in safety to Detroit. Some time after this event, Captain Dalzell's detachment, on their way to Detroit, stopped at the place, and found, close to the ruined fort, the hair of several of the men, which had been shorn off, as a preliminary step in the process of painting and bedecking them like Indian warriors. From this it appears that some of the unfortunate soldiers were adopted on the spot into the tribes of their conquerors. In a previous chapter, a detailed account has been given of the defence of Presqu' Isle, and its capture.

Gray informed Captain Ecuyer that, a few days before the attack on the garrison, they had seen a schooner on the lake, approaching from the westward. She had sent a boat to shore with the tidings that Detroit had been beleaguered, for more than six weeks, by many hundred Indians, and that a detachment of ninety-six men had been attacked near that place, of whom only about thirty had escaped, the rest being either killed on the spot or put to death by slow torture. The panic-stricken soldier, in his flight from Presqu' Isle, had passed the spots where lately had stood the little forts of Le Bœuf and Venango. Both were burnt to the ground, and he surmised that the whole of their wretched garrisons had fallen victims.[1] The disaster proved less fatal than his fears led him to suspect; for, on the same day on which he arrived, Ensign Price, the officer commanding at Le Bœuf, was seen approaching along the bank of the Alleghany, followed by seven haggard and half-famished soldiers.[2] He and his men told the following story: —

[1] MS. Letter — *Ecuyer to Bouquet*, June 26.

[2] Extract from a Letter — *Fort Pitt*, June 26 (*Penn. Gaz.* No. 1802).

"This Morning, Ensign Price, of the Royal Americans, with Part of his Garrison, arrived here, being separated from the rest in the night. — The Enemy attacked his Post, and set it on Fire, and while they watched the Door of the House, he got out on the other side, and the Indians continued firing a long Time afterwards, imagining that the Garrison was in it, and that they were consumed with the House. — He touched at Venango, found the Fort burnt to the Ground, and saw one of our Expresses lying killed on the Road.

"Four o'clock in the Afternoon. Just now came in one of the Soldiers from Presque Isle, who says, Mr. Christie fought two Days; that the Enemy Fifty times set Fire to the Blockhouse, but that they as often put it out: That they then undermined the House, and was ready to blow it up, when they offered Mr. Christie Terms, who accepted them, viz., That he, and his Garrison, was to be conducted to this Place. — The

The available defences of Fort Le Bœuf consisted, at the time, of a single ill-constructed blockhouse, occupied by the ensign, with two corporals and eleven privates. They had only about twenty rounds of ammunition each; and the powder, moreover, was in a damaged condition. At nine or ten o'clock, on the morning of the eighteenth of June, a soldier told Price that he saw Indians approaching from the direction of Presqu' Isle. Price ran to the door, and, looking out, saw one of his men, apparently much frightened, shaking hands with five Indians. He held open the door till the man had entered, the five Indians following close, after having, in obedience to a sign from Price, left their weapons behind. They declared that they were going to fight the Cherokees, and begged for powder and ball. This being refused, they asked leave to sleep on the ground before the blockhouse. Price assented, on which one of them went off, but very soon returned with thirty more, who crowded before the window of the blockhouse, and begged for a kettle to cook their food. Price tried to give them one through the window, but the aperture proved too narrow, and they grew clamorous that he should open the door again. This he refused.

Soldier also says, he suspected they intended to put them all to Death; and that on hearing a Woman scream out, he supposed they were murdering her; upon which he and another Soldier came immediately off, but knows nothing of the rest: That the Vessel from Niagara was in Sight, but believes she had no Provisions, as the Indians told them they had cut off Little Niagara, and destroyed 800 Barrels: And that he thinks, by what he saw, Venango had capitulated."

The soldier here spoken of was no doubt Gray, who was mentioned above, though his story is somewhat differently given in the letter of Captain Ecuyer, just cited.

They then went to a neighboring storehouse, pulled out some of the foundation stones, and got into the cellar; whence, by knocking away one or two planks immediately above the sill of the building, they could fire on the garrison in perfect safety, being below the range of shot from the loopholes of the blockhouse, which was not ten yards distant. Here they remained some hours, making their preparations, while the garrison waited in suspense, cooped up in their wooden citadel. Towards evening, they opened fire, and shot such a number of burning arrows against the side and roof of the blockhouse, that three several times it was in flames. But the men worked desperately, and each time the fire was extinguished. A fourth time the alarm was given; and now the men on the roof came down in despair, crying out that they could not extinguish it, and calling on their officer for God's sake to let them leave the building, or they should all be burnt alive. Price behaved with great spirit. "We must fight as long as we can, and then die together," was his answer to the entreaties of his disheartened men.[1] But he could not revive their drooping courage, and meanwhile the fire spread beyond all hope of mastering it. They implored him to let them go, and at length the brave young officer told them to save themselves if they could. It was time, for they were suffocating in their burning prison. There was a narrow window in the back of the blockhouse, through which, with the

[1] *Record of Court of Inquiry, Evidence of Corporal Fisher.* The statement is supported by all the rest of the men examined

help of axes, they all got out; and, favored by the darkness, — for night had closed in, — escaped to the neighboring pine-swamp, while the Indians, to make assurance doubly sure, were still showering fire-arrows against the front of the blazing building. As the fugitives groped their way, in pitchy darkness, through the tangled intricacies of the swamp, they saw the sky behind them lurid with flames, and heard the reports of the Indians' guns, as these painted demons were leaping and yelling in front of the flaming blockhouse, firing into the loopholes, and exulting in the thought that their enemies were suffering the agonies of death within.

Presqu' Isle was but fifteen miles distant; but, from the direction in which his assailants had come, Price rightly judged that it had been captured, and therefore resolved to make his way, if possible, to Venango, and reinforce Lieutenant Gordon, who commanded there. A soldier named John Dortinger, who had been sixteen months at Le Bœuf, thought that he could guide the party, but lost the way in the darkness; so that, after struggling all night through swamps and forests, they found themselves at daybreak only two miles from their point of departure. Just before dawn, several of the men became separated from the rest. Price and those with him waited for some time, whistling, coughing, and making such other signals as they dared, to attract their attention, but without success, and they were forced to proceed without them. Their only provisions were three biscuits to a man.

They pushed on all day, and reached Venango at one o'clock of the following night. Nothing remained but piles of smouldering embers, among which lay the half-burned bodies of its hapless garrison. They now continued their journey down the Alleghany. On the third night their last biscuit was consumed, and they were half dead with hunger and exhaustion before their eyes were gladdened at length by the friendly walls of Fort Pitt. Of those who had straggled from the party, all eventually appeared but two, who, spent with starvation, had been left behind, and no doubt perished.[1]

Not a man remained alive to tell the fate of Venango. An Indian, who was present at its destruction, long afterwards described the scene to Sir William Johnson. A large body of Senecas gained entrance under pretence of friendship, then closed the gates, fell upon the garrison, and butchered them all except the commanding officer, Lieutenant Gordon, whom they forced to write, from their dictation, a statement of the grievances which had driven them to arms, and then tortured over a slow fire for several successive nights, till he expired.

[1] On the 27th of June, Price wrote to Colonel Bouquet from Fort Pitt, announcing his escape; and again on the 28th, giving an account of the affair. Both letters are before me; but the most satisfactory evidence is furnished by the record of the court of inquiry held at Fort Pitt on the 12th of September, to ascertain the circumstances of the loss of Presqu' Isle and Le Bœuf. This embraces the testimony of most of the survivors; namely, Ensign George Price, Corporals Jacob Fisher and John Nash, and privates John Dogood, John Nigley, John Dortinger, and Uriah Trunk. All the men bear witness to the resolution of their officer. One of them declared that it was with the utmost difficulty that they could persuade him to leave the blockhouse with them.

This done, they burned the place to the ground, and departed.[1]

While Le Bœuf and Venango were thus assailed, Fort Ligonier was also attacked by a large body of Indians, who fired upon it with great fury and per tinacity, but were beaten off after a hard day's fighting. Fort Augusta, on the Susquehanna, was at the same time menaced; but the garrison being strengthened by a timely re-enforcement, the Indians abandoned their purpose. Carlisle, Bedford, and the small intermediate posts, all experienced some effects of savage hostility;[2] while among the settlers, whose houses were scattered throughout the adjacent valleys, outrages were perpetrated,

[1] MS. *Johnson Papers.* Not many years since, some traces of Fort Venango were yet visible. The following description of them is from the *Historical Collections of Pennsylvania:*—

"Its ruins plainly indicate its destruction by fire. Burnt stone, melted glass and iron, leave no doubt of this. All through the groundworks are to be found great quantities of mouldering bones. Amongst the ruins, knives, gun-barrels, locks, and musket-balls have been frequently found, and still continue to be found. About the centre of the area are seen the ruins of the magazine, in which, with what truth I cannot vouch, is said to be a well. The same tradition also adds, 'And in that well there is a cannon;' but no examination has been made for it."

[2] Extract from a Letter—*Fort Bedford, June* 30, 1763 (*Penn. Gaz.* No. 1802).

"This Morning a Party of the Enemy attacked fifteen Persons, who were mowing in Mr. Croghan's Field, within a Mile of the Garrison; and News is brought in of two Men being killed.—Eight o'clock. Two Men are brought in, alive, tomahawked and scalped more than Half the Head over—Our Parade just now presents a Scene of bloody and savage Cruelty; three Men, two of which are in the Bloom of Life, the other an old man, lying scalped (two of them still alive) thereon: Any thing feigned in the most fabulous Romance, cannot parallel the horrid Sight now before me; the Gashes the poor People bear are most terrifying.—Ten o'clock. They are just expired—One of them, after being tomahawked and scalped, ran a little way, and got on a Loft in Mr. Croghan's House, where he lay till found by a Party of the Garrison."

and sufferings endured, which defy all attempt at description.

At Fort Pitt, every preparation was made to repel the attack which was hourly expected. A part of the rampart, undermined by the spring floods, had fallen into the ditch; but, by dint of great labor, this injury was repaired. A line of palisades was erected along the ramparts; the barracks were made shot-proof, to protect the women and children; and, as the interior buildings were all of wood, a rude fire-engine was constructed, to extinguish any flames which might be kindled by the burning arrows of the Indians. Several weeks, however, elapsed without any determined attack from the enemy, who were engaged in their bloody work among the settlements and smaller posts. From the beginning of July until towards its close, nothing occurred except a series of petty and futile attacks, by which the Indians abundantly exhibited their malicious intentions, without doing harm to the garrison. During the whole of this time, the communication with the settlements was completely cut off, so that no letters were written from the fort, or, at all events, none reached their destination; and we are therefore left to depend upon a few meagre official reports, as our only sources of information.

On the twenty-sixth of July, a small party of Indians was seen approaching the gate, displaying a flag, which one of them had some time before received as a present from the English commander On the strength of this token, they were admitted, and proved to be chiefs of distinction; among whom were Shingas, Turtle's Heart, and others, who had hitherto maintained an appearance of friendship. Being admitted to a council, one of them addressed Captain Ecuyer and his officers to the following effect: —

"Brothers, what we are about to say comes from our hearts, and not from our lips.

"Brothers, we wish to hold fast the chain of friendship — that ancient chain which our forefathers held with their brethren the English. You have let your end of the chain fall to the ground, but ours is still fast within our hands. Why do you complain that our young men have fired at your soldiers, and killed your cattle and your horses? You yourselves are the cause of this. You marched your armies into our country, and built forts here, though we told you, again and again, that we wished you to remove. My Brothers, this land is ours, and not yours.

"My Brothers, two days ago we received a great belt of wampum from the Ottawas of Detroit, and the message they sent us was in these words: —

"'Grandfathers the Delawares, by this belt we inform you that in a short time we intend to pass, in a very great body, through your country, on our way to strike the English at the forks of the Ohio. Grandfathers, you know us to be a headstrong people. We are determined to stop at nothing; and as we expect to be very hungry, we will seize and eat up every thing that comes in our way.'[1]

"Brothers, you have heard the words of the

[1] This is a common Indian metaphor. To destroy an enemy is, in their phrase, to eat him.

Ottawas. If you leave this place immediately, and go home to your wives and children, no harm will come of it; but if you stay, you must blame yourselves alone for what may happen. Therefore we desire you to remove."

To the not wholly unreasonable statement of wrongs contained in this speech, Captain Ecuyer replied, by urging the shallow pretence that the forts were built for the purpose of supplying the Indians with clothes and ammunition. He then absolutely refused to leave the place. "I have," he said, "warriors, provisions, and ammunition, to defend it three years against all the Indians in the woods; and we shall never abandon it as long as a white man lives in America. I despise the Ottawas, and am very much surprised at our brothers the Delawares, for proposing to us to leave this place and go home. This is our home. You have attacked us without reason or provocation; you have murdered and plundered our warriors and traders; you have taken our horses and cattle; and at the same time you tell us your hearts are good towards your brethren the English. How can I have faith in you? Therefore, now, Brothers, I will advise you to go home to your towns, and take care of your wives and children. Moreover, I tell you that if any of you appear again about this fort, I will throw bombshells, which will burst and blow you to atoms, and fire cannon among you, loaded with a whole bag full of bullets. Therefore take care, for I don't want to hurt you." [1]

[1] MS. *Report of Conference with the Indians at Fort Pitt*, July 26, 1763

The chiefs departed, much displeased with their reception. Though nobody in his senses could blame the course pursued by Captain Ecuyer, and though the building of forts in the Indian country could not be charged as a crime, except by the most overstrained casuistry, yet we cannot refrain from sympathizing with the intolerable hardship to which the progress of civilization subjected the unfortunate tenants of the wilderness, and which goes far to extenuate the perfidy and cruelty that marked their conduct throughout the whole course of the war.

Disappointed of gaining a bloodless possession of the fort, the Indians now, for the first time, began a general attack. On the night succeeding the conference, they approached in great numbers, under cover of the darkness, and completely surrounded it; many of them crawling under the banks of the two rivers, and, with incredible perseverance, digging, with their knives, holes in which they were completely sheltered from the fire of the fort. On one side, the whole bank was lined with these burrows, from each of which a bullet or an arrow was shot out whenever a soldier chanced to expose his head. At daybreak, a general fire was opened from every side, and continued without intermission until night, and through several succeeding days. No great harm was done, however. The soldiers lay close behind their parapet of logs, watching the movements of their subtle enemies, and paying back their shot with interest. The red uniforms of the Royal Americans mingled with the gray homespun of the border riflemen, or the fringed hunting-frocks of old Indian fighters, wary and adroit as the red-skinned warriors themselves. They liked the sport, and were eager to sally from behind their defences, and bring their assailants to close quarters; but Ecuyer was too wise to consent. He was among them, as well pleased as they, directing, encouraging, and applauding them in his broken English. An arrow flew over the rampart and wounded him in the leg; but, it seems, with no other result than to extort a passing execration. The Indians shot fire-arrows, too, from their burrows, but not one of them took effect. The yelling at times was terrific, and the women and children in the crowded barracks clung to each other in terror; but there was more noise than execution, and the assailants suffered more than the assailed. Three or four days after, Ecuyer wrote in French to his colonel, "They were all well under cover, and so were we. They did us no harm: nobody killed; seven wounded, and I myself slightly. Their attack lasted five days and five nights. We are certain of having killed and wounded twenty of them, without reckoning those we could not see. I let nobody fire till he had marked his man; and not an Indian could show his nose without being pricked with a bullet, for I have some good shots here. . . . Our men are doing admirably, regulars and the rest. All that they ask is to go out and fight. I am fortunate to have the honor of commanding such brave men. I only wish the Indians had ventured an assault. They would have remembered it to the thousandth generation! . . . I forgot to tell you that they threw fire-arrows to burn our works, but they could not reach the buildings, nor even the rampart. Only two arrows came into the fort, one of which had the insolence to make free with my left leg."

This letter was written on the second of August. On the day before the Indians had all decamped. An event, soon to be described, had put an end to the attack, and relieved the tired garrison of their presence.[1]

[1] Extract from a MS. Letter — *Colonel Bouquet to Sir J. Amherst:* -

"Fort Pitt, 11th Aug. 1763.

"Sir:

"We Arrived here Yesterday, without further Opposition than Scattered Shots along the Road.

"The Delawares, Shawnese, Wiandots, & Mingoes had closely Beset, and Attacked this Fort from the 27th July, to the First Instant, when they Quitted it to March against us.

"The Boldness of those Savages is hardly Credible; they had taken Post under the Banks of Both Rivers, Close to the Fort, where Digging Holes, they kept an Incessant Fire, and threw Fire Arrows: They are good Marksmen, and though our People were under Cover, they Killed one, & Wounded seven. — Captain Ecuyer is Wounded in the Leg by an Arrow. — I Would not Do Justice to that Officer, should I omit to Inform Your Excellency, that, without Engineer, or any other Artificers than a few Ship Wrights, he has Raised a Parapet of Logs round the Fort, above the Old One, which having not been Finished, was too Low, and Enfiladed; he has Fraised the Whole; Palisadoed the Inside of the Aria, Constructed a Fire Engine; and in short, has taken all Precautions, which Art and Judgment could suggest for the Preservation of this Post, open before on the three sides, which had suffered by the Floods."

CHAPTER XIX.

1763.

THE WAR ON THE BORDERS.

Along the western frontiers of Pennsylvania, Maryland, and Virginia, terror reigned supreme. The Indian scalping-parties were ranging everywhere, laying waste the settlements, destroying the harvests, and butchering men, women, and children, with ruthless fury. Many hundreds of wretched fugitives flocked for refuge to Carlisle and the other towns of the border, bringing tales of inconceivable horror. Strong parties of armed men, who went out to reconnoitre the country, found every habitation reduced to cinders, and the half-burned bodies of the inmates lying among the smouldering ruins; while here and there was seen some miserable wretch, scalped and tomahawked, but still alive and conscious. One writing from the midst of these scenes declares that, in his opinion, a thousand families were driven from their homes; that, on both sides of the Susquehanna, the woods were filled with fugitives, without shelter and with out food; and that, unless the havoc were speedily checked, the western part of Pennsylvania would be totally deserted, and Lancaster become the frontier town.[1]

While these scenes were enacted on the borders of Pennsylvania and the more southern provinces, the settlers in the valley of the Mohawk, and even along the Hudson, were menaced with destruction. Had not the Six Nations been kept tranquil by the exertions of Sir William Johnson, the most disastrous results must have ensued. The Senecas and a few of the Cayugas were the only members of the confederacy who took part in the war. Venango, as we have seen, was destroyed by a party of Senecas, who soon after made a feeble attack upon Niagara. They blockaded it for a few days, with no other effect than that of confining the garrison within the walls, and, soon despairing of success, abandoned the attempt.

In the mean time, Sir Jeffrey Amherst, the Commander-in-chief, was in a position far from enviable. He had reaped laurels; but if he hoped to enjoy them in peace, he was doomed to disappointment. A miserable war was suddenly thrown on his hands, barren of honors and fruitful of troubles; and this, too, at a time when he was almost bereft of resources. The armies which had conquered Canada were, as we have seen, disbanded or sent home, and nothing remained but a few fragments and skeletons of regiments lately arrived from the West Indies, enfeebled by disease and hard service. In one particular, however, he had reason to congratulate himself, — the character of the offi-

[1] *Penn. Gaz.* No. 1805–1809.

cers who commanded under his orders in Pennsylvania, Virginia, and Maryland. Colonel Henry Bouquet was a Swiss, of the Canton of Berne, who had followed the trade of war from boyhood. He had served first the King of Sardinia, and afterwards the republic of Holland; and when the French war began in 1755, he accepted the commission of lieutenant-colonel, in a regiment newly organized, under the direction of the Duke of Cumberland, expressly for American service. The commissions were to be given to foreigners as well as to Englishmen and provincials; and the ranks were to be filled chiefly from the German emigrants in Pennsylvania and other provinces.[1] The men and officers of this regiment, known as the "Royal American," had now, for more than six

[1] "The next object of the immediate attention of Parliament in this session was the raising of a new regiment of foot in North America, for which purpose the sum of £81,178 16*s.* was voted. This regiment, which was to consist of four battalions of 1000 men each, was intended to be raised chiefly out of the Germans and Swiss, who, for many years past, had annually transported themselves in great numbers to British plantations in America, where waste lands had been assigned them upon the frontiers of the provinces; but, very injudiciously, no care had been taken to intermix them with the English inhabitants of the place, so that very few of them, even of those who have been born there, have yet learned to speak or understand the English tongue. However, as they were all zealous Protestants, and in general strong, hardy men, accustomed to the climate, it was judged that a regiment of good and faithful soldiers might be raised out of them, particularly proper to oppose the French; but to this end it was necessary to appoint some officers, especially subalterns, who understood military discipline and could speak the German language; and as a sufficient number of such could not be found among the English officers, it was necessary to bring over and grant commissions to several German and Swiss officers and engineers. But as this step, by the Act of Settlement, could not be taken without the authority of Parliament, an act was now passed for enabling his Majesty to grant commissions to a certain number of foreign Protestants, who had

years, been engaged in the rough and lonely service of the frontiers and forests; and when the Indian war broke out, it was chiefly they, who, like military hermits, held the detached outposts of the West. Bouquet, however, who was at this time colonel of the first battalion, had his headquarters at Philadelphia, where he was held in great esteem. His person was fine, and his bearing composed and dignified; perhaps somewhat austere, for he is said to have been more respected than loved by his officers. Nevertheless, their letters to him are very far from indicating any want of cordial relations. He was fond of the society of men of science, and wrote English better than most British officers of the time. Here and there, however, a passage in his letters suggests the inference, that the character of the gallant mercenary was toned to his profession, and to the unideal epoch in which he lived. Yet he was not the less an excellent soldier; indefatigable, faithful, full of resource, and without those arrogant prejudices which had impaired the efficiency of many good British officers, in the recent war, and of which Sir Jeffrey Amherst was a conspicuous example. He had acquired a practical knowledge of Indian warfare; and it is said that, in the course of the hazardous partisan service in which he was often engaged, when it was necessary to penetrate dark

served abroad as officers or engineers, to act and rank as officers or engineers in America only." — Smollett, *England*, III. 475.

The Royal American Regiment is now the 60th Rifles. Its ranks, at the time of the Pontiac war, were filled by provincials of English as well as of German descent.

defiles and narrow passes, he was sometimes known to advance before his men, armed with a rifle, and acting the part of a scout.[1]

Sir Jeffrey had long and persistently flattered himself that the Indian uprising was but a temporary ebullition, which would soon subside. Bouquet sent him, on the fourth of June, a copy of a letter from Captain Ecuyer,[2] at Fort Pitt, reporting the disturbances in that quarter. On the next day Bouquet wrote again, in a graver strain; and Amherst replied, from New York, on the sixth: "I gave immediate orders for completing the light infantry companies of the 17th, 42d, and 77th regiments. They are to assemble without loss of time, and to encamp on Staten Island, under Major Campbell, of the 42d. . . . Although I have thought proper to assemble this force, which I judge more than sufficient to quell any disturbances the whole Indian strength could raise, yet I am persuaded the alarm will end in nothing more than a rash attempt of what the Senecas have been threatening, and which we have heard of for some time past. As to their cutting off defenceless families, or even some of the small posts, it is certainly at all times in their power to effect such enterprises. . . . The post of Fort Pitt, or any of the others commanded by officers, can certainly never be in danger from such a wretched enemy. . . .

[1] There is a sketch of Bouquet's life prefixed to the French translation of the *Account of Bouquet's Expedition*. See also the reprint in the first volume of Clarke's "Ohio Valley Historical Series."

[2] An extract from this letter, which is dated May 30, is given on page 374.

I am only sorry that when such outrages are committed, the guilty should escape; for I am fully convinced the only true method of treating the savages is to keep them in proper subjection, and punish, without exception, the transgressors. . . . As I have no sort of dependence on the Assembly of Pennsylvania, I have taken such measures as will fully enable me to chastise any nation or tribe of Indians that dare to commit hostilities on his Majesty's subjects. I only wait to hear from you what farther steps the savages have taken; for I still think it cannot be any thing general, but the rash attempt of that turbulent tribe, the Senecas, who richly deserve a severe chastisement from our hands, for their treacherous behavior on many occasions."

On receiving this letter, Bouquet immediately wrote to Ecuyer at Fort Pitt: "The General has taken the necessary measures to chastise those infamous villains, and defers only to make them feel the weight of his resentment till he is better informed of their intentions." And having thus briefly despatched the business in hand, he proceeds to touch on the news of the day: "I give you joy of the success of our troops at the Manilla, where Captain George Ourry hath acquired the two best things in this world, glory and money. We hear of a great change in the ministry," etc. . . . "P. S. I have lent three pounds to the express. Please to stop it for me. The General expects that Mr. Croghan will proceed directly to Fort Pitt, when he will soon discover the causes of this sudden rupture and the intentions of these rascals."

Scarcely had Bouquet sent off the express-rider with this letter, when another came from Ecuyer with worse reports from the west. He forwarded it to Amherst, who wrote on receiving it: "I find by the intelligence enclosed in your letter that the affair of the Indians appears to be more general than I had apprehended, although I believe nothing of what is mentioned regarding the garrison of the Detroit being cut off. It is extremely inconvenient at this time; . . . but I cannot defer sending you a reinforcement for the communication." Accordingly he ordered two companies of the 42d and 77th regiments to join Bouquet at Philadelphia. "If you think it necessary," he adds, "you will yourself proceed to Fort Pitt, that you may be the better enabled to put in execution the requisite orders for securing the communication and reducing the Indians to reason."

Amherst now bestirred himself to put such troops as he had into fighting order. The 80th regiment, Hopkins's company of Rangers, and a portion of the Royal Americans, were disbanded, and the men drafted to complete other broken corps. His plan was to push forward as many troops as possible to Niagara by way of Oswego, and to Presqu' Isle by way of Fort Pitt, and thence to send them up the lakes to take vengeance on the offending tribes.

Bouquet, recognizing at length the peril of the small outlying posts, like Venango and Le Bœuf, proposed to abandon them, and concentrate at Fort Pitt and Presqu' Isle; a movement which, could it have been executed in time, would have saved both blood and trouble. But Amherst would not consent. "I cannot think," he writes, "of giving them up at this time, if we can keep them, as such a step would give the Indians room to think themselves more formidable than they really are; and it would be much better we never attempted to take posts in what they call their country, if, upon every alarm, we abandon them. . . . It remains at present for us to take every precaution we can, by which we may put a stop, as soon as possible, to their committing any farther mischief, and to bring them to a proper subjection; for, without *that*, I never do expect that they will be quiet and orderly, as every act of kindness and generosity to those barbarians is looked upon as proceeding from our fears."

Bouquet next writes to report that, with the help of the two companies sent him, he has taken steps which he hopes will secure the communication to Fort Pitt and allay the fears of the country people, who are deserting their homes in a panic, though the enemy has not yet appeared east of the mountains. A few days later, on the twenty-third of June, Amherst writes, boiling with indignation. He had heard from Gladwyn of the investment of Detroit, and the murder of Sir Robert Davers and Lieutenant Robertson. "The villains after this," he says, "had the assurance to come with a *Pipe of Peace*, desiring admittance into the fort." He then commends the conduct of Gladwyn, but pursues: "I only regret that when the chief of the Ottawas and the other villains returned with the *Pipe of Peace*, they were not instantly put to *death*.[1] I conclude Major Gladwyn was not apprised of the murder of Sir Robert Davers, Lieutenant Robertson, etc., at that time, or he certainly would have revenged their deaths by that method; and, indeed, I cannot but wish that whenever we have any of the savages in our power, who have in so treacherous a way committed any barbarities on our people, a quick retaliation may be made without the least exception or hesitation. I am determined," he continues, "to take every measure in my power, not only for securing and keeping entire possession of the country, but for punishing those barbarians who have thus perfidiously massacred his Majesty's subjects. To effect this most essential service, I intend to collect, agreeable to what I wrote you in my last, all the force I can at Presqu' Isle and Niagara, that I may push them forwards as occasion may require. I have therefore ordered the remains of the 42d and 77th regiments — the first consisting of two hundred and fourteen men, including officers, and the latter of one hundred and thirty-three, officers included — to march this evening or early to-morrow morning, under the command of Major Campbell of the 42d, who has my orders to send an officer before to acquaint you of his being on the march, and to obey such further directions as he may receive from you. . . . You will observe that I

[1] The italics and capitals are Sir Jeffrey's.

have now forwarded from hence every man that was here; for the small remains of the 17th regiment are already on their march up the Mohawk, and I have sent such of the 42d and 77th as were not able to march, to Albany, to relieve the company of the 55th at present there, who are to march immediately to Oswego."

Two days after, the twenty-fifth of June, he writes again to Bouquet: "All the troops from hence that could be collected are sent you; so that should the whole race of Indians take arms against us, I can do no more." [1]

On the same day, Bouquet, who was on his way to the frontier, wrote to Amherst, from Lancaster: "I had this moment the honor of your Excellency's letter of the twenty-third instant, with the most welcome news of the preservation of the Detroit from the infernal treachery of the vilest of brutes. I regret sincerely the brave men they have so basely massacred, but hope that we shall soon take an adequate revenge on the barbarians. The reinforcement you have ordered this way, so considerable by the additional number of officers, will fully enable me to crush the little opposition they may dare to make along the road, and secure that part of the country against all their future attempts, till you think proper to order us to act in conjunction with the rest of your forces to extirpate that vermin from a country they have forfeited, and, with it, all claim to the rights of humanity."

[1] On the 29th of July following, the fragments of five more regiments arrived from Havana, numbering in all 982 men and officers fit for duty — *Official Returns.*

Three days later the express-rider delivered the truculent letter, from which the above is taken, to Amherst at New York. He replied: "Last night I received your letter of the twenty-fifth, the contents of which please me very much, — your sentiments agreeing exactly with my own regarding the treatment the savages deserve from us. . . I need only add that I wish to hear of *no prisoners*, should any of the villains be met with in arms; and whoever of those who were concerned in the murder of Sir Robert Davers, Lieutenant Robertson, etc., or were at the attack of the detachment going to the Detroit,[1] and that may be hereafter taken, shall certainly be put to *death.*"[2]

Bouquet was now busy on the frontier in preparations for pushing forward to Fort Pitt with the troops sent him. After reaching the fort, with his wagon-trains of ammunition and supplies, he was to proceed to Venango and Le Bœuf, reinforce and provision them; and thence advance to Presqu' Isle to wait Amherst's orders for the despatch of his troops westward to Detroit, Michillimackinac, and the other distant garrisons, the fate of which was still unknown. He was encamped near Carlisle when, on the third of July, he heard what he styles the "fatal account of the loss of our

[1] *i. e.*, Cuyler's detachment.

[2] Amherst wrote again on the 16th of July: "My former orders for putting such of the Indians as are or have been in arms against us, and that fall in our power, to death, remain in full force; as the barbarities they have committed on the late commanding officer at Venango" (Gordon, whom they roasted alive during several nights) "and his unfortunate garrison fully prove that no punishment we can inflict is adequate to the crimes of those inhuman villains."

posts at Presqu' Isle, Le Bœuf, and Venango." He at once sent the news to Amherst; who, though he persisted in his original plan of operations, became at length convinced of the formidable nature of the Indian outbreak, and felt bitterly the slenderness of his own resources. His correspondence, nevertheless, breathes a certain thick-headed, blustering arrogance, worthy of the successor of Braddock.[1] In his contempt for the Indians, he finds fault with Captain Ecuyer at Fort Pitt for condescending to fire cannon at them, and with Lieutenant Blane at Fort Ligonier for burning some outhouses, under cover of which "so despicable an enemy" were firing at his garrison. This despicable enemy had, however, pushed him to such straits that he made, in a postscript to Bouquet, the following detestable suggestion: —

"Could it not be contrived to send the *Small Pox* among those disaffected tribes of Indians? We must on this occasion use every stratagem in our power to reduce them."

(Signed) J. A.

[1] The following is a characteristic example. He is writing to Johnson, 27 Aug. 1763: "I shall only say that it Behoves the Whole Race of Indians to Beware (for I Fear the best of them have in some Measure been privy to, and Concerned in the Late Mischief) of Carrying Matters much farther against the English, or Daring to form Conspiracys; as the Consequence will most Certainly occasion Measures to be taken, that, in the End, will put a most Effectual Stop to their Very Being."

The following is his view of the Indians, in a letter to Bouquet, 7 Aug. 1763: —

"I wish there was not an Indian Settlement within a thousand miles of our Country, for they are only fit to live with the Inhabitants of the woods: (i.e., *wild beasts*), being more allied to the *Brute* than the *human* Creation"

Bouquet replied, also in postscript: —

"I will try to inoculate the ——— with some blankets that may fall in their hands, and take care not to get the disease myself. As it is a pity to expose good men against them, I wish we could make use of the Spanish method, to hunt them with English dogs, supported by rangers and some light horse, who would, I think, effectually extirpate or remove that vermin."

Amherst rejoined: "You will do well to try to inoculate the Indians by means of blankets, as well as to try every other method that can serve to extirpate this execrable race. I should be very glad your scheme for hunting them down by dogs could take effect, but England is at too great a distance to think of that at present.

(Signed) J. A.[1]

[1] This correspondence is among the manuscripts of the British Museum, *Bouquet and Haldimand Papers*, No. 21,634. The first postscript by Amherst is on a single leaf of foolscap, written at the top of the page, and addressed on the back, —

"On His Majesty's Service.
"To Colonel BOUQUET,
"etc."

"JEFF. AMHERST."

The postscript seems to belong to a letter written on the first leaf of the foolscap sheet, which is lost or destroyed. The other postscript by Amherst has neither indorsement nor address, but that of Bouquet is appended to a letter dated Carlisle, 13 July, 1763, and addressed to "His Excellency, Sir Jeffrey Amherst." It appears from a letter of Capt. Ecuyer that the small-pox had lately broken out at Fort Pitt, which would have favored the execution of the plan. We hear nothing more of it; but, in the following spring, Gershom Hicks, who had been among the Indians, reported at Fort Pitt that the small-pox had been raging for some time among them, and that sixty or eighty Mingoes and Delawares, besides some Shawanoes, had died of it.

The suggestion of using dogs against the Indians did not originate

There is no direct evidence that Bouquet carried into effect the shameful plan of infecting the Indians though, a few months after, the small-pox was known to have made havoc among the tribes of the Ohio. Certain it is, that he was perfectly capable of dealing with them by other means, worthy of a man and a soldier; and it is equally certain, that in relations with civilized men he was in a high degree honorable, humane, and kind.

with Bouquet. Just before he wrote, he received a letter from one John Hughes, dated Lancaster, July 11, in which an elaborate plan is laid down for conquering the Indians with the help of canine allies.

The following is the substance of the proposal, which is set forth under eight distinct heads: 1st, Each soldier to have a dog, which he is to lead on the march by a strap three feet long. 2d, All the dogs to be held fast by the straps, except one or two on each flank and as many in advance, to discover the enemy in ambush. 3d, When you are fired upon, let loose all the dogs, which will rush at the concealed Indians, and force them in self-defence to expose themselves and fire at their assailants, with so little chance of hitting them, that, in the words of the letter, "if 1000 Indians fired on 300 dogs, there would be at least 200 dogs left, besides all the soldiers' fires, which must put the Indians to flight very soon.' 4th, If you come to a swamp, thicket, or the like, "only turn loose 3 or 4 dogs extraordinary, and you are immediately convinced what you have to fear." 5th, "No Indian can well conceal himself in a swamp or thicket as a spy, for yr dogs will discover him, and may soon be learnt to destroy him too." 6th, "The leading the dogs makes them more fierce, and keeps them from being tired in running after wild beasts or fighting one another." 7th, Expatiates on the advantages of having the leading-straps short. 8th, "The greater the number of dogs, the more fierce they will be by a great deal, and the more terrible to the Indians; and if, when you get to Bedford, a few scouting parties were sent out with dogs, and one or two Indians killed and the dogs put at them to tear them to pieces, you would soon see the good effects of it; and I could almost venture my life that 500 men with 500 dogs would be much more dreadful to 2000 Indians than an army of some thousand of brave men in the regular way.

"JN HUGHES.

"COLONEL BOUQUET."

Probably there is no man who ever had occasion to fight Indians in the woods who would object to a dog as an ally.

The scenes which daily met his eye might well have moved him to pity as well as indignation When he reached Carlisle, at the end of June, he found every building in the fort, every house, barn, and hovel, in the little town, crowded with the families of settlers, driven from their homes by the terror of the tomahawk. Wives made widows, children made orphans, wailed and moaned in anguish and despair. On the thirteenth of July he wrote to Amherst: "The list of the people known to be killed increases very fast every hour. The desolation of so many families, reduced to the last extremity of want and misery; the despair of those who have lost their parents, relations, and friends, with the cries of distracted women and children, who fill the streets, — form a scene painful to humanity, and impossible to describe."[1] Rage alternated with grief. A Mohican and a Cayuga Indian, both well known as friendly and peaceable, came with their squaws and children to claim protection from the soldiers. "It was with the utmost difficulty," pursues Bouquet, "that I could prevail with the enraged multitude not to massacre them. I don't think them very safe in the gaol. They ought to be removed to Philadelphia."

Bouquet, on his part, was full of anxieties. On the road from Carlisle to Fort Pitt was a chain of four or five small forts, of which the most advanced and the most exposed were Fort Bedford and Fort

[1] This is the letter in which he accepts Amherst's proposal to infect the Indians. His just indignation at the atrocities which had caused so much misery is his best apology.

Ligonier; the former commanded by Captain Lewis Ourry, and the latter by Lieutenant Archibald Blane. These officers kept up a precarious correspondence with him and each other, by means of express-riders, a service dangerous to the last degree and soon to become impracticable. It was of the utmost importance to hold these posts, which contained stores and munitions, the capture of which by the Indians would have led to the worst consequences. Ourry had no garrison worth the name; but at every Indian alarm the scared inhabitants would desert their farms, and gather for shelter around his fort, to disperse again when the alarm was over.

On the third of June, he writes to Bouquet: "No less than ninety-three families are now come in here for refuge, and more hourly arriving. I expect ten more before night." He adds that he had formed the men into two militia companies. "My returns," he pursues, "amount already to a hundred and fifty-five men. My regulars are increased by expresses, etc., to three corporals and nine privates; no despicable garrison!"

On the seventh, he sent another letter. . . . "As to myself, I find I can bear a good deal. Since the alarm I never lie down till about twelve, and am walking about the fort between two and three in the morning, turning out the guards and sending out patrols, before I suffer the gates to remain open. . . . My greatest difficulty is to keep my militia from straggling by twos and threes to their dear plantations, thereby exposing themselves to be scalped, and weakening my garrison by such numbers absenting themselves. They are still in good spirits, but they don't know all the bad news. I shall use all means to prevail on them to stay till some troops come up. I long to see my Indian scouts come in with intelligence; but I long more to hear the Grenadiers' March, and see some more red-coats."

Ten days later, the face of affairs had changed. "I am now, as I foresaw, entirely deserted by the country people. No accident having happened here, they have gradually left me to return to their plantations; so that my whole force is reduced to twelve Royal Americans to guard the fort, and seven Indian prisoners. I should be very glad to see some troops come to my assistance. A fort with five bastions cannot be guarded, much less defended, by a dozen men; but I hope God will protect us."

On the next day, he writes again: "This moment I return from the parade. Some scalps taken up Dening's Creek yesterday, and to-day some families murdered and houses burnt, have restored me my militia. . . . Two or three other families are missing, and the houses are seen in flames. The people are all flocking in again."

Two days afterwards, he says that, while the countrymen were at drill on the parade, three Indians attempted to seize two little girls, close to the fort, but were driven off by a volley. "This," he pursues, "has added greatly to the panic of the people. With difficulty I can restrain them from murdering the Indian prisoners." And he concludes: "I can't help thinking that the enemy will collect, after cutting off the little posts one after another, leaving Fort Pitt as too tough a morsel, and bend their whole force upon the frontiers."

On the second of July, he describes an attack by about twenty Indians on a party of mowers, several of whom were killed. "This accident," he says, "has thrown the people into a great consternation, but such is their stupidity that they will do nothing right for their own preservation."

It was on the next day that he sent a mounted soldier to Bouquet with news of the loss of Presqu' Isle and its sister posts, which Blane, who had received it from Fort Pitt, had contrived to send him; though he himself, in his feeble little fort of Ligonier, buried in a sea of forests, hardly dared hope to maintain himself. Bouquet was greatly moved at the tidings, and his vexation betrayed him into injustice towards the defender of Presqu' Isle. "Humanity makes me hope that Christie is dead, as his scandalous capitulation, for a post of that consequence and so impregnable to savages, deserves the most severe punishment."[1] He is equally vehement in regard to Blane, who appears to have intimated, in writing to Ourry, that he had himself had thoughts of capitulating, like Christie. "I shivered when you hinted to me Lieutenant Bl—'s intentions. Death and infamy would have

[1] The blockhouse at Presqu' Isle had been built under the direction of Bouquet. Being of wood, it was not fire-proof; and he urged upon Amherst that it should be re-built of brick with a slate roof, thus making it absolutely proof against Indians.

been the reward he would expect, instead of the honor he has obtained by his prudence, courage, and resolution. . . . This is a most trying time. . . . You may be sure that all the expedition possible will be used for the relief of the few remaining posts."[1]

As for Blane, the following extracts from his letters will show his position; though, when his affairs were at the worst, nothing was heard from him, as all his messengers were killed. On the fourth of June, he writes: "Thursday last my garrison was attacked by a body of Indians, about five in the morning; but as they only fired upon us from the skirts of the woods, I contented myself with giving them three cheers, without spending a single shot upon them. But as they still continued their popping upon the side next the town, I sent the sergeant of the Royal Americans, with a proper detachment, to fire the houses, which effectually disappointed them in their plan."

On the seventeenth, he writes to Bouquet: "I hope soon to see yourself, and live in daily hopes of a reinforcement. . . . Sunday last, a man straggling out was killed by the Indians; and Monday night three of them got under the n——house, but were discovered. The darkness secured them their retreat. . . . I believe the communication between Fort Pitt and this is entirely cut off, having heard nothing from them since the thirtieth of May,

[1] Bouquet had the strongest reasons for wishing that Fort Ligonier should hold out. As the event showed, its capture would probably have entailed the defeat and destruction of his entire command.

though two expresses have gone from Bedford by this post."

On the twenty-eighth, he explains that he has not been able to report for some time, the road having been completely closed by the enemy. "On the twenty-first," he continues, "the Indians made a second attempt in a very serious manner, for near two hours, but with the like success as the first. They began with attempting to cut off the retreat of a small party of fifteen men, who, from their impatience to come at four Indians who showed themselves, in a great measure forced me to let them out. In the evening, I think above a hundred lay in ambush by the side of the creek, about four hundred yards from the fort; and, just as the party was returning pretty near where they lay, they rushed out, when they undoubtedly must have succeeded, had it not been for a deep morass which intervened. Immediately after, they began their attack; and I dare say they fired upwards of one thousand shot. Nobody received any damage. So far, my good fortune in dangers still attends me."

And here one cannot but give a moment's thought to those whose desperate duty it was to be the bearers of this correspondence of the officers of the forest outposts with their commander. They were usually soldiers, sometimes backwoodsmen, and occasionally a friendly Indian, who, disguising his attachment to the whites, could pass when others would infallibly have perished. If white men, they were always mounted; and it may well be supposed that their horses did not lag by the way. The profound solitude; the silence, broken only by the moan of the wind, the caw of the crow, or the cry of some prowling tenant of the waste; the mystery of the verdant labyrinth, which the anxious wayfarer strained his eyes in vain to penetrate; the consciousness that in every thicket, behind every rock, might lurk a foe more fierce and subtle than the cougar or the lynx; and the long hours of darkness, when, stretched on the cold ground, his excited fancy roamed in nightmare visions of a horror but too real and imminent, — such was the experience of many an unfortunate who never lived to tell it. If the messenger was an Indian, his greatest danger was from those who should have been his friends. Friendly Indians were told, whenever they approached a fort, to make themselves known by carrying green branches thrust into the muzzles of their guns; and an order was issued that the token should be respe ted. This gave them tolerable security as regarded soldiers, but not as regarded the enraged backwoodsmen, who would shoot without distinction at any thing with a red skin.

To return to Bouquet, who lay encamped at Carlisle, urging on his preparations, but met by obstacles at every step. Wagons and horses had been promised, but promises were broken, and all was vexation and delay. The province of Pennsylvania, from causes to be shown hereafter, would do nothing to aid the troops who were defending it; and even the people of the frontier, partly from the apathy and confusion of terror, and partly, it seems, from dislike and jealousy of the regulars, were backward and sluggish in co-operating with them. "I hope," writes Bouquet to Sir Jeffrey Amherst, "that we shall be able to save that infatuated people from destruction, notwith standing all their endeavors to defeat your vigorous measures. I meet everywhere with the same backwardness, even among the most exposed of the inhabitants, which makes every thing move on heavily, and is disgusting to the last degree." And again: "I find myself utterly abandoned by the very people I am ordered to protect. . . . I have borne very patiently the ill-usage of this province, having still hopes that they will do something for us; and therefore have avoided to quarrel with them."

While, vexed and exasperated, Bouquet labored at his thankless task, remonstrated with provincial officials, or appealed to refractory farmers, the terror of the country people increased every day. When on Sunday, the third of July, Ourry's express rode into Carlisle with the disastrous news from Presqu' Isle and the other outposts, he stopped for a moment in the village street to water his horse. A crowd of countrymen were instantly about him, besieging him with questions. He told his ill-omened story; and added as, remounting, he rode towards Bouquet's tent, "The Indians will be here soon." All was now excitement and consternation. Messengers hastened out to spread the tidings; and every road and pathway leading into Carlisle was beset with the flying settlers, flocking thither for refuge. Soon rumors were heard that the Indians were come. Some of the fugitives had seen the smoke of burning houses rising from the valleys; and these reports were fearfully confirmed by the appearance of miserable wretches, who, half frantic with grief and dismay, had fled from blazing dwellings and slaughtered families. A party of the inhabitants armed themselves and went out, to warn the living and bury the dead. Reaching Shearman's Valley, they found fields laid waste, stacked wheat on fire, and the houses yet in flames; and they grew sick with horror at seeing a group of hogs tearing and devouring the bodies of the dead.[1] As they advanced up the valley, every thing betokened the recent presence of the enemy, while columns of smoke, rising among the surrounding mountains, showed how general was the work of destruction.

On the preceding day, six men, assembled for reaping the harvest, had been seated at dinner at the house of Campbell, a settler on the Juniata Four or five Indians suddenly burst the door, fired among them, and then beat down the survivors with the butts of their rifles. One young man leaped from his seat, snatched a gun which stood in a corner, discharged it into the breast of the warrior who was rushing upon him, and, leaping through an open window, made his escape. He fled through the forest to a settlement at some distance, where he related his story. Upon this, twelve young men volunteered to cross the mountain, and warn the

[1] *Penn. Gaz.* No. 1804.

inhabitants of the neighboring Tuscarora valley. On entering it, they found that the enemy had been there before them. Some of the houses were on fire, while others were still standing, with no tenants but the dead. Under the shed of a farmer, the Indians had been feasting on the flesh of the cattle they had killed, and the meat had not yet grown cold. Pursuing their course, the white men found the spot where several detached parties of the enemy had united almost immediately before; and they boldly resolved to follow, in order to ascertain what direction the marauders had taken. The trail led them up a deep and woody pass of the Tuscarora. Here the yell of the war-whoop and the din of fire-arms suddenly greeted them, and five of their number were shot down. Thirty warriors rose from their ambuscade, and rushed upon them. They gave one discharge, scattered, and ran for their lives. One of them, a boy named Charles Eliot, as he fled, plunging through the thickets, heard an Indian tearing the boughs behind him, in furious pursuit. He seized his powder-horn, poured the contents at random down the muzzle of his gun, threw in a bullet after them, without using the ramrod, and, wheeling about, discharged the piece into the breast of his pursuer. He saw the Indian shrink back and roll over into the bushes. He continued his flight; but a moment after, a voice called his name. Turning to the spot, he saw one of his comrades stretched helpless upon the ground. This man had been mortally wounded at the first fire, but had fled a few rods from the scene of blood, before his strength gave out. Eliot approached him. "Take my gun," said the dying frontiersman. "Whenever you see an Indian, kill him with it, and then I shall be satisfied."[1] Eliot, with several others of the party, escaped, and finally reached Carlisle, where his story excited a spirit of uncontrollable wrath and vengeance among the fierce backwoodsmen. Several parties went out; and one of them, commanded by the sheriff of the place, encountered a band of Indians, routed them after a sharp fight, and brought in several scalps.[2]

The surrounding country was by this time completely abandoned by the settlers, many of whom, not content with seeking refuge at Carlisle, continued their flight to the eastward, and, headed by the clergyman of that place, pushed on to Lancaster, and even to Philadelphia.[3] Carlisle presented

[1] Robison, *Narrative.* Robison was one of the party, and his brother was mortally wounded at the first fire.

[2] Extract from a Letter — *Carlisle,* July 13 (*Penn. Gaz.* No. 1804): —

"Last Night Colonel Armstrong returned. He left the Party, who pursued further, and found several dead, whom they buried in the best manner they could, and are now all returned in. — From what appears, the Indians are travelling from one Place to another, along the Valley, burning the Farms, and destroying all the People they meet with. — This Day gives an Account of six more being killed in the Valley, so that, since last Sunday Morning to this Day, Twelve o'clock, we have a pretty authentic Account of the Number slain, being Twenty-five, and four or five wounded. — The Colonel, Mr. Wilson, and Mr. Alricks, are now on the Parade, endeavouring to raise another Party, to go out and succour the Sheriff and his Party, consisting of Fifty Men, which marched Yesterday, and hope they will be able to send off immediately Twenty good Men. — The People here, I assure you, want nothing but a good Leader, and a little Encouragement, to make a very good Defence."

[3] Extract from a Letter — *Carlisle,* July 5 (*Haz. Pa. Reg.* IV. 390): —

"Nothing could exceed the terror which prevailed from house to

a most deplorable spectacle. A multitude of the refugees, unable to find shelter in the town, had encamped in the woods or on the adjacent fields, erecting huts of branches and bark, and living on such charity as the slender means of the towns-people could supply. Passing among them, one would have witnessed every form of human misery. In these wretched encampments were men, women, and children, bereft at one stroke of friends, of home, and the means of supporting life. Some stood aghast and bewildered at the sudden and fatal blow; others were sunk in the apathy of despair; others were weeping and moaning with irrepressible anguish. With not a few, the craven passion of fear drowned all other emotion, and day and night they were haunted with visions of the bloody knife and the reeking scalp; while in others, every faculty was absorbed by the burning thirst for vengeance, and mortal hatred against the whole Indian race.[1]

house, from town to town. The road was near covered with women and children, flying to Lancaster and Philadelphia. The Rev. —— ——, Pastor of the Episcopal Church, went at the head of his congregation, to protect and encourage them on the way. A few retired to the Breast works for safety. The alarm once given could not be appeased. We have done all that men can do to prevent disorder. All our hopes are turned upon Bouquet."

[1] Extract from a Letter — *Carlisle,* July 12 (*Penn. Gaz.* No. 1804): —

"I embrace this first Leisure, since Yesterday Morning, to transmit you a brief Account of our present State of Affairs here, which indeed is very distressing; every Day, almost, affording some fresh Object to awaken the Compassion, alarm the Fears, or kindle into Resentment and Vengeance every sensible Breast, while flying Families, obliged to abandon House and Possession, to save their Lives by an hasty Escape; mourning Widows, bewailing their Husbands surprised and massacred by savage Rage; tender Parents, lamenting the Fruits of their own Bodies, cropt in the very Bloom of Life by a barbarous Hand; with Relations and Acquaintances, pouring out Sorrow for murdered Neighbours and Friends, present a varied Scene of mingled Distress.

"To-day a British Vengeance begins to rise in the Breasts of our Men. — One of them that fell from among the 12, as he was just expiring, said to one of his Fellows, Here, take my Gun, and kill the first Indian vou see, and all shall be well."

CHAPTER XX.

1763.

THE BATTLE OF BUSHY RUN.

THE miserable multitude were soon threatened with famine, and gathered in crowds around the tents of Bouquet, begging relief, which he had not the heart to refuse. After a delay of eighteen days, the chief obstacles were overcome. Wagons and draught animals had, little by little, been collected, and provisions gathered among the settlements to the eastward. At length all was ready, and Bouquet broke up his camp, and began his march. The force under his command did not exceed five hundred men, of whom the most effective were the Highlanders of the 42d regiment. The remnant of the 77th, which was also with him, was so enfeebled by West Indian exposures, that Amherst had at first pronounced it fit only for garrison duty, and nothing but necessity had induced him to employ it on this arduous service. As the heavy wagons of the convoy lumbered along the street of Carlisle, guarded by the bare-legged Highlanders, in kilts and plaids, the crowd gazed in anxious silence; for they knew that their all was at stake on the issue of this dubious enterprise. There was little to reassure them in the thin frames and haggard look of the worn-out veterans; still less in the sight of sixty invalid soldiers, who, unable to walk, were carried in wagons, to furnish a feeble reinforcement to the small garrisons along the route.[1] The desponding rustics watched the last gleam of the bayonets, the last flutter of the tartans, as the rear files vanished in the woods; then returned to their hovels, prepared for tidings of defeat, and ready, when they heard them, to abandon the country, and fly beyond the Susquehanna.

In truth, the adventure was no boy's play. In that gloomy wilderness lay the bones of Braddock and the hundreds that perished with him. The number of the slain on that bloody day exceeded Bouquet's whole force; while the strength of the assailants was inferior to that of the swarms who now infested the forests. Bouquet's troops were, for the most part, as little accustomed to the backwoods as those of Braddock; but their commander had served seven years in America, and perfectly understood his work. He had attempted to engage a body of frontiersmen to join him on the march; but they preferred to remain for the defence of their families. He was therefore forced to employ the Highlanders as flankers, to protect his line of march and prevent surprise; but, singularly enough, these mountaineers were sure to lose themselves in the woods, and therefore proved useless.[2] For a few days, however, his progress would be tolerably

[1] *Account of Bouquet's Expedition; Introduction,* vi.

[2] "I cannot send a Highlander out of my sight without running the

secure, at least from serious attack. His anxieties centred on Fort Ligonier, and he resolved to hazard the attempt to throw a reinforcement into it. Thirty of the best Highlanders were chosen, furnished with guides, and ordered to push forward with the utmost speed, avoiding the road, travelling by night on unfrequented paths, and lying close by day. The attempt succeeded. After resting several days at Bedford, where Ourry was expecting an attack, they again set out, found Fort Ligonier beset by Indians, and received a volley as they made for the gate; but entered safely, to the unspeakable relief of Blane and his beleaguered men.

Meanwhile, Bouquet's little army crept on its slow way along the Cumberland valley. Passing here and there a few scattered cabins, deserted or burnt to the ground, they reached the hamlet of Shippensburg, somewhat more than twenty miles from their point of departure. Here, as at Carlisle, was gathered a starving multitude, who had fled from the knife and the tomahawk.[1] Beyond lay a solitude whence every settler had fled. They reached Fort Loudon, on the declivity of Cove Mountain, and climbed the wood-encumbered defiles beyond.

risk of losing the man, which exposes me to surprise from the skulking villains I have to deal with." — MS. Letter — *Bouquet to Amherst*, 26 July, 1763.

[1] "Our Accounts from the westward are as follows, viz.: —

"On the 25th of July there were in Shippensburg 1384 of our poor distressed Back Inhabitants, viz. Men, 301; Women, 345; Children, 738; Many of whom were obliged to lie in Barns, Stables, Cellars, and under old leaky Sheds, the Dwelling-houses being all crowded." — *Penn. Gaz.* No. 1806.

Far on their right stretched the green ridges of the Tuscarora; and, in front, mountain beyond mountain was piled against the sky. Over rocky heights and through deep valleys, they reached at length Fort Littleton, a provincial post, in which, with incredible perversity, the government of Pennsylvania had refused to place a garrison.[1] Not far distant was the feeble little post of the Juniata, empty like the other; for the two or three men who held it had been withdrawn by Ourry.[2] On the twenty-fifth of July, they reached Bedford, hemmed in by encircling mountains. It was the frontier village and the centre of a scattered border population, the whole of which was now clustered in terror in and around the fort; for the neighboring woods were full of prowling savages. Ourry reported that for several weeks nothing had been heard from the westward, every messenger having been killed and the communication completely cut off. By the last intelligence Fort Pitt had been surrounded by Indians, and daily threatened with a general attack.

At Bedford, Bouquet had the good fortune to engage thirty backwoodsmen to accompany him.[3]

[1] "The government of Pennsylvania having repeatedly refused to garrison Fort Lyttleton (a provincial fort), even with the kind of troops they have raised, I have stationed some inhabitants of the neighborhood in it, with some provisions and ammunition, to prevent the savages burning it." — MS. Letter — *Bouquet to Amherst*, 26 July, 1763.

[2] MS. Letter — *Ourry to Bouquet*, 20 June, 1763.

[3] Extract from a *Letter of Bouquet to Amherst, Bedford*, July 26th, 1763:

"The troops & Convoy arrived here yesterday. . . . Three men have been massacred near Shippensburg since we left, but we have not perceived yet any of the Villains. . . . Having observed in our march that the Highlanders lose themselves in the woods as soon as they go out of

He lay encamped three days to rest men and animals, and then, leaving his invalids to garrison the fort, put out again into the sea of savage verdure that stretched beyond. The troops and convoy defiled along the road made by General Forbes in 1758, if the name of road can be given to a rugged track, hewn out by axemen through forests and swamps and up the steep acclivities of rugged mountains; shut in between impervious walls of trunks, boughs, and matted thickets, and overarched by a canopy of restless leaves. With difficulty and toil, the wagons dragged slowly on, by hill and hollow, through brook and quagmire, over roots, rocks, and stumps. Nature had formed the country for a war of ambuscades and surprises, and no pains were spared to guard against them. A band of backwoodsmen led the way, followed closely by the pioneers; the wagons and the cattle were in the centre, guarded by the regulars; and a rear guard of backwoodsmen closed the line of march. Frontier riflemen scoured the woods far in front and on either flank, and made surprise impossible. Thus they toiled heavily on till the main ridge of the Alleghanies, a mighty wall of green, rose up before them; and they began their zigzag progress up the woody heights amid the sweltering heats of July. The tongues of the panting oxen hung lolling from their jaws; while the pine-trees, scorching in the hot sun, diffused their resinous

the road, and cannot on that account be employed as Flankers, I have commissioned a person here to procure me about thirty woodsmen to march with us. . . . This is very irregular, but the circumstances render it so absolutely necessary that I hope you will approve it."

odors through the sultry air. At length from the windy summit the Highland soldiers could gaze around upon a boundless panorama of forest-covered mountains, wilder than their own native hills. Descending from the Alleghanies, they entered upon a country less rugged and formidable in itself, but beset with constantly increasing dangers. On the second of August, they reached Fort Ligonier, about fifty miles from Bedford, and a hundred and fifty from Carlisle. The Indians who were about the place vanished at their approach; but the garrison could furnish no intelligence of the motions and designs of the enemy, having been completely blockaded for weeks. In this uncertainty, Bouquet resolved to leave behind the oxen and wagons, which formed the most cumbrous part of the convoy, in order to advance with greater celerity, and oppose a better resistance in case of attack. Thus relieved, the army resumed its march on the fourth, taking with them three hundred and fifty pack horses and a few cattle, and at nightfall encamped at no great distance from Ligonier. Within less than a day's march in advance lay the dangerous defiles of Turtle Creek, a stream flowing at the bottom of a deep hollow, flanked by steep declivities, along the foot of which the road at that time ran for some distance. Fearing that the enemy would lay an ambuscade at this place, Bouquet resolved to march on the following day as far as a small stream called Bushy Run; to rest here until night, and then, by a forced march, to cross Turtle Creek under cover of the darkness.

On the morning of the fifth, the tents were struck at an early hour, and the troops began their march through a country broken with hills and deep hollows, covered with the tall, dense forest, which spread for countless leagues around. By one o'clock, they had advanced seventeen miles; and the guides assured them that they were within half a mile of Bushy Run, their proposed resting-place. The tired soldiers were pressing forward with renewed alacrity, when suddenly the report of rifles from the front sent a thrill along the ranks; and, as they listened, the firing thickened into a fierce, sharp rattle; while shouts and whoops, deadened by the intervening forest, showed that the advance guard was hotly engaged. The two foremost companies were at once ordered forward to support it; but, far from abating, the fire grew so rapid and furious as to argue the presence of an enemy at once numerous and resolute. At this, the convoy was halted, the troops formed into line, and a general charge ordered. Bearing down through the forest with fixed bayonets, they drove the yelping assailants before them, and swept the ground clear. But at the very moment of success, a fresh burst of whoops and firing was heard from either flank; while a confused noise from the rear showed that the convoy was attacked. It was necessary instantly to fall back for its support. Driving off the assailants, the troops formed in a circle around the crowded and terrified horses. Though they were new to the work, and though the numbers and movements of the enemy, whose yelling resounded on every side, were concealed by the thick forest, yet no man lost his composure; and all displayed a steadiness which nothing but implicit confidence in their commander could have inspired. And now ensued a combat of a nature most harassing and discouraging. Again and again, now on this side and now on that, a crowd of Indians rushed up, pouring in a heavy fire, and striving, with furious outcries, to break into the circle. A well-directed volley met them, followed by a steady charge of the bayonet. They never waited an instant to receive the attack, but, leaping backwards from tree to tree, soon vanished from sight, only to renew their attack with unabated ferocity in another quarter. Such was their activity, that very few of them were hurt; while the British, less expert in bush-fighting, suffered severely. Thus the fight went on, without intermission, for seven hours, until the forest grew dark with approaching night. Upon this, the Indians grad ually slackened their fire, and the exhausted soldiers found time to rest.

It was impossible to change their ground in the enemy's presence, and the troops were obliged to encamp upon the hill where the combat had taken place, though not a drop of water was to be found there. Fearing a night attack, Bouquet stationed numerous sentinels and outposts to guard against it; while the men lay down upon their arms, preserving the order they had maintained during the fight. Having completed the necessary arrangements, Bouquet, doubtful of surviving the battle of the morrow, wrote to Sir Jeffrey Amherst, in a few clear, concise words, an account of the day's events. His letter concludes as follows: "Whatever our fate may be, I thought it necessary to give your Excellency this early information, that you may, at all events, take such measures as you will think proper with the provinces, for their own safety, and the effectual relief of Fort Pitt; as, in case of another engagement, I fear insurmountable difficulties in protecting and transporting our provisions, being already so much weakened by the losses of this day, in men and horses, besides the additional necessity of carrying the wounded, whose situation is truly deplorable."

The condition of these unhappy men might well awaken sympathy. About sixty soldiers, besides several officers, had been killed or disabled. A space in the centre of the camp was prepared for the reception of the wounded, and surrounded by a wall of flour-bags from the convoy, affording some protection against the bullets which flew from all sides during the fight. Here they lay upon the ground, enduring agonies of thirst, and waiting, passive and helpless, the issue of the battle. Deprived of the animating thought that their lives and safety depended on their own exertions; surrounded by a wilderness, and by scenes to the horror of which no degree of familiarity could render the imagination callous, they must have endured mental sufferings, compared to which the pain of their wounds was slight. In the probable event of defeat, a fate inexpressibly horrible awaited them; while even victory would not ensure their safety, since any great increase in their numbers would render it impossible for their comrades to transport them. Nor was the condition of those who had hitherto escaped an enviable one. Though they were about equal in number to their assailants, yet the dexterity and alertness of the Indians, joined to the nature of the country, gave all the advantages of a greatly superior force. The enemy were, moreover, exulting in the fullest confidence of success; for it was in these very forests that, eight years before, they had nearly destroyed twice their number of the best British troops. Throughout the earlier part of the night, they kept up a dropping fire upon the camp; while, at short intervals, a wild whoop from the thick surrounding gloom told with what fierce eagerness they waited to glut their vengeance on the morrow. The camp remained in darkness, for it would have been dangerous to build fires within its precincts, to direct the aim of the lurking marksmen. Surrounded by such terrors, the men snatched a disturbed and broken sleep, recruiting their exhausted strength for the renewed struggle of the morning.

With the earliest dawn of day, and while the damp, cool forest was still involved in twilight, there rose around the camp a general burst of those horrible cries which form the ordinary prelude of an Indian battle. Instantly, from every side at once, the enemy opened their fire, approaching under cover of the trees and bushes, and levelling with a close and deadly aim. Often, as on the previous day, they would rush up with furious impetuosity, striving to break into the ring of troops. They were repulsed at every point; but the British, though constantly victorious, were beset with undiminished perils, while the violence of the enemy seemed every moment on the increase. True to their favorite tactics, they would never stand their ground when attacked, but vanish at the first gleam of the levelled bayonet, only to appear again the moment the danger was past. The troops, fatigued by the long march and equally long battle of the previous day, were maddened by the torments of thirst, "more intolerable," says their commander, "than the enemy's fire." They were fully conscious of the peril in which they stood, of wasting away by slow degrees beneath the shot of assailants at once so daring, so cautious, and so active, and upon whom it was impossible to inflict any decisive injury. The Indians saw their distress, and pressed them closer and closer, redoubling their yells and howlings; while some of them, sheltered behind trees, assailed the troops, in bad English, with abuse and derision.

Meanwhile the interior of the camp was a scene of confusion. The horses, secured in a crowd near the wall of flour-bags which covered the wounded, were often struck by the bullets, and wrought to the height of terror by the mingled din of whoops, shrieks, and firing. They would break away by half scores at a time, burst through the ring of troops and the outer circle of assailants, and scour madly up and down the hill-sides; while many of the drivers, overcome by the terrors of a scene in which they could bear no active part, hid themselves among the bushes, and could neither hear nor obey orders.

It was now about ten o'clock. Oppressed with heat, fatigue, and thirst, the distressed troops still maintained a weary and wavering defence, encircling the convoy in a yet unbroken ring. They were fast falling in their ranks, and the strength and spirits of the survivors had begun to flag. If the fortunes of the day were to be retrieved, the effort must be made at once; and happily the mind of the commander was equal to the emergency. In the midst of the confusion he conceived a masterly stratagem. Could the Indians be brought together in a body, and made to stand their ground when attacked, there could be little doubt of the result; and, to effect this object, Bouquet determined to increase their confidence, which had already mounted to an audacious pitch. Two companies of infantry, forming a part of the ring which had been exposed to the hottest fire, were ordered to fall back into the interior of the camp; while the troops on either hand joined their files across the vacant space, as if to cover the retreat of their comrades. These orders, given at a favorable moment, were executed with great promptness. The thin line of troops who took possession of the deserted part of the circle were, from their small numbers, brought closer in towards the centre. The Indians mistook these movements for a retreat. Confident that their time was come, they leaped up on all sides, from behind the trees and bushes, and with infernal screeches, rushed headlong towards the spot, pouring in a heavy and galling fire. The shock was too violent to be long endured. The men struggled to maintain their posts; but the Indians seemed on the point of breaking into the heart of the camp, when the aspect of affairs was suddenly reversed. The two companies, who had apparently abandoned their position, were in fact destined to begin the attack; and they now sallied out from the circle at a point where a depression in the ground, joined to the thick growth of trees, concealed them from the eyes of the Indians. Making a short *détour* through the woods, they came round upon the flank of the furious assailants, and fired a close volley into the midst of the crowd. Numbers were seen to fall; yet though completely surprised, and utterly at a loss to understand the nature of the attack, the Indians faced about with the greatest intrepidity, and returned the fire. But the Highlanders, with yells as wild as their own, fell on them with the bayonet. The shock was irresistible, and they fled before the charging ranks in a tumultuous throng. Orders had been given to two other companies, occupying a contiguous part of the circle, to support the attack whenever a favorable moment should occur; and they had therefore advanced a little from their position, and lay close crouched in ambush. The fugitives, pressed by the Highland bayonets, passed directly across their front; upon which they rose, and poured among them a second volley, no less destructive than the first. This completed the rout. The four companies, uniting, drove the flying savages through the woods, giving them no time to rally or reload their empty rifles, killing many, and scattering the rest in hopeless confusion.

While this took place at one part of the circle, the troops and the savages had still maintained their respective positions at the other; but when the latter perceived the total rout of their comrades, and saw the troops advancing to assail them, they also lost heart, and fled. The discordant outcries which had so long deafened the ears of the English soon ceased altogether, and not a living Indian remained near the spot. About sixty corpses lay scattered over the ground. Among them were found those of several prominent chiefs, while the blood which stained the leaves of the bushes showed that numbers had fled wounded from the field. The soldiers took but one prisoner, whom they shot to death like a captive wolf. The loss of the Brit ish in the two battles surpassed that of the enemy, amounting to eight officers and one hundred and fifteen men.[1]

[1] MS. Letters — *Bouquet to Amherst*, Aug. 5, 6. *Penn. Gaz.* 1809–1810 *Gent. Mag.* XXXIII. 487. *London Mag.* for 1763, 545. *Account of Bouquet's Expedition. Annual Register* for 1763, 28. Mante, 493.

The accounts of this action, published in the journals of the day, excited much attention, from the wild and novel character of this species of warfare. A well-written description of the battle, together with a journal of Bouquet's expedition of the succeeding year, was published in a thin quarto, with illustrations from the pencil of West. The writer was Dr. William Smith, of Philadelphia, and not, as has usually been thought, the geographer Thomas Hutchins. See the reprint, *Clarke's Historical Series*, Vol. I. A French translation of the narrative was published at Amsterdam in 1769.

Having been for some time detained by the necessity of making litters for the wounded, and destroying the stores which the flight of most of the horses made it impossible to transport, the army moved on, in the afternoon, to Bushy Run. Here they had scarcely formed their camp, when they were again fired upon by a body of Indians, who, however, were soon repulsed. On the next day they resumed their progress towards Fort Pitt, distant about twenty-five miles; and, though frequently annoyed on the march by petty attacks, they reached their destination, on the tenth, without serious loss. It was a joyful moment both to the troops and to the garrison. The latter, it will be remembered, were left surrounded and hotly pressed by the Indians, who had beleaguered the place from the twenty-eighth of July to the first of August, when, hearing of Bouquet's approach, they

Extract from a Letter — *Fort Pitt*, August 12 (*Penn. Gaz.* No. 1810): —

"We formed a Circle round our Convoy and Wounded; upon which the Savages collected themselves, and continued whooping and popping at us all the Evening. Next Morning, having mustered all their Force, they began the War-whoop, attacking us in Front, when the Colonel feigned a Retreat, which encouraged the Indians to an eager Pursuit, while the Light Infantry and Grenadiers rushed out on their Right and Left Flanks, attacking them where they little expected it; by which Means a great Number of them were killed; and among the rest, Keelyuskung, a Delaware Chief, who the Night before, and that Morning, had been Blackguarding us in English: We lost one Man in the Rear, on our March the Day after.

"In other Letters from Fort Pitt, it is mentioned that, to a Man, they were resolved to defend the Garrison (if the Troops had not arrived), as long as any Ammunition, and Provision to support them, were left; and that then they would have fought their Way through, or died in the Attempt, rather than have been made Prisoners by such perfidious, cruel, and Blood-thirsty Hell-hounds."

See Appendix, D.

had abandoned the siege, and marched to attack him. From this time, the garrison had seen nothing of them until the morning of the tenth, when, shortly before the army appeared, they had passed the fort in a body, raising the scalp-yell, and displaying their disgusting trophies to the view of the English.[1]

The battle of Bushy Run was one of the best contested actions ever fought between white men and Indians. If there was any disparity of numbers, the advantage was on the side of the troops;

[1] Extract from a Letter — *Fort Pitt*, August 12 (*Penn. Gaz.* No. 1810): "As you will probably have the Accounts of these Engagements from the Gentlemen that were in them, I shall say no more than this, that it is the general Opinion, the Troops behaved with the utmost Intrepidity, and the Indians were never known to behave so fiercely. You may be sure the Sight of the Troops was very agreeable to our poor Garrison, being penned up in the Fort from the 27th of May to the 9th Instant, and the Barrack Rooms crammed with Men, Women, and Children, tho' providentially no other Disorder ensued than the Small-pox. — From the 16th of June to the 28th of July, we were pestered with the Enemy; sometimes with their Flags, demanding Conferences; at other Times threatening, then soothing, and offering their Cordial Advice, for us to evacuate the Place; for that they, the Delawares, tho' our dear Friends and Brothers, could no longer protect us from the Fury of Legions of other Nations, that were coming from the Lakes, &c., to destroy us. But, finding that neither had any Effect on us, they mustered their whole force, in Number about 400, and began a most furious Fire from all Quarters on the Fort, which they continued for four Days, and great Part of the Nights, viz., from the 28th of July to the last. — Our Commander was wounded by an Arrow in the Leg, and no other Person, of any Note, hurt, tho' the Balls were whistling very thick about our Ears. Nine Rank and File wounded, and one Hulings having his Leg broke, was the whole of our Loss during this hot Firing; tho' we have Reason to think that we killed several of our loving Brethren, notwithstanding their Alertness in skulking behind the Banks of the Rivers, &c. — These Gentry, seeing they could not take the Fort, sheered off, and we heard no more of them till the Account of the above Engagements came to hand, when we were convinced that our good Brothers did us this second Act of Friendship. — What they intend next, God knows, but am afraid they will disperse in small Parties, among the Inhabitants, if not well defended."

and the Indians had displayed throughout a fierceness and intrepidity matched only by the steady valor with which they were met. In the provinces, the victory excited equal joy and admiration, especially among those who knew the incalculable difficulties of an Indian campaign. The Assembly of Pennsylvania passed a vote expressing their sense of the merits of Bouquet, and of the service he had rendered to the province. He soon after received the additional honor of the formal thanks of the King.[1]

In many an Indian village, the women cut away their hair, gashed their limbs with knives, and uttered their dismal howlings of lamentation for the fallen. Yet, though surprised and dispirited, the rage of the Indians was too deep to be quenched, even by so signal a reverse; and their outrages upon the frontier were resumed with unabated ferocity. Fort Pitt, however, was effectually relieved; while the moral effect of the victory enabled the frontier settlers to encounter the enemy with a spirit which would have been wanting, had Bouquet sustained a defeat.

[1] Extract from a MS. Letter — *Sir J. Amherst to Colonel Bouquet:* —

"New York, 31st August, 1763.

"The Disposition you made for the Reception of the Indians, the Second Day, was indeed very wisely Concerted, and as happily Executed; I am pleased with Every part of your Conduct on the Occasion, which being so well seconded by the Officers and Soldiers under your Command, Enabled you not only to Protect your Large Convoy, but to rout a Body of Savages that would have been very formidable against any Troops but such as you had with you."

CHAPTER XXI.

1763.

THE IROQUOIS.—AMBUSCADE OF THE DEVIL'S HOLE.

WHILE Bouquet was fighting the battle of Bushy Run, and Dalzell making his fatal sortie against the camp of Pontiac, Sir William Johnson was engaged in the more pacific yet more important task of securing the friendship and alliance of the Six Nations. After several preliminary conferences, he sent runners throughout the whole confederacy to invite deputies of the several tribes to meet him in council at Johnson Hall. The request was not declined. From the banks of the Mohawk; from the Oneida, Cayuga, and Tuscarora villages; from the valley of Onondaga, where, from immemorial time, had burned the great council-fire of the confederacy,—came chiefs and warriors, gathering to the place of meeting. The Senecas alone, the warlike tenants of the Genesee valley, refused to attend; for they were already in arms against the English. Besides the Iroquois, deputies came from the tribes dwelling along the St. Lawrence, and within the settled parts of Canada.

The council opened on the seventh of September. Despite their fair words, their attachment was doubtful; but Sir William Johnson, by a dexterous mingling of reasoning, threats, and promises, allayed their discontent, and banished the thoughts of war. They winced, however, when he informed them that, during the next season, an English army must pass through their country, on its way to punish the refractory tribes of the West. "Your foot is broad and heavy," said the speaker from Onondaga; "take care that you do not tread on us." Seeing the improved temper of his auditory, Johnson was led to hope for some farther advantage than that of mere neutrality. He accordingly urged the Iroquois to take up arms against the hostile tribes, and concluded his final harangue with the following figurative words: "I now deliver you a good English axe, which I desire you will give to the warriors of all your nations, with directions to use it against these covenant-breakers, by cutting off the bad links which have sullied the chain of friendship."

These words were confirmed by the presentation of a black war-belt of wampum, and the offer of a hatchet, which the Iroquois did not refuse to accept. That they would take any very active and strenuous part in the war, could not be expected; yet their bearing arms at all would prove of great advantage, by discouraging the hostile Indians who had looked upon the Iroquois as friends and abettors. Some months after the council, several small parties actually took the field; and, being stimulated by the prospect of reward, brought in a considerable number of scalps and prisoners.[1]

[1] MS. *Minutes of Conference with the Six Nations and others, at Johnson Hall*, Sept. 1763. *Letters of Sir William Johnson.*

Upon the persuasion of Sir William Johnson, the tribes of Canada were induced to send a message to the western Indians, exhorting them to bury the hatchet, while the Iroquois despatched an embassy of similar import to the Delawares on the Susquehanna. "Cousins the Delawares," — thus ran the message, — "we have heard that many wild Indians in the West, who have tails like bears, have let fall the chain of friendship, and taken up the hatchet against our brethren the English. We desire you to hold fast the chain, and shut your ears against their words." [1]

In spite of the friendly disposition to which the Iroquois had been brought, the province of New York suffered not a little from the attacks of the hostile tribes who ravaged the borders of Ulster, Orange, and Albany counties, and threatened to destroy the upper settlements of the Mohawk.[2] Sir William Johnson was the object of their especial enmity, and he several times received intimations that he was about to be attacked. He armed his tenantry, surrounded his seat of Johnson Hall with

[1] MS. *Harrisburg Papers.*

[2] Extract from a MS. Letter — *Sir W. Johnson to Sir J. Amherst:* —

"Johnson Hall, July 8th, 1763.

"I Cannot Conclude without Representing to Your Excellency the great Panic and uneasiness into which the Inhabitants of these parts are cast, which I have endeavored to Remove by every Method in my power, to prevent their Abandoning their Settlements from their apprehensions of the Indians: As they in General Confide much in my Residence, they are hitherto Prevented from taking that hasty Measure, but should I be Obliged to retire (which I hope will not be the case), not only my Own Tenants, who are upwards of 120 Families, but all the Rest would Immediately follow the Example, which I am Determined against doing 'till the last Extremity, as I know it would prove of general bad Consequence."

a stockade, and garrisoned it with a party of soldiers, which Sir Jeffrey Amherst had ordered thither for his protection.

About this time, a singular incident occurred near the town of Goshen. Four or five men went out among the hills to shoot partridges, and, chancing to raise a large covey, they all fired their guns at nearly the same moment. The timorous inhabitants, hearing the reports, supposed that they came from an Indian war-party, and instantly fled in dismay, spreading the alarm as they went. The neighboring country was soon in a panic. The farmers cut the harness of their horses, and, leaving their carts and ploughs behind, galloped for their lives. Others, snatching up their children and their most valuable property, made with all speed for New England, not daring to pause until they had crossed the Hudson. For several days the neighborhood was abandoned, five hundred families having left their habitations and fled.[1] Not long after this absurd affair, an event occurred of a widely different character. Allusion has before been made to the carrying-place of Niagara, which formed an essential link in the chain of communication between the province of New York and the interior country. Men and military stores were conveyed in boats up the River Niagara, as far as the present site of Lewiston. Thence a portage road, several miles in length, passed along the banks of the stream, and terminated at Fort Schlosser, above the cataract. This road traversed a region whose sub-

[1] *Penn. Gaz.* No. 1809.

lime features have gained for it a world-wide renown. The River Niagara, a short distance below the cataract, assumes an aspect scarcely less remarkable than that stupendous scene itself. Its channel is formed by a vast ravine, whose sides, now bare and weather-stained, now shaggy with forest-trees, rise in cliffs of appalling height and steepness. Along this chasm pour all the waters of the lakes, heaving their furious surges with the power of an ocean and the rage of a mountain torrent. About three miles below the cataract, the precipices which form the eastern wall of the ravine are broken by an abyss of awful depth and blackness, bearing at the present day the name of the Devil's Hole. In its shallowest part, the precipice sinks sheer down to the depth of eighty feet, where it meets a chaotic mass of rocks, descending with an abrupt declivity to unseen depths below. Within the cold and damp recesses of the gulf, a host of forest-trees have rooted themselves; and, standing on the perilous brink, one may look down upon the mingled foliage of ash, poplar, and maple, while, above them all, the spruce and fir shoot their sharp and rigid spires upward into sunlight. The roar of the convulsed river swells heavily on the ear; and, far below, its headlong waters, careering in foam, may be discerned through the openings of the matted foliage.

On the thirteenth of September, a numerous train of wagons and pack-horses proceeded from the lower landing to Fort Schlosser; and on the following morning set out on their return, guarded by an escort of twenty-four soldiers. They pursued their slow progress until they reached a point where the road passed along the brink of the Devil's Hole. The gulf yawned on their left, while on their right the road was skirted by low densely wooded hills. Suddenly they were greeted by the blaze and clatter of a hundred rifles. Then followed the startled cries of men, and the bounding of maddened horses. At the next instant, a host of Indians broke screeching from the woods, and rifle-butt and tomahawk finished the bloody work. All was over in a moment. Horses leaped the precipice; men were driven shrieking into the abyss; teams and wagons went over, crashing to atoms among the rocks below. Tradition relates that the drummer-boy of the detachment was caught, in his fall, among the branches of a tree, where he hung suspended by his drum-strap. Being but slightly injured, he disengaged himself, and, hiding in the recesses of the gulf, finally escaped. One of the teamsters also, who was wounded at the first fire, contrived to crawl into the woods, where he lay concealed till the Indians had left the place. Besides these two, the only survivor was Stedman, the conductor of the convoy; who, being well mounted, and seeing the whole party forced helpless towards the precipice, wheeled his horse, and resolutely spurred through the crowd of Indians. One of them, it is said, seized his bridle; but he freed himself by a dexterous use of his knife, and plunged into the woods, untouched by the bullets which whistled about his head. Flying at full speed through the forest, he reached Fort Schlosser in safety.

The distant sound of the Indian rifles had been heard by a party of soldiers, who occupied a small fortified camp near the lower landing. Forming in haste, they advanced eagerly to the rescue. In anticipation of this movement, the Indians, who were nearly five hundred in number, had separated into two parties, one of which had stationed itself at the Devil's Hole, to waylay the convoy, while the other formed an ambuscade upon the road, a mile nearer the landing-place. The soldiers, marching precipitately, and huddled in a close body, were suddenly assailed by a volley of rifles, which stretched half their number dead upon the road. Then, rushing from the forest, the Indians cut down the survivors with merciless ferocity. A small remnant only escaped the massacre, and fled to Fort Niagara with the tidings. Major Wilkins, who commanded at this post, lost no time in marching to the spot, with nearly the whole strength of his garrison. Not an Indian was to be found. At the two places of ambuscade, about seventy dead bodies were counted, naked, scalpless, and so horribly mangled that many of them could not be recognized. All the wagons had been broken to pieces, and such of the horses as were not driven over the precipice had been carried off, laden, doubtless, with the plunder. The ambuscade of the Devil's Hole has gained a traditionary immortality, adding fearful interest to a scene whose native horrors need no aid from the imagination.[1]

The Seneca warriors, aided probably by some of the western Indians, were the authors of this un expected attack. Their hostility did not end here. Several weeks afterwards, Major Wilkins, with a force of six hundred regulars, collected with great effort throughout the provinces, was advancing to

[1] MS. Letter — *Amherst to Egremont,* October 13. Two anonymous letters from officers at Fort Niagara, September 16 and 17. *Life of Mary Jemison,* Appendix. MS. *Johnson Papers.*

One of the actors in the tragedy, a Seneca warrior, named Blacksnake, was living a few years since at a very advanced age. He described the scene with great animation to a friend of the writer; and, as he related how the English were forced over the precipice, his small eyes glittered like those of the serpent whose name he bore.

Extract from a Letter — *Niagara,* September 16 (*Penn. Gaz.* No. 1815):

"On the first hearing of the Firing by the Convoy, Capt. Johnston, and three Subalterns, marched with about 80 Men, mostly of Gage's Light Infantry, who were in a little Camp adjacent; they had scarce Time to form when the Indians appeared at the above Pass; our People fired briskly upon them, but was instantly surrounded, and the Captain who commanded mortally wounded the first Fire; the 3 Subalterns also were soon after killed, on which a general Confusion ensued. The Indians rushed in on all Sides and cut about 60 or 70 Men in Pieces, including the Convoy: Ten of our Men are all we can yet learn have made their Escape; they came here through the Woods Yesterday. From many Circumstances, it is believed the Senecas have a chief Hand in this Affair."

Extract from a Letter — *Niagara,* September 17 (*Penn. Gaz.* No. 1815):

"Wednesday the 14th Inst. a large Body of Indians, some say 300 others 4 or 500, came down upon the Carrying-Place, attacked the Waggon Escort, which consisted of a Serjeant and 24 Men. This small Body immediately became a Sacrifice, only two Waggoners escaped. Two Companies of Light Infantry (the General's and La Hunt's), that were encamped at the Lower Landing, hearing the Fire, instantly rushed out to their Relief, headed by Lieuts. George Campbell, and Frazier, Lieutenant Rosco, of the Artillery, and Lieutenant Deaton, of the Provincials; this Party had not marched above a Mile and Half when they were attacked, surrounded, and almost every Man cut to Pieces; the Officers were all killed, it is reported, on the Enemy's first Fire; the Savages rushed down upon them in three Columns."

the relief of Detroit. As the boats were slowly forcing their way upwards against the swift current above the falls of Niagara, they were assailed by a mere handful of Indians, thrown into confusion, and driven back to Fort Schlosser with serious loss. The next attempt was more fortunate, the boats reaching Lake Erie without farther attack; but the inauspicious opening of the expedition was followed by results yet more disastrous. As they approached their destination, a violent storm overtook them in the night. The frail bateaux, tossing upon the merciless waves of Lake Erie, were overset, driven ashore, and many of them dashed to pieces. About seventy men perished, all the ammunition and stores were destroyed, and the shattered flotilla was forced back to Niagara.[1]

[1] MS. *Diary of an officer in Wilkins's Expedition against the Indians at Detroit.*

CHAPTER XXII.

1763.

DESOLATION OF THE FRONTIERS.

The advancing frontiers of American civilization have always nurtured a class of men of striking and peculiar character. The best examples of this character have, perhaps, been found among the settlers of Western Virginia, and the hardy progeny who have sprung from that generous stock. The Virginian frontiersman was, as occasion called, a farmer, a hunter, and a warrior, by turns. The well-beloved rifle was seldom out of his hand; and he never deigned to lay aside the fringed frock, moccasons, and Indian leggins, which formed the appropriate costume of the forest ranger. Concerning the business, pleasures, and refinements of cultivated life, he knew little, and cared nothing; and his manners were usually rough and obtrusive to the last degree. Aloof from mankind, he lived in a world of his own, which, in his view, contained all that was deserving of admiration and praise. He looked upon himself and his compeers as models of prowess and manhood, nay, of all that is elegant and polite; and the forest gallant regarded with peculiar complacency his own half-savage dress, his swaggering gait, and his backwoods jargon. He was wilful, headstrong, and quarrelsome; frank, straightforward, and generous; brave as the bravest, and utterly intolerant of arbitrary control. His self-confidence mounted to audacity. Eminently capable of heroism, both in action and endurance, he viewed every species of effeminacy with supreme contempt; and, accustomed as he was to entire self-reliance, the mutual dependence of conventional life excited his especial scorn. With all his ignorance, he had a mind by nature quick, vigorous, and penetrating; and his mode of life, while it developed the daring energy of his character, wrought some of his faculties to a high degree of acuteness. Many of his traits have been reproduced in his offspring. From him have sprung those hardy men whose struggles and sufferings on the bloody ground of Kentucky will always form a striking page in American history; and that band of adventurers before whose headlong charge, in the valley of Chihuahua, neither breastworks, nor batteries, nor fivefold odds could avail for a moment.

At the period of Pontiac's war, the settlements of Virginia had extended as far as the Alleghanies, and several small towns had already sprung up beyond the Blue Ridge. The population of these beautiful valleys was, for the most part, thin and scattered; and the progress of settlement had been greatly retarded by Indian hostilities, which, during the early years of the French war, had thrown these borders into total confusion. They had contributed, however, to enhance the martial temper of the people, and give a warlike aspect to the whole frontier. At intervals, small stockade forts, containing houses and cabins, had been erected by the joint labor of the inhabitants; and hither, on occasion of alarm, the settlers of the neighborhood congregated for refuge, remaining in tolerable security till the danger was past. Many of the inhabitants were engaged for a great part of the year in hunting; an occupation upon which they entered with the keenest relish.[1] Well versed in woodcraft, unsurpassed as marksmen, and practised in all the wiles of Indian war, they would have formed, under a more stringent organization, the best possible defence against a savage enemy; but each man came and went at his own sovereign will, and discipline and obedience were repugnant to all his habits.

The frontiers of Maryland and Virginia closely resembled each other; but those of Pennsylvania had peculiarities of their own. The population of this province was of a most motley complexion, being made up of members of various nations, and

[1] "I have often seen them get up early in the morning at this season, walk hastily out, and look anxiously to the woods, and snuff the autumnal winds with the highest rapture; then return into the house, and cast a quick and attentive look at the rifle, which was always suspended to a joist by a couple of buck's horns, or little forks. His hunting dog, understanding the intentions of his master, would wag his tail, and, by every blandishment in his power, express his readiness to accompany him to the woods." — Doddridge, *Notes on Western Va. and Pa.*, 124.

For a view of the state of the frontier, see also Kercheval, *Hist. of the Valley of Virginia;* and Smyth, *Travels in America.*

numerous religious sects: English, Irish, German, Swiss, Welsh, and Dutch; Quakers, Presbyterians, Lutherans, Dunkers, Mennonists, and Moravians. Nor is this catalogue by any means complete. The Quakers, to whose peaceful temper the rough frontier offered no attraction, were confined to the eastern parts of the province. Cumberland County, which lies west of the Susquehanna, and may be said to have formed the frontier, was then almost exclusively occupied by the Irish and their descendants; who, however, were neither of the Roman faith nor of Celtic origin, being emigrants from the colony of Scotch which forms a numerous and thrifty population in the north of Ireland. In religious faith, they were stanch and zealous Presbyterians. Long residence in the province had modified their national character, and imparted many of the peculiar traits of the American backwoodsman; yet the nature of their religious tenets produced a certain rigidity of temper and demeanor, from which the Virginian was wholly free. They were, nevertheless, hot-headed and turbulent, often setting law and authority at defiance. The counties east of the Susquehanna supported a mixed population, among which was conspicuous a swarm of German peasants; who had been inundating the country for many years past, and who for the most part were dull and ignorant boors, like some of their descendants. The Swiss and German sectaries called Mennonists, who were numerous in Lancaster County, professed, like the Quakers, principles of non-resistance, and refused to bear arms.[1]

It was upon this mingled population that the storm of Indian war was now descending with appalling fury, — a fury unparalleled through all past and succeeding years. For hundreds of miles from north to south, the country was wasted with fire and steel. It would be a task alike useless and revolting to explore, through all its details, this horrible monotony of blood and havoc.[2] The

[1] For an account of the population of Pennsylvania, see Rupp's two histories of York and Lancaster, and of Lebanon and Berks Counties. See also the *History of Cumberland County*, and the *Penn. Hist. Coll.*

[2] "There are many Letters in Town, in which the Distresses of the Frontier Inhabitants are set forth in a most moving and striking Manner; but as these Letters are pretty much the same, and it would be endless to insert the whole, the following is the Substance of some of them, as near as we can recollect, viz.: —

"That the Indians had set Fire to Houses, Barns, Corn, Hay, and, in short, to every Thing that was combustible, so that the whole Country seemed to be in one general Blaze — That the Miseries and Distresses of the poor People were really shocking to Humanity, and beyond the Power of Language to describe — That Carlisle was become the Barrier, not a single Individual being beyond it — That every Stable and Hovel in the Town was crowded with miserable Refugees, who were reduced to a State of Beggary and Despair; their Houses, Cattle and Harvest destroyed; and from a plentiful, independent People, they were become real Objects of Charity and Commiseration — That it was most dismal to see the Streets filled with People, in whose Countenances might be discovered a Mixture of Grief, Madness and Despair; and to hear, now and then, the Sighs and Groans of Men, the disconsolate Lamentations of Women, and the Screams of Children, who had lost their nearest and dearest Relatives: And that on both Sides of the Susquehannah, for some Miles, the Woods were filled with poor Families, and their Cattle, who make Fires, and live like the Savages." — *Penn. Gaz.* No. 1805.

Extract from a MS. Letter, signature erased — *Staunton*, July 26: —

"Since the reduction of the Regiment, I have lived in the country, which enables me to enform yr Hon^r of some particulars, I think it is a duty incumbent on me to do. I can assert that in eight years' service, I never knew such a general consternation as the late irruption of Indians has occasioned. Should they make a second attempt, I am assured the

country was filled with the wildest dismay. The people of Virginia betook themselves to their forts for refuge. Those of Pennsylvania, ill supplied with such asylums, fled by thousands, and crowded in upon the older settlements. The ranging parties who visited the scene of devastation beheld, among the ruined farms and plantations, sights of unspeakable horror; and discovered, in the depths of the forest, the half-consumed bodies of men and women, still bound fast to the trees, where they had perished in the fiery torture.[1]

Among the numerous war-parties which were now ravaging the borders, none was more destructive than a band, about sixty in number, which

country will be laid desolate, which I attribute to the following reasons The sudden, great, and unexpected slaughter of the people; their being destitute of arms and ammunition; the country Lieut. being at a distance and not exerting himself, his orders are neglected; the most of the militia officers being unfit persons, or unwilling, not to say afraid to meet an Enemy; too busy with their harvest to run a risk in the field. The Inhabitants left without protection, without a person to stead them, have nothing to do but fly, as the Indians are saving and caressing all the negroes they take; should it produce an insurrection, it may be attended with the most serious consequences."

1 "*To Col. Francis Lee, or, in his Absence, to the next Commanding Officer in Loudoun County.*" (*Penn. Gaz.* No. 1805).

"I examined the Express that brought this Letter from Winchester to Loudoun County, and he informed me that he was employed as an Express from Fort Cumberland to Winchester, which Place he left the 4th Instant, and that passing from the Fort to Winchester, he saw lying on the Road a Woman, who had been just scalped, and was then in the Agonies of Death, with her Brains hanging over her Skull; his Companions made a Proposal to knock her on the Head, to put an End to her Agony, but this Express apprehending the Indians were near at Hand, and not thinking it safe to lose any Time, rode off, and left the poor Woman in the Situation they found her."

The circumstances referred to in the text are mentioned in several pamphlets of the day, on the authority of James Smith, a prominent leader of the rangers.

ascended the Kenawha, and pursued its desolating course among the settlements about the sources of that river. They passed valley after valley, sometimes attacking the inhabitants by surprise, and sometimes murdering them under the mask of friendship, until they came to the little settlement of Greenbrier, where nearly a hundred of the people were assembled at the fortified house of Archibald Glendenning. Seeing two or three Indians approach, whom they recognized as former acquaintances, they suffered them to enter without distrust; but the new-comers were soon joined by others, until the entire party were gathered in and around the buildings. Some suspicion was now awakened; and, in order to propitiate the danger ous guests, they were presented with the carcass of an elk lately brought in by the hunters. They immediately cut it up, and began to feast upon it. The backwoodsmen, with their families, were assembled in one large room; and finding themselves mingled among the Indians, and embarrassed by the presence of the women and children, they remained indecisive and irresolute. Meanwhile, an old woman, who sat in a corner of the room, and who had lately received some slight accidental injury, asked one of the warriors if he could cure the wound. He replied that he thought he could, and, to make good his words, killed her with his tomahawk. This was the signal for a scene of general butchery. A few persons made their escape; the rest were killed or captured. Glendenning snatched up one of his children, and rushed from the house, but was shot dead as he leaped the fence. A negro woman gained a place of concealment, whither she was followed by her screaming child; and, fearing lest the cries of the boy should betray her, she turned and killed him at a blow. Among the prisoners was the wife of Glendenning, a woman of a most masculine spirit, who, far from being overpowered by what she had seen, was excited to the extremity of rage, charged her captors with treachery, cowardice, and ingratitude, and assailed them with a tempest of abuse. Neither the tomahawk, which they brandished over her head, nor the scalp of her murdered husband, with which they struck her in the face, could silence the undaunted virago. When the party began their retreat, bearing with them a great quantity of plunder packed on the horses they had stolen, Glendenning's wife, with her infant child, was placed among a long train of captives guarded before and behind by the Indians. As they defiled along a narrow path which led through a gap in the mountains, she handed the child to the woman behind her, and, leaving it to its fate,[1] slipped into the bushes and escaped. Being well acquainted with the woods, she succeeded, before nightfall, in reaching the spot where the ruins of her dwelling had not yet ceased to burn. Here she sought out the body of her husband, and covered it with fence-

[1] Her absence was soon perceived, on which one of the Indians remarked that he would bring the cow back to her calf, and, seizing the child, forced it to scream violently. This proving ineffectual, he dashed out its brains against a tree. This was related by one of the captives who was taken to the Indian villages and afterwards redeemed.

rails, to protect it from the wolves. When her task was complete, and when night closed around her, the bold spirit which had hitherto borne her up suddenly gave way. The recollection of the horrors she had witnessed, the presence of the dead, the darkness, the solitude, and the gloom of the surrounding forest, wrought upon her till her terror rose to ecstasy; and she remained until daybreak, crouched among the bushes, haunted by the threatening apparition of an armed man, who, to her heated imagination, seemed constantly approaching to murder her.[1]

Some time after the butchery at Glendenning's house, an outrage was perpetrated, unmatched, in its fiend-like atrocity, through all the annals of the war. In a solitary place, deep within the settled limits of Pennsylvania, stood a small school-house, one of those rude structures of logs which, to this day, may be seen in some of the remote northern districts of New England. A man chancing to pass by was struck by the unwonted silence; and, pushing open the door, he looked in. In the centre lay the master, scalped and lifeless, with a Bible clasped in his hand; while around the room were strewn the bodies of his pupils, nine in number, miserably mangled, though one of them still retained a spark of life. It was afterwards known that the deed was committed by three or four warriors from a village near the Ohio; and it is but just

[1] Doddridge, *Notes*, 221. MS. *Narrative*, written by Colonel Stuart from the relation of Glendenning's wife.

to observe that, when they returned home, their conduct was disapproved by some of the tribe.[1]

Page after page might be filled with records like these, for the letters and journals of the day are replete with narratives no less tragical. Districts were depopulated, and the progress of the country put back for years. Those small and scattered settlements which formed the feeble van of advancing civilization were involved in general destruction, and the fate of one may stand for the fate of all. In many a woody valley of the Alleghanies, the axe and fire-brand of the settlers had laid a wide space open to the sun. Here and there, about the clearing, stood rough dwellings of logs, surrounded by enclosures and cornfields; while, farther out towards the verge of the woods, the fallen trees still cumbered the ground. From the clay-built chimneys the smoke rose in steady columns against the dark verge of the forest; and the afternoon sun, which brightened the tops of the mountains,

[1] Gordon, *Hist. Penn.* Appendix. Bard, *Narrative.*

"Several small parties went on to different parts of the settlements: it happened that three of them, whom I was well acquainted with, came from the neighborhood of where I was taken from — they were young fellows, perhaps none of them more than twenty years of age, — they came tc a school-house, where they murdered and scalped the master, and all the scholars, except one, who survived after he was scalped, a boy about ten years old, and a full cousin of mine. I saw the Indians when they returned home with the scalps; some of the old Indians were very much displeased at them for killing so many children, especially *Neep-paugh-whese,* or Night Walker, an old chief, or half king, — he ascribed it to cowardice, which was the greatest affront he could offer them." — M'Cullough, *Narrative.*

Extract from an anonymous Letter — *Philadelphia,* August 30, 1764:

"The Lad found alive in the School, and said to be since dead, is, I am informed, yet alive, and in a likely Way to recover."

had already left the valley in shadow. Before many hours elapsed, the night was lighted up with the glare of blazing dwellings, and the forest rang with the shrieks of the murdered inmates.[1]

Among the records of that day's sufferings and disasters, none are more striking than the narratives of those whose lives were spared that they might be borne captive to the Indian villages. Exposed to the extremity of hardship, they were urged forward with the assurance of being tomahawked or burnt in case their strength should fail them. Some made their escape from the clutches of their tormentors; but of these not a few found reason to

[1] Extract from a MS. Letter — *Thomas Cresap to Governor Sharpe:* —

"Old Town, July 15th, 1763.

"May it please yr Excellency:

"I take this opportunity in the height of confusion to acquaint you with our unhappy and most wretched situation at this time, being in hourly expectation of being massacred by our barbarous and inhuman enemy the Indians, we having been three days successively attacked by them, viz. the 13th, 14th, and this instant. . . . I have enclosed a list of the desolate men and women, and children who have fled to my house, which is enclosed by a small stockade for safety, by which you see what a number of poor souls, destitute of every necessary of life, are here penned up, and likely to be butchered without immediate relief and assistance, and can expect none, unless from the province to which they belong. I shall submit to your wiser judgment the best and most effectual method for such relief, and shall conclude with hoping we shall have it in time."

Extract from a Letter — *Frederick Town,* July 19, 1763 (*Penn. Gaz.* No. 1807): —

"Every Day, for some Time past, has offered the melancholy Scene of poor distressed Families driving downwards, through this Town, with their Effects, who have deserted their Plantations, for Fear of falling into the cruel Hands of our Savage Enemies, now daily seen in the Woods. And never was Panic more general or forcible than that of the Back Inhabitants, whose Terrors, at this Time, exceed what followed on the Defeat of General Braddock, when the Frontiers lay open to the Incursions of both French and Indians."

repent their success, lost in a trackless wilderness, and perishing miserably from hunger and exposure. Such attempts could seldom be made in the neighborhood of the settlements. It was only when the party had penetrated deep into the forest that their vigilance began to relax, and their captives were bound and guarded with less rigorous severity. Then, perhaps, when encamped by the side of some mountain brook, and when the warriors lay lost in sleep around their fire, the prisoner would cut or burn asunder the cords that bound his wrists and ankles, and glide stealthily into the woods. With noiseless celerity he pursues his flight over the fallen trunks, through the dense undergrowth, and the thousand pitfalls and impediments of the forest; now striking the rough, hard trunk of a tree, now tripping among the insidious network of vines and brambles. All is darkness around him, and through the black masses of foliage above he can catch but dubious and uncertain glimpses of the dull sky. At length, he can hear the gurgle of a neighboring brook; and, turning towards it, he wades along its pebbly channel, fearing lest the soft mould and rotten wood of the forest might retain traces enough to direct the bloodhound instinct of his pursuers. With the dawn of the misty and cloudy morning, he is still pushing on his way, when his attention is caught by the spectral figure of an ancient birch-tree, which, with its white bark hanging about it in tatters, seems wofully familiar to his eye. Among the neighboring bushes, a blue smoke curls faintly upward; and, to his horror and amazement, he recognizes the very fire from which he had fled a few hours before, and the piles of spruce boughs upon which the warriors had slept. They have gone, however, and are ranging the forest, in keen pursuit of the fugitive, who, in his blind flight amid the darkness, had circled round to the very point whence he set out; a mistake not uncommon with careless or inexperienced travellers in the woods. Almost in despair, he leaves the ill-omened spot, and directs his course eastward with greater care; the bark of the trees, rougher and thicker on the northern side, furnishing a precarious clew for his guidance. Around and above him nothing can be seen but the same endless monotony of brown trunks and green leaves, closing him in with an impervious screen. He reaches the foot of a mountain, and toils upwards against the rugged declivity; but when he stands on the summit, the view is still shut out by impenetrable thickets. High above them all shoots up the tall, gaunt stem of a blasted pine-tree; and, in his eager longing for a view of the surrounding objects, he strains every muscle to ascend. Dark, wild, and lonely, the wilderness stretches around him, half hidden in clouds, half open to the sight, mountain and valley, crag and glistening stream; but nowhere can he discern the trace of human hand or any hope of rest and harborage. Before he can look for relief, league upon league must be passed, without food to sustain or weapon to defend him. He descends the mountain, forcing his way through the undergrowth of laurel-bushes; while the clouds sink lower, and a storm of sleet and rain descends upon the waste. Through such scenes, and under such exposures, he presses onward, sustaining life with the aid of roots and berries or the flesh of reptiles. Perhaps, in the last extremity, some party of Rangers find him, and bring him to a place of refuge; perhaps, by his own efforts, he reaches some frontier post, where rough lodging and rough fare seem to him unheard-of luxury; or perhaps, spent with fatigue and famine, he perishes in despair, a meagre banquet for the wolves.

Within two or three weeks after the war had broken out, the older towns and settlements of Pennsylvania were crowded with refugees from the deserted frontier, reduced, in many cases, to the extremity of destitution.[1] Sermons were preached in their behalf at Philadelphia; the religious societies united for their relief, and liberal contributions were added by individuals. While private aid was thus generously bestowed upon the sufferers, the government showed no such promptness in arrest-

[1] Extract from a Letter — *Winchester, Virginia,* June 22d (*Penn. Gaz.* No. 1801): —

"Last Night I reached this Place. I have been at Fort Cumberland several Days, but the Indians having killed nine People, and burnt several Houses near Fort Bedford, made me think it prudent to remove from those Parts, from which, I suppose, near 500 Families have run away within this week. — I assure you it was a most melancholy Sight, to see such Numbers of poor People, who had abandoned their Settlements in such Consternation and Hurry, that they had hardly any thing with them but their Children. And what is still worse, I dare say there is not Money enough amongst the whole Families to maintain a fifth Part of them till the Fall; and none of the poor Creatures can get a Hovel to shelter them from the Weather, but lie about scattered in the Woods."

ing the public calamity. Early in July, Governor Hamilton had convoked the Assembly, and, representing the distress of the borders, had urged them to take measures of defence.[1] But the provincial government of Pennsylvania was more conducive to prosperity in time of peace than to efficiency in time of war. The Quakers, who held a majority in the Assembly, were from principle and practice the reverse of warlike, and, regarding the Indians with a blind partiality, were reluctant to take measures against them. Proud, and with some reason, of the justice and humanity which had marked their conduct towards the Indian race, they had learned to regard themselves as its advocates and patrons, and their zeal was greatly sharpened by opposition and political prejudice. They now pretended that the accounts from the frontier were grossly exaggerated; and, finding this ground untenable, they alleged, with better show of reason, that the Indians were driven into hostility by the ill-treatment of the proprietaries and their partisans. They recognized, however, the necessity of defensive measures, and accordingly passed a bill for raising and equipping a force of seven hundred men, to be composed of frontier farmers, and to be kept in pay only during the time of harvest. They were not to leave the settled parts of the province to engage in offensive operations of any kind, nor even to perform garrison duty; their sole object being to enable the people to gather in their crops unmolested.

[1] *Votes of Assembly*, V. 259

This force was divided into numerous small detached parties, who were stationed here and there at farm-houses and hamlets on both sides of the Susquehanna, with orders to range the woods daily from post to post, thus forming a feeble chain of defence across the whole frontier. The two companies assigned to Lancaster County were placed under the command of a clergyman, John Elder, pastor of the Presbyterian Church of Paxton; a man of worth and education, and held in great respect upon the borders. He discharged his military functions with address and judgment, drawing a cordon of troops across the front of the county, and preserving the inhabitants free from attack for a considerable time.[1]

The feeble measures adopted by the Pennsylvania Assembly highly excited the wrath of Sir Jeffrey Amherst, and he did not hesitate to give his feelings an emphatic expression. "The conduct of the Pennsylvania legislature," he writes, "is altogether so infatuated and stupidly obstinate, that I want words to express my indignation thereat;

[1] Extract from a MS. Letter — *John Elder to Governor Penn:* —

"Paxton, 4th August, 1763.

"Sir:

"The service your Honr was pleased to appoint me to, I have performed to the best of my power; tho' not with success equal to my desires. However, both companies will, I imagine, be complete in a few days: there are now upwards of 30 men in each, exclusive of officers, who are now and have been employed since their enlistment in such service as is thought most safe and encouraging to the Frontier inhabitants, who are here and everywhere else in the back countries quite sunk and dispirited, so that it's to be feared that on any attack of the enemy, a considerable part of the country will be evacuated, as all seem inclinable to seek safety rather in flight than in opposing the Savage Foe."

but the colony of Virginia, I hope, will have the honor of not only driving the enemy from its own settlements, but that of protecting those of its neighbors who have not spirit to defend themselves."

Virginia did, in truth, exhibit a vigor and activity not unworthy of praise. Unlike Pennsylvania, she had the advantage of an existing militia law; and the House of Burgesses was neither embarrassed by scruples against the shedding of blood, nor by any peculiar tenderness towards the Indian race. The House, however, was not immediately summoned together; and the governor and council, without waiting to consult the Burgesses, called out a thousand of the militia, five hundred of whom were assigned to the command of Colonel Stephen, and an equal number to that of Major Lewis.[1] The presence of these men, most of whom were woodsmen and hunters, restored order and confidence to the distracted borders; and the inhabitants, before pent up in their forts, or flying before the enemy, now took the field, in conjunction with the militia. Many severe actions were fought, but it seldom happened that the Indians could stand their ground against the border riflemen. The latter were uniformly victorious until the end of the summer; when Captains Moffat and Phillips, with sixty men, were lured into an ambuscade, and routed, with the loss of half their number. A few weeks after, they took an ample revenge. Learning by their scouts that more than a hundred

[1] Sparks, *Writings of Washington*, II. 340.

warriors were encamped near Jackson's River, preparing to attack the settlements, they advanced secretly to the spot, and set upon them with such fury that the whole party broke away and fled; leaving weapons, provisions, articles of dress, and implements of magic, in the hands of the victors.

Meanwhile the frontier people of Pennsylvania, finding that they could hope for little aid from government, bestirred themselves with admirable spirit in their own defence. The march of Bouquet, and the victory of Bushy Run, caused a temporary lull in the storm, thus enabling some of the bolder inhabitants, who had fled to Shippensburg, Carlisle, and other places of refuge, to return to their farms, where they determined, if possible, to remain. With this resolution, the people of the Great Cove, and the adjacent valleys beyond Shippensburg, raised among themselves a small body of riflemen, which they placed under the command of James Smith; a man whose resolute and daring character, no less than the native vigor of his intellect, gave him great popularity and influence with the borderers. Having been, for several years, a prisoner among the Indians, he was thoroughly acquainted with their mode of fighting. He trained his men in the Indian tactics and discipline, and directed them to assume the dress of warriors, and paint their faces red and black, so that, in appearance, they were hardly distinguishable from the enemy.[1] Thus equipped, they

[1] *Petition of the Inhabitants of the Great Cove.* Smith, *Narrative.* This is a highly interesting account of the writer's captivity among the Indians

scoured the woods in front of the settlements, had various skirmishes with the enemy, and discharged their difficult task with such success that the inhabitants of the neighborhood were not again driven from their homes.

The attacks on the Pennsylvania frontier were known to proceed, in great measure, from several Indian villages, situated high up the west branch of the Susquehanna, and inhabited by a debauched rabble composed of various tribes, of whom the most conspicuous were Delawares. To root out this nest of banditti would be the most effectual means of protecting the settlements, and a hundred and ten men offered themselves for the enterprise. They marched about the end of August; but on their way along the banks of the Susquehanna, they encountered fifty warriors, advancing against the borders. The Indians had the first fire, and drove in the van-guard of the white men. A hot fight ensued. The warriors fought naked, painted black from head to foot; so that, as they leaped among the trees, they seemed to their opponents like demons of the forest. They were driven back with heavy loss; and the volunteers returned in triumph, though without accomplishing the

and his adventures during several succeeding years. In the war of the Revolution, he acted the part of a zealous patriot. He lived until the year 1812, about which time, the western Indians having broken out into hostility, he gave his country the benefit of his ample experience, by publishing a treatise on the Indian mode of warfare. In Kentucky, where he spent the latter part of his life, he was much respected, and several times elected to the legislature. This narrative may be found in Drake's *Tragedies of the Wilderness*, and in several other similar collections.

object of the expedition; for which, indeed, their numbers were scarcely adequate.[1]

Within a few weeks after their return, Colonel Armstrong, a veteran partisan of the French war, raised three hundred men, the best in Cumberland County, with a view to the effectual destruction of the Susquehanna villages. Leaving their rendezvous at the crossings of the Juniata, about the first of October, they arrived on the sixth at the Great Island, high up the west branch. On or near this island were situated the principal villages of the enemy. But the Indians had vanished, abandoning their houses, their cornfields, their stolen horses and cattle, and the accumulated spoil of the settlements. Leaving a detachment to burn the towns and lay waste the fields, Armstrong, with the main body of his men, followed close on the trail of the fugitives; and, pursuing them through a rugged and difficult country, soon arrived at another village, thirty miles above the former. His scouts informed him that the place was full of Indians; and his men, forming a circle around it, rushed in upon the cabins at a given signal. The Indians were gone, having stolen away in such haste that the hominy and bear's meat, prepared for their meal, were found smoking upon their dishes of birch-bark. Having burned the place to the ground, the party returned to the Great Island; and, rejoining their companions, descended the Susquehanna, reaching Fort Augusta in a wretched condition,

[1] *Penn Gaz.* No. 1811.

fatigued, half famished, and quarrelling among themselves.[1]

Scarcely were they returned, when another expedition was set on foot, in which a portion of them were persuaded to take part. During the previous year, a body of settlers from Connecticut had possessed themselves of the valley of Wyoming, on the east branch of the Susquehanna, in defiance of the government of Pennsylvania, and to the great displeasure of the Indians. The object of the expedition was to remove these settlers, and destroy their corn and provisions, which might otherwise fall into the hands of the enemy. The party, com posed chiefly of volunteers from Lancaster County, set out from Harris's Ferry, under the command of Major Clayton, and reached Wyoming on the seventeenth of October. They were too late. Two days before their arrival, a massacre had been perpetrated, the fitting precursor of that subsequent scene of blood which, embalmed in the poetic romance of Campbell, has made the name of Wyoming a household word. The settlement was a pile of ashes and cinders, and the bodies of its miserable inhabitants offered frightful proof of the cruelties inflicted upon them.[2] A large war-party had fallen upon the place, killed and carried off more than twenty of the people, and driven the rest,

[1] *Penn. Gaz.* Nos. 1816–1818 MS. Letter — *Graydon to Bird,* October 12.

[2] Extract from a MS. Letter — *Paxton,* October 23 : —

"The woman was roasted, and had two hinges in her hands, supposed to be put in red hot, and several of the men had awls thrust into their eyes, and spears, arrows, pitchforks, etc., sticking in their bodies."

men, women, and children, in terror to the mountains. Gaining a point which commanded the whole expanse of the valley below, the fugitives looked back, and saw the smoke rolling up in volumes from their burning homes; while the Indians could be discerned roaming about in quest of plunder, or feasting in groups upon the slaughtered cattle. One of the principal settlers, a man named Hopkins, was separated from the rest, and driven into the woods. Finding himself closely pursued, he crept into the hollow trunk of a fallen tree, while the Indians passed without observing him. They soon returned to the spot, and ranged the surrounding woods like hounds at fault; two of them approaching so near, that, as Hopkins declared, he could hear the bullets rattle in their pouches. The search was unavailing; but the fugitive did not venture from his place of concealment until extreme hunger forced him to return to the ruined settlement in search of food. The Indians had abandoned it some time before; and, having found means to restore his exhausted strength, he directed his course towards the settlements of the Delaware, which he reached after many days of wandering.[1]

Having buried the dead bodies of those who had fallen in the massacre, Clayton and his party returned to the settlements. The Quakers, who seemed resolved that they would neither defend the people of the frontier nor allow them to defend themselves, vehemently inveighed against the several

[1] MS. *Elder Papers.* Chapman, *Hist. Wyoming,* 70. Miner, *Hist Wyoming,* 56.

expeditions up the Susquehanna, and denounced them as seditious and murderous. Urged by their blind prejudice in favor of the Indians, they insisted that the bands of the Upper Susquehanna were friendly to the English ; whereas, with the single exception of a few Moravian converts near Wyoming, who had not been molested by the whites, there could be no rational doubt that these savages nourished a rancorous and malignant hatred against the province. But the Quakers, removed by their situation from all fear of the tomahawk, securely vented their spite against the borderers, and doggedly closed their ears to the truth.[1] Meanwhile, the people of the frontier besieged the Assembly with petitions for relief; but little heed was given to their complaints.

Sir Jeffrey Amherst had recently resigned his office of commander-in-chief; and General Gage, a man of less efficiency than his predecessor, was appointed to succeed him. Immediately before his departure for England, Amherst had reluctantly condescended to ask the several provinces for troops to march against the Indians early in the spring, and the first act of Gage was to confirm this requisition. New York was called upon to furnish fourteen hundred men, and New Jersey six

It has already been stated that the Quakers were confined to the eastern parts of the province. That their security was owing to their local situation, rather than to the kind feeling of the Indians towards them, is shown by the fact, that, of the very few of their number who lived in exposed positions, several were killed. One of them in particular, John Fincher, seeing his house about to be attacked, went out to meet the warriors, declared that he was a Quaker, and begged for mercy. The Indians laughed, and struck him dead with a tomahawk.

hundred.[1] The demand was granted, on condition that the New England provinces should also contribute a just proportion to the general defence. This condition was complied with, and the troops were raised.

Pennsylvania had been required to furnish a thousand men; but in this quarter many difficulties intervened. The Assembly of the province, never prompt to vote supplies for military purposes, was now embroiled in that obstinate quarrel with the proprietors, which for years past had clogged all the wheels of government. The proprietors insisted on certain pretended rights, which the Assembly strenuously opposed; and the governors, who represented the proprietary interest, were bound by imperative instructions to assert these claims, in spite of all opposition. On the present occasion, the chief point of dispute related to the taxation of the proprietary estates; the governor, in conformity with his instructions, demanding that

[1] MS. *Gage Papers.*

Extract from a MS. Letter — *William Smith, Jr., to* —— : —

"New York, 22d Nov. 1763.

"Is not Mr. Amherst the happiest of men to get out of this Trouble so seasonably? At last he was obliged to submit, to give the despised Indians so great a mark of his Consideration, as to confess he could not defend us, and to make a requisition of 1400 Provincials by the Spring — 600 more he demands from New Jersey. Our People refused all but a few for immediate Defence, conceiving that all the Northern Colonies ought to contribute equally, and upon an apprehension that he has called for too insufficient an aid. . . .

"Is not Gage to be pitied? The war will be a tedious one, nor can it be glorious, even tho' attended with Success. Instead of decisive Battles, woodland skirmishes — instead of Colours and Cannon, our Trophies will be stinking scalps. — Heaven preserve you, my Friend, from a War conducted by a spirit of Murder rather than of brave and generous offence."

they should be assessed at a lower rate than other lands of equal value in the province. The Assembly stood their ground, and refused to remove the obnoxious clauses in the supply bill. Message after message passed between the House and the governor; mutual recrimination ensued, and ill blood was engendered. The frontiers might have been left to their misery but for certain events which, during the winter, threw the whole province into disorder, and acted like magic on the minds of the stubborn legislators.

These events may be ascribed, in some degree, to the renewed activity of the enemy; who, during a great part of the autumn, had left the borders in comparative quiet. As the winter closed in, their attacks became more frequent; and districts, repeopled during the interval of calm, were again made desolate. Again the valleys were illumined by the flames of burning houses, and families fled shivering through the biting air of the winter night, while the fires behind them shed a ruddy glow upon the snow-covered mountains. The scouts, who on snowshoes explored the track of the marauders, found the bodies of their victims lying in the forest, stripped naked, and frozen to marble hardness. The distress, wrath, and terror of the borderers produced results sufficiently remarkable to deserve a separate examination.

CHAPTER XXIII.

1763–1764.

THE INDIANS RAISE THE SIEGE OF DETROIT.

I RETURN to the long-forgotten garrison of Detroit, which was left still beleaguered by an increasing multitude of savages, and disheartened by the defeat of Captain Dalzell's detachment. The schooner, so boldly defended by her crew against a force of more than twenty times their number, brought to the fort a much-needed supply of provisions. It was not, however, adequate to the wants of the garrison; and the whole were put upon the shortest possible allowance.

It was now the end of September. The Indians, with unexampled pertinacity, had pressed the siege since the beginning of May; but at length their constancy began to fail. The tidings had reached them that Major Wilkins, with a strong force, was on his way to Detroit. They feared the consequences of an attack, especially as their ammunition was almost exhausted; and, by this time, most of them were inclined to sue for peace, as the easiest mode of gaining safety for themselves, and at the same time lulling the English into security.[1] They

[1] MS. Letter —*Gage to Johnson,* Dec. 25, 1763. *Penn. Gaz.* No. 1827.

thought that by this means they might retire unmolested to their wintering grounds, and renew the war with good hope of success in the spring.

Accordingly, on the twelfth of October, Wapocomoguth, great chief of the Mississaugas, a branch of the Ojibwas, living within the present limits of Upper Canada, came to the fort with a pipe of peace. He began his speech to Major Gladwyn, with the glaring falsehood that he and his people had always been friends of the English. They were now, he added, anxious to conclude a formal treaty of lasting peace and amity. He next declared that he had been sent as deputy by the Pottawattamies, Ojibwas, and Wyandots, who had instructed him to say that they sincerely repented of their bad conduct, asked forgiveness, and humbly begged for peace. Gladwyn perfectly understood the hollowness of these professions, but the circumstances in which he was placed made it expedient to listen to their overtures. His garrison was threatened with famine, and it was impossible to procure provisions while completely surrounded by hostile Indians. He therefore replied, that, though he was not empowered to grant peace, he would still consent to a truce. The Mississauga deputy left the fort with this reply, and Gladwyn immediately took advantage of this lull in the storm to collect provisions among the Canadians; an attempt in which he succeeded so well that the fort was soon furnished with a tolerable supply for the winter

The Ottawas alone, animated by Pontiac, had refused to ask for peace, and still persisted in a course of petty hostilities. They fired at intervals on the English foraging parties, until, on the thirty-first of October, an unexpected blow was given to the hopes of their great chief. French messengers came to Detroit with a letter from M. Neyon, commandant of Fort Chartres, the principal post in the Illinois country. This letter was one of those which, on demand of General Amherst, Neyon, with a very bad grace, had sent to the different Indian tribes. It assured Pontiac that he could expect no assistance from the French; that they and the English were now at peace, and regarded each other as brothers; and that the Indians had better abandon hostilities which could lead to no good result.[1] The emotions of Pontiac at receiving this message may be conceived. His long-cherished hopes of assistance from the French were swept away at once, and he saw himself and his people thrown back upon their own slender resources. His cause was lost. At least, there was no present hope for him but in dissimulation. True to his Indian nature, he would put on a mask of peace, and bide his time. On the day after the arrival of the message from Neyon, Gladwyn wrote as follows to Amherst: "This moment I received a message from Pondiac, telling me that he should send to all the nations concerned in the war to

[1] MS. *Lettre de M. Neyon de la Vallière, à tous les nations de la Belle Rivière et du Lac,* etc

bury the hatchet; and he hopes your Excellency will forget what has passed."[1]

Having soothed the English commander with these hollow overtures, Pontiac withdrew with some of his chiefs to the Maumee, to stir up the Indians in that quarter, and renew the war in the spring.

About the middle of November, not many days after Pontiac's departure, two friendly Wyandot Indians from the ancient settlement at Lorette, near Quebec, crossed the river, and asked admittance into the fort. One of them then unslung his powder-horn, and, taking out a false bottom, disclosed a closely folded letter, which he gave to Major Gladwyn. The letter was from Major Wilkins,

[1] The following is Pontiac's message to Gladwyn, written for him by a Canadian: "Mon Frère, — La Parole que mon Père m'a envoyée, pour faire la paix, je l'ai acceptée, tous nos jeunes gens ont enterré leurs Casse-têtes. Je pense que tu oublieras les mauvaises choses qui sont passées il y a long-temps; de même j'oublierai ce que tu peux m'avoir fait pour ne penser que de bonnes, moi, les Saulteurs (*Ojibwas*), les Hurons, nous devons t'aller parler quand tu nous demanderas. Fais moi la réponse. Je t'envoyes ce conseil (*Q. collier?*) afin que tu le voyes. Si tu es bien comme moi, tu me feras réponse. Je te souhaite le bonjour.

(Signé) "PONDIAC.

Gladwyn's answer is also in French. He says that he will communicate the message to the General; and doubts not that if he, Pontiac, is true to his words, all will be well.

The following is from the letter in which Gladwyn announces the overtures of peace to Amherst (Detroit, Nov. 1): "Yesterday M. Dequindre, a volunteer, arrived with despatches from the Commandant of the Illinois, copies of which I enclose you. . . . The Indians are pressing for peace. . . . I don't imagine there will be any danger of their breaking out again, provided some examples are made of our good subjects, the French, who set them on. . . . They have lost between 80 and 90 of their best warriors; but if y^r Excellency still intends to punish them further for their barbarities, *it may easily be done without any expense to the Crown, by permitting a free sale of rum, which will destroy them more effectually than fire and sword.*"

and contained the disastrous news that the detachment under his command had been overtaken by a storm, that many of the boats had been wrecked, that seventy men had perished, that all the stores and ammunition had been destroyed, and the detachment forced to return to Niagara. This intelligence had an effect upon the garrison which rendered the prospect of the cold and cheerless winter yet more dreary and forlorn.

The summer had long since drawn to a close, and the verdant landscape around Detroit had undergone an ominous transformation. Touched by the first October frosts, the forest glowed like a bed of tulips; and, all along the river bank, the painted foliage, brightened by the autumnal sun, reflected its mingled colors upon the dark water below. The western wind was fraught with life and exhilaration; and in the clear, sharp air, the form of the fish-hawk, sailing over the distant headland, seemed almost within range of the sportsman's gun.

A week or two elapsed, and then succeeded that gentler season which bears among us the name of the Indian summer; when a light haze rests upon the morning landscape, and the many-colored woods seem wrapped in the thin drapery of a veil; when the air is mild and calm as that of early June, and at evening the sun goes down amid a warm, voluptuous beauty, that may well outrival the softest tints of Italy. But through all the still and breathless afternoon the leaves have fallen fast in the woods, like flakes of snow; and every thing betokens that the last melancholy change is at hand. And, in truth, on the morrow the sky is overspread with cold and stormy clouds; and a raw, piercing wind blows angrily from the north-east. The shivering sentinel quickens his step along the rampart, and the half-naked Indian folds his tattered blanket close around him. The shrivelled leaves are blown from the trees, and soon the gusts are whistling and howling amid gray, naked twigs and mossy branches. Here and there, indeed, the beech-tree, as the wind sweeps among its rigid boughs, shakes its pale assemblage of crisp and rustling leaves. The pines and firs, with their rough tops of dark evergreen, bend and moan in the wind; and the crow caws sullenly, as, struggling against the gusts, he flaps his black wings above the denuded woods.

The vicinity of Detroit was now almost abandoned by its besiegers, who had scattered among the forests to seek sustenance through the winter for themselves and their families. Unlike the buffalo-hunting tribes of the western plains, they could not at this season remain together in large bodies. The comparative scarcity of game forced them to separate into small bands, or even into single families. Some steered their canoes far northward, across Lake Huron; while others turned westward, and struck into the great wilderness of Michigan. Wandering among forests, bleak, cheerless, and choked with snow, now famishing with want, now cloyed with repletion, they passed the dull, cold winter. The chase yielded their only subsistence; and the slender lodges, borne on the backs of the squaws, were their only shelter Encamped at intervals by the margin of some frozen lake, surrounded by all that is most stern and dreary in the aspects of nature, they were subjected to every hardship, and endured all with stubborn stoicism. Sometimes, during the frosty night, they were gathered in groups about the flickering lodge-fire, listening to traditions of their forefathers, and wild tales of magic and incantation. Perhaps, before the season was past, some bloody feud broke out among them; perhaps they were assailed by their ancient enemies the Dahcotah; or perhaps some sinister omen or evil dream spread more terror through the camp than the presence of an actual danger would have awakened. With the return of spring, the scattered parties once more united, and moved towards Detroit, to indulge their unforgotten hatred against the English.

Detroit had been the central point of the Indian operations; its capture had been their favorite project; around it they had concentrated their greatest force, and the failure of the attempt proved disastrous to their cause. Upon the Six Nations, more especially, it produced a marked effect. The friendly tribes of this confederacy were confirmed in their friendship, while the hostile Senecas began to lose heart. Availing himself of this state of things, Sir William Johnson, about the middle of the winter, persuaded a number of Six Nation warriors, by dint of gifts and promises, to go out against the enemy. He stimulated their zeal by offering rewards of fifty dollars for the heads of the two principal Delaware chiefs.[1] Two hundred of them, accompanied by a few provincials, left the Oneida country during the month of February, and directed their course southward. They had been out but a few days, when they found an encampment of forty Delawares, commanded by a formidable chief, known as Captain Bull, who, with his warriors, was on his way to attack the settlements. They surrounded the camp undiscovered, during the night, and at dawn of day raised the war-whoop and rushed in. The astonished Delawares had no time to snatch their arms. They were all made prisoners, taken to Albany, and thence sent down to New York, where they were conducted, under a strong guard, to the common jail; the mob crowding round them as they passed, and admiring the sullen ferocity of their countenances. Not long after this success, Captain Montour, with a party of provincials and Six Nation warriors, destroyed the town of Kanestio, and other hostile villages, on the upper branches of the Susquehanna. This blow, inflicted by supposed friends,

[1] Extract from a MS. Letter — *Sir W. Johnson to* —— : —

"For God's Sake exert yourselves like Men whose Honour & every thing dear to them is now at stake; the General has great Expectations from the success of your Party, & indeed so have all People here, & I hope they will not be mistaken, — in Order to Encourage your party I will, out of my own Pocket, pay to any of the Party 50 Dollars for the Head Men of the Delawares there, viz., Onuperaquedra, and 50 Dollars more for the Head of Long Coat, alias ——, in which case they must either bring them alive or their whole Heads; the Money shall be paid to the Man who takes or brings me them, or their Heads, — this I would have you tell to the Head men of the Party, as it will make them more eager."

produced more effect upon the enemy than greater reverses would have done, if encountered at the hands of the English alone.[1]

The calamities which overwhelmed the borders of the middle provinces were not unfelt at the south. It was happy for the people of the Carolinas that the Cherokees, who had broken out against them three years before, had at that time received a chastisement which they could never forget, and from which they had not yet begun to recover. They were thus compelled to remain comparatively quiet; while the ancient feud between them and the northern tribes would, under any circumstances, have prevented their uniting with the latter. The contagion of the war reached them, however, and they perpetrated numerous murders; while the neighboring nation of the Creeks rose in open hostility, and committed formidable ravages. Towards the north, the Indian tribes were compelled, by their position, to remain tranquil, yet they showed many signs of uneasiness; and those of Nova Scotia caused great alarm, by mustering in large bodies in the neighborhood of Halifax. The excitement among them was temporary, and they dispersed without attempting mischief.

[1] MS. *Johnson Papers.*

CHAPTER XXIV.

1763.

THE PAXTON MEN.

Along the thinly settled borders, two thousand persons had been killed, or carried off, and nearly an equal number of families driven from their homes.[1] The frontier people of Pennsylvania, goaded to desperation by long-continued suffering, were divided between rage against the Indians, and resentment against the Quakers, who had yielded them cold sympathy and inefficient aid. The horror and fear, grief and fury, with which these men looked upon the mangled remains of friends and relatives, set language at defiance. They were of a rude and hardy stamp, hunters, scouts, rangers, Indian traders, and backwoods farmers, who had grown up with arms in their hands, and been

[1] Extract from a MS. Letter — *George Croghan to the Board of Trade:*

"They can with great ease enter our colonies, and cut off our frontier settlements, and thereby lay waste a large tract of country, which indeed they have effected in the space of four months, in Virginia, Maryland, Pennsylvania, and the Jerseys, on whose frontiers they have killed and captivated not less than two thousand of his Majesty's subjects, and drove some thousands to beggary and the greatest distress, besides burning to the ground nine forts or blockhouses in the country, and killing a number of his Majesty's troops and traders."

trained under all the influences of the warlike frontier. They fiercely complained that they were interposed as a barrier between the rest of the province and a ferocious enemy; and that they were sacrificed to the safety of men who looked with indifference on their miseries, and lost no opportunity to extenuate and smooth away the cruelties of their destroyers.[1] They declared that the Quakers would go farther to befriend a murdering Delaware than to succor a fellow-countryman; that they loved red blood better than white, and a pagan better than a Presbyterian. The Pennsylvania borderers were, as we have seen, chiefly the descendants of Presbyterian emigrants from the north of Ireland. They had inherited some portion of their forefathers' sectarian zeal, which, while it did nothing to soften the barbarity of their manners, served to inflame their animosity against the Quakers, and added bitterness to their just complaints. It supplied, moreover, a convenient sanction for the indulgence of their hatred and vengeance; for, in the general turmoil of their passions, fanaticism too was awakened, and they interpreted the command that Joshua should destroy

[1] Extract from the *Declaration of Lazarus Stewart:*—

"Did we not brave the summer's heat and the winter's cold, and the savage tomahawk, while the Inhabitants of Philadelphia, Philadelphia county, Bucks, and Chester, 'ate, drank, and were merry'?

"If a white man kill an Indian, it is a murder far exceeding any crime upon record; he must not be tried in the county where he lives, or where the offence was committed, but in Philadelphia, that he may be tried, convicted, sentenced and hung without delay. If an Indian kill a white man, it was the act of an ignorant Heathen, perhaps in liquor; alas, poor innocent! he is sent to the *friendly Indians* that he may be made a *Christian.*"

the heathen[1] into an injunction that they should exterminate the Indians.

The prevailing excitement was not confined to the vulgar. Even the clergy and the chief magistrates shared it; and while they lamented the excess of the popular resentment, they maintained that the general complaints were founded in justice. Viewing all the circumstances, it is not greatly to be wondered at that some of the more violent class were inflamed to the commission of atrocities which bear no very favorable comparison with those of the Indians themselves.

It is not easy for those living in the tranquillity of polished life fully to conceive the depth and force of that unquenchable, indiscriminate hate, which Indian outrages can awaken in those who have suffered them. The chronicles of the American borders are filled with the deeds of men, who, having lost all by the merciless tomahawk, have lived for vengeance alone; and such men will never cease to exist so long as a hostile tribe remains within striking distance of an American settlement.[2] Never was this hatred more deep or more general than on the Pennsylvania frontier at this period; and never, perhaps, did so many collateral causes unite to inflame it to madness. It was not long in finding a vent.

Near the Susquehanna, and at no great distance

1 "And when the Lord thy God shall deliver them before thee, thou shalt smite them, and utterly destroy them; thou shalt make no covenant with them, nor show mercy unto them." — *Deuteronomy*, vii. 2.

2 So promising a theme has not escaped the notice of novelists, and it has been adopted by Dr. Bird in his spirited story of *Nick of the Woods*.

from the town of Lancaster, was a spot known as the Manor of Conestoga; where a small band of Indians, speaking the Iroquois tongue, had been seated since the first settlement of the province. William Penn had visited and made a treaty with them, which had been confirmed by several succeeding governors, so that the band had always remained on terms of friendship with the English. Yet, like other Indian communities in the neighborhood of the whites, they had dwindled in numbers and prosperity, until they were reduced to twenty persons; who inhabited a cluster of squalid cabins, and lived by beggary and the sale of brooms, baskets, and wooden ladles, made by the women. The men spent a small part of their time in hunting, and lounged away the rest in idleness. In the immediate neighborhood, they were commonly regarded as harmless vagabonds; but elsewhere a more unfavorable opinion was entertained, and they were looked upon as secretly abetting the enemy, acting as spies, giving shelter to scalping-parties, and even aiding them in their depredations. That these suspicions were not wholly unfounded is shown by a conclusive mass of evidence, though it is probable that the treachery was confined to one or two individuals.[1] The exasperated frontiersmen were not in a mood to discriminate, and the innocent were destined to share the fate of the guilty.[2]

[1] See Appendix, E.

[2] For an account of the Conestoga Indians, see *Penn. Hist. Coll.* 390. It is extremely probable, as shown by Mr. Shea, that they were the remnant of the formidable people called Andastes, who spoke a dialect of the Iroquois, but were deadly enemies of the Iroquois proper, or Five Nations, by whom they were nearly destroyed about the year 1672.

On the east bank of the Susquehanna, at some distance above Conestoga, stood the little town of Paxton; a place which, since the French war, had occupied a position of extreme exposure. In the year 1755 the Indians had burned it to the ground, killing many of the inhabitants, and reducing the rest to poverty. It had since been rebuilt; but its tenants were the relatives of those who had perished, and the bitterness of the recollection was enhanced by the sense of their own more recent sufferings. Mention has before been made of John Elder, the Presbyterian minister of this place; a man whose worth, good sense, and superior education gave him the character of counsellor and director throughout the neighborhood, and caused him to be known and esteemed even in Philadelphia. His position was a peculiar one. From the rough pulpit of his little church, he had often preached to an assembly of armed men, while scouts and sentinels were stationed without, to give warning of the enemy's approach.[1] The men of Paxton, under the auspices of their pastor, formed themselves into a body of rangers, who became noted for their zeal and efficiency in defending the borders. One of their principal leaders was Matthew Smith, a man who had influence and popu-

[1] On one occasion, a body of Indians approached Paxton on Sunday, and sent forward one of their number, whom the English supposed to be a friend, to reconnoitre. The spy reported that every man in the church, including the preacher, had a rifle at his side; upon which the enemy withdrew, and satisfied themselves with burning a few houses in the neighborhood. The papers of Mr. Elder were submitted to the writer's examination by his son, an aged and esteemed citizen of Harrisburg.

larity among his associates, and was not without pretensions to education; while he shared a full proportion of the general hatred against Indians, and suspicion against the band of Conestoga.

Towards the middle of December, a scout came to the house of Smith, and reported that an Indian, known to have committed depredations in the neighborhood, had been traced to Conestoga. Smith's resolution was taken at once. He called five of his companions; and, having armed and mounted, they set out for the Indian settlement. They reached it early in the night; and Smith, leaving his horse in charge of the others, crawled forward, rifle in hand, to reconnoitre; when he saw, or fancied he saw, a number of armed warriors in the cabins. Upon this discovery he withdrew, and rejoined his associates. Believing themselves too weak for an attack, the party returned to Paxton. Their blood was up, and they determined to extirpate the Conestogas. Messengers went abroad through the neighborhood; and, on the following day, about fifty armed and mounted men, chiefly from the towns of Paxton and Donegal, assembled at the place agreed upon. Led by Matthew Smith, they took the road to Conestoga, where they arrived a little before daybreak, on the morning of the fourteenth. As they drew near, they discerned the light of a fire in one of the cabins, gleaming across the snow. Leaving their horses in the forest, they separated into small parties, and advanced on several sides at once. Though they moved with some caution, the sound of their footsteps or their voices caught the ear of an Indian; and they saw him issue from one of the cabins, and walk forward in the direction of the noise. He came so near that one of the men fancied that he recognized him. "He is the one that killed my mother," he exclaimed with an oath; and, firing his rifle, brought the Indian down. With a general shout the furious ruffians burst into the cabins, and shot, stabbed, and hacked to death all whom they found there. It happened that only six Indians were in the place; the rest, in accordance with their vagrant habits, being scattered about the neighborhood. Thus baulked of their complete vengeance, the murderers seized upon what little booty they could find, set the cabins on fire, and departed at dawn of day.[1]

The morning was cold and murky. Snow was falling, and already lay deep upon the ground; and, as they urged their horses through the drifts, they were met by one Thomas Wright, who, struck by their appearance, stopped to converse with them. They freely told him what they had done; and, on his expressing surprise and horror, one of them

[1] The above account of the massacre is chiefly drawn from the narrative of Matthew Smith himself. This singular paper was published by Mr. Redmond Conyngham, of Lancaster, in the *Lancaster Intelligencer* for 1843. Mr. Conyngham states that he procured it from the son of Smith, for whose information it had been written. The account is partially confirmed by incidental allusions, in a letter written by another of the Paxton men, and also published by Mr. Conyngham. This gentleman employed himself with most unwearied diligence in collecting a voluminous mass of documents, comprising, perhaps, every thing that could contribute to extenuate the conduct of the Paxton men; and to these papers, as published from time to time in the above-mentioned newspaper, reference will often be made

demanded if he believed in the Bible, and if the Scripture did not command that the heathen should be destroyed.

They soon after separated, dispersing among the farm-houses, to procure food for themselves and their horses. Several rode to the house of Robert Barber, a prominent settler in the neighborhood; who, seeing the strangers stamping their feet and shaking the snow from their blanket coats, invited them to enter, and offered them refreshment. Having remained for a short time seated before his fire, they remounted and rode off through the snow-storm. A boy of the family, who had gone to look at the horses of the visitors, came in and declared that he had seen a tomahawk, covered with blood, hanging from each man's saddle; and that a small gun, belonging to one of the Indian children, had been leaning against the fence.[1] Barber at once guessed the truth, and, with several of his neighbors, proceeded to the Indian settlement, where they found the solid log cabins still on fire. They buried the remains of the victims, which Barber compared in appearance to half-burnt logs. While they were thus engaged, the sheriff of Lancaster, with a party of men, arrived on the spot; and the first care of the officer was to send through the neighborhood to collect the Indians, fourteen in number, who had escaped the massacre. This was soon accomplished. The un happy survivors, learning the fate of their friends and relatives, were in great terror for their own

[1] *Haz. Pa. Reg.* IX. 114.

lives, and earnestly begged protection. They were conducted to Lancaster, where, amid great excitement, they were lodged in the county jail, a strong stone building, which it was thought would afford the surest refuge.

An express was despatched to Philadelphia with news of the massacre; on hearing which, the governor issued a proclamation denouncing the act, and offering a reward for the discovery of the perpetrators. Undaunted by this measure, and enraged that any of their victims should have escaped, the Paxton men determined to continue the work they had begun. In this resolution they were confirmed by the prevailing impression, that an Indian known to have murdered the relatives of one of their number was among those who had received the protection of the magistrates at Lancaster. They sent forward a spy to gain intelligence, and, on his return, once more met at their rendezvous. On this occasion, their nominal leader was Lazarus Stewart, who was esteemed upon the borders as a brave and active young man; and who, there is strong reason to believe, entertained no worse design than that of seizing the obnoxious Indian, carrying him to Carlisle, and there putting him to death, in case he should be identified as the murderer.[1] Most of his followers, however, hardened amidst war and bloodshed, were bent on indiscriminate slaughter; a purpose which they concealed from their more moderate associates.

Early on the twenty-seventh of December, the

[1] Papers published by Mr Conyngham in the *Lancaster Intelligencer*

party, about fifty in number, left Paxton on their desperate errand. Elder had used all his influence to divert them from their design; and now, seeing them depart, he mounted his horse, overtook them, and addressed them with the most earnest remonstrance. Finding his words unheeded, he drew up his horse across the narrow road in front, and charged them, on his authority as their pastor, to return. Upon this, Matthew Smith rode forward, and, pointing his rifle at the breast of Elder's horse, threatened to fire unless he drew him aside, and gave room to pass. The clergyman was forced to comply, and the party proceeded.[1]

At about three o'clock in the afternoon, the rioters, armed with rifle, knife, and tomahawk, rode at a gallop into Lancaster; turned their horses into the yard of the public house, ran to the jail, burst open the door, and rushed tumultuously in. The fourteen Indians were in a small yard adjacent to the building, surrounded by high stone walls. Hearing the shouts of the mob, and startled by the apparition of armed men in the doorway, two or three of them snatched up billets of wood in self defence. Whatever may have been the purpose of the Paxton men, this show of resistance banished every thought of forbearance; and the foremost, rushing forward, fired their rifles among the crowd of Indians. In a moment more, the yard was filled with ruffians, shouting, cursing, and firing upon the cowering wretches; holding

[1] This anecdote was told to the writer by the son of Mr. Elder, and is also related by Mr. Conyngham.

the muzzles of their pieces, in some instances, so near their victims' heads that the brains were scattered by the explosion. The work was soon finished. The bodies of men, women, and children, mangled with outrageous brutality, lay scattered about the yard; and the murderers were gone.[1]

When the first alarm was given, the magistrates were in the church, attending the Christmas service, which had been postponed on the twenty-fifth. The door was flung open, and the voice of a man half breathless was heard in broken exclamations, "Murder — the jail — the Paxton Boys — the Indians."

The assembly broke up in disorder, and Shippen, the principal magistrate, hastened towards the scene of riot; but, before he could reach it, all

[1] *Deposition of Felix Donolly,* keeper of Lancaster jail. *Declaration of Lazarus Stewart,* published by Mr. Conyngham. Rupp, *Hist. of York and Lancaster Counties,* 358. Heckewelder, *Narrative of Moravian Missions,* 79. See Appendix, E.

Soon after the massacre, Franklin published an account of it at Philadelphia, which, being intended to strengthen the hands of government by exciting a popular sentiment against the rioters, is more rhetorical than accurate. The following is his account of the consummation of the act: —

"When the poor wretches saw they had no protection nigh, nor could possibly escape, they divided into their little families, the children clinging to the parents; they fell on their knees, protested their innocence, declared their love to the English, and that, in their whole lives, they had never done them injury; and in this posture they all received the hatchet!"

This is a pure embellishment of the fancy. The only persons present were the jailer and the rioters themselves, who unite in testifying that the Indians died with the stoicism which their race usually exhibit under such circumstances; and indeed, so sudden was the act, that there was no time for enacting the scene described by Franklin

was finished, and the murderers were galloping in a body from the town.[1] The sheriff and the coroner had mingled among the rioters, aiding and abetting them, as their enemies affirm, but, according to their own statement, vainly risking their lives to restore order.[2] A company of Highland soldiers, on their way from Fort Pitt to Philadelphia, were encamped near the town. Their commander, Captain Robertson, afterwards declared that he put himself in the way of the magistrates, expecting that they would call upon him to aid the civil authority; while, on the contrary, several of the inhabitants testify, that, when they urged him to interfere, he replied with an oath that his men had suffered enough from Indians already, and should not stir hand or foot to save them. Be this as it may, it seems certain that neither soldiers nor

[1] Extract from a MS. Letter — *Edward Shippen to Governor Penn:* —

"Lancaster, 27th Dec., 1763, P.M.

"Honoured Sir: —

"I am to acquaint your Honour that between two and three of the Clock this afternoon, upwards of a hundred armed men from the Westward rode very fast into Town, turned their Horses into Mr. Slough's (an Innkeeper's) yard, and proceeded with the greatest precipitation to the Work-House, stove open the door and killed all the Indians, and then took to their Horses and rode off: all their business was done, & they were returning to their Horses before I could get half way down to the Work-House. The Sheriff and Coroner however, and several others, got down as soon as the rioters, but could not prevail with them to stop their hands. Some people say they heard them declare they would proceed to the Province Island, & destroy the Indians there."

[2] Extract from a MS. Letter — *John Hay, the sheriff, to Governor Penn:* —

"They in a body left the town without offering any insults to the Inhabitants, & without putting it in the power of any one to take or molest any of them without danger of life to the person attempting it; of which both myself and the Coroner, by our opposition, were in great danger."

magistrates, with their best exertions, could have availed to prevent the massacre; for so well was the plan concerted, that, within ten or twelve minutes after the alarm, the Indians were dead, and the murderers mounted to depart.

The people crowded into the jail-yard to gaze upon the miserable spectacle; and, when their curiosity was sated, the bodies were gathered together, and buried not far from the town, where they reposed three quarters of a century; until, at length, the bones were disinterred in preparing the foundation for a railroad.

The tidings of this massacre threw the country into a ferment. Various opinions were expressed; but, in the border counties, even the most sober and moderate regarded it, not as a wilful and deliberate crime, but as the mistaken act of rash men, fevered to desperation by wrongs and sufferings.[1]

When the news reached Philadelphia, a clamorous outcry rose from the Quakers, who could find no

[1] Extract from a Letter — *Rev. Mr. Elder to Colonel Burd:* —

"Paxton, 1764.

"Lazarus Stewart is still threatened by the Philadelphia party; he and his friends talk of leaving — if they do, the province will lose some of their truest friends, and that by the faults of others, not their own; for if any cruelty was practised on the Indians at Conestogue or at Lancaster, it was not by his, or their hands. There is a great reason to believe that much injustice has been done to all concerned. In the contrariness of accounts, we must infer that much rests for support on the imagination or interest of the witness. The characters of Stewart and his friends were well established. Ruffians nor brutal they were not; humane, liberal and moral, nay, religious. It is evidently not the wish of the party to give Stewart a fair hearing. All he desires, is to be put on trial, at Lancaster, near the scenes of the horrible butcheries, committed by the Indians at Tulpehocken, &c., when he can have the testimony of the Scouts or Rangers, men whose services can never be sufficiently rewarded."

words to express their horror and detestation. They assailed not the rioters only, but the whole Presbyterian sect, with a tempest of abuse, not the less virulent for being vented in the name of philanthropy and religion. The governor again issued a proclamation, offering rewards for the detection and arrest of the murderers; but the latter, far from shrinking into concealment, proclaimed their deed in the face of day, boasted the achievement, and defended it by reason and Scripture. So great was the excitement in the frontier counties, and so deep the sympathy with the rioters, that to arrest them would have required the employment of a strong military force, an experiment far too dangerous to be tried. Nothing of the kind was attempted until nearly eight years afterwards, when Lazarus Stewart was apprehended on the charge of murdering the Indians of Conestoga. Learning that his trial was to take place, not in the county where the act was committed, but in Philadelphia, and thence judging that his condemnation was certain, he broke jail and escaped. Having written a declaration to justify his conduct, he called his old associates around him, set the provincial government of Pennsylvania at defiance, and withdrew to Wyoming with his band. Here he joined the settlers recently arrived from Connecticut, and thenceforth played a conspicuous part in the eventful history of that remarkable spot.[1]

[1] Papers published by Mr. Conyngham.

Extract from the *Declaration of Lazarus Stewart*: —

"What I have done was done for the security of hundreds of settlers on the frontiers. The blood of a thousand of my fellow-creatures called

After the massacre at Conestoga, the excitement in the frontier counties, far from subsiding, increased in violence daily; and various circumstances conspired to inflame it. The principal of these was the course pursued by the provincial government towards the Christian Indians attached to the Moravian missions. Many years had elapsed since the Moravians began the task of converting the Indians of Pennsylvania, and their steadfast energy and regulated zeal had been crowned with success. Several thriving settlements of their converts had sprung up in the valley of the Lehigh, when the opening of the French war, in 1755, involved them in unlooked-for calamities. These unhappy neutrals, between the French and Indians on the one side, and the English on the other, excited the enmity of both; and while from the west they were threatened by the hatchets of their own countrymen, they were menaced on the east by the no less formidable vengeance of the white settlers, who, in their distress and terror, never doubted that the Moravian converts were in league with the enemy. The popular rage against them at length grew so furious, that their destruction was resolved upon. The settlers assembled and advanced against the Moravian community of Gnadenhutten; but the French and Indians gained

for vengeance. As a Ranger, I sought the post of danger, and now you ask my life. Let me be tried where prejudice has not prejudged my case. Let my brave Rangers, who have stemmed the blast nobly, and never flinched; let them have an equitable trial; they were my friends in the hour of danger — to desert them now were cowardice! What remains is to leave our cause with our God, and our guns."

the first blow, and, descending upon the doomed settlement, utterly destroyed it. This disaster, deplorable as it was in itself, proved the safety of the other Moravian settlements, by making it fully apparent that their inhabitants were not in league with the enemy. They were suffered to remain unmolested for several years; but with the murders that ushered in Pontiac's war, in 1763, the former suspicion revived, and the expediency of destroying the Moravian Indians was openly debated. Towards the end of the summer, several outrages were committed upon the settlers in the neighborhood, and the Moravian Indians were loudly accused of taking part in them. These charges were never fully confuted; and, taking into view the harsh treatment which the converts had always experienced from the whites, it is highly probable that some of them were disposed to sympathize with their heathen countrymen, who are known to have courted their alliance. The Moravians had, however, excited in their converts a high degree of religious enthusiasm; which, directed as it was by the teachings of the missionaries, went farther than any thing else could have done to soften their national prejudices, and wean them from their warlike habits.

About three months before the massacre at Conestoga, a party of drunken Rangers, fired by the general resentment against the Moravian Indians murdered several of them, both men and women whom they found sleeping in a barn. Not long after, the same party of Rangers were, in their turn, surprised and killed, some peaceful settlers of the neighborhood sharing their fate. This act was at once ascribed, justly or unjustly, to the vengeance of the converted Indians, relatives of the murdered; and the frontier people, who, like the Paxton men, were chiefly Scotch and Irish Presbyterians, resolved that the objects of their suspicion should live no longer. At this time, the Moravian converts consisted of two communities, those of Nain and Wecquetank, near the Lehigh; and to these may be added a third, at Wyalusing, near Wyoming. The latter, from its distant situation, was, for the present, safe; but the two former were in imminent peril, and the inhabitants, in mortal terror for their lives, stood day and night on the watch.

At length, about the tenth of October, a gang of armed men approached Wecquetank, and encamped in the woods, at no great distance. They intended to make their attack under favor of the darkness; but before evening a storm, which to the missionaries seemed providential, descended with such violence, that the fires of the hostile camp were extinguished in a moment, the ammunition of the men wet, and the plan defeated.[1]

After so narrow an escape, it was apparent that flight was the only resource. The terrified congregation of Wecquetank broke up on the following day; and, under the charge of their missionary, Bernard Grube, removed to the Moravian town of

[1] Loskiel, *Hist. Moravian Missions*, Part II. 211.

Nazareth, where it was hoped they might remain in safety.[1]

In the mean time, the charges against the Mora vian converts had been laid before the provincial Assembly; and, to secure the safety of the frontier people, it was judged expedient to disarm the sus pected Indians, and remove them to a part of the province where it would be beyond their power to do mischief.[2] The motion was passed in the Assembly with little dissent; the Quakers supporting it from regard to the safety of the Indians, and their opponents from regard to the safety of the whites. The order for removal reached its destination on the sixth of November; and the Indians, reluctantly yielding up their arms, prepared for departure. When a sermon had been preached before the united congregations, and a hymn sung in which all took part, the unfortunate exiles set out on their forlorn pilgrimage; the aged, the young, the sick, and the blind, borne in wagons, while the rest journeyed on foot.[3] Their total number, including the band from Wyalusing, which joined them after they reached Philadelphia, was about a hundred and forty. At every village and hamlet which they passed on their way, they were greeted with threats and curses; nor did the temper of the people improve as they advanced, for, when they came to Germantown, the mob could scarcely be restrained from attacking them. On reaching Phil-

[1] MS. Letter — *Bernard Grube to Governor Hamilton*, Oct. 13.

[2] *Votes of Assembly*, V. 284.

[3] Loskiel, *Hist. Moravian Missions*, Part II. 214. Heckewelder, *Narrative of Missions*, 75.

adelphia, they were conducted, amidst the yells and hootings of the rabble, to the barracks, which had been intended to receive them; but the soldiers, who outdid the mob in their hatred of Indians, refused to admit them, and set the orders of the governor at defiance. From ten o'clock in the morning until three in the afternoon, the persecuted exiles remained drawn up in the square before the barracks, surrounded by a multitude who never ceased to abuse and threaten them; but wherever the broad hat of a Quaker was seen in the crowd, there they felt the assurance of a friend,—a friend, who, both out of love for them, and aversion to their enemies, would spare no efforts in their behalf. The soldiers continued refractory, and the Indians were at length ordered to proceed. As they moved down the street, shrinking together in their terror, the mob about them grew so angry and clamorous, that to their missionaries they seemed like a flock of sheep in the midst of howling wolves.[1] A body-guard of Quakers gathered around, protecting them from the crowd, and speaking words of sympathy and encouragement. Thus they proceeded to Province Island, below the city, where they were lodged in waste buildings, prepared in haste for their reception, and where the Quakers still attended them, with every office of kindness and friendship.

[1] Loskiel, Part II. 216.

CHAPTER XXV.

1764.

THE RIOTERS MARCH ON PHILADELPHIA.

THE Conestoga murders did not take place until some weeks after the removal of the Moravian converts to Philadelphia; and the rioters, as they rode, flushed with success, out of Lancaster, after the achievement of their exploit, were heard to boast that they would soon visit the city and finish their work, by killing the Indians whom it had taken under its protection. It was soon but too apparent that this design was seriously entertained by the people of the frontier. They had tasted blood, and they craved more. It seemed to them intolerable, that, while their sufferings were unheeded, and their wounded and destitute friends uncared for, they should be taxed to support those whom they regarded as authors of their calamities, or, in their own angry words, "to maintain them through the winter, that they may scalp and butcher us in the spring."[1] In their blind rage, they would

[1] *Remonstrance* of the Frontier People to the Governor and Assembly. See *Votes of Assembly*, V. 313.

The "Declaration," which accompanied the "Remonstrance," contains the following passage: "To protect and maintain these Indians at the public expense, while our suffering brethren on the frontiers are almost

not see that the Moravian Indians had been removed to Philadelphia, in part, at least, with a view to the safety of the borders. To their enmity against Indians was added a resentment, scarcely less vehement, against the Quakers, whose sectarian principles they hated and despised. They complained, too, of political grievances, alleging that the five frontier counties were inadequately represented in the Assembly, and that from thence arose the undue influence of the Quakers in the councils of the province.

The excited people soon began to assemble at taverns and other places of resort, recounting their grievances, real or imaginary; relating frightful stories of Indian atrocities, and launching fierce invectives against the Quakers.[1] Political agita-

destitute of the necessaries of life, and are neglected by the public, is sufficient to make us mad with rage, and tempt us to do what nothing but the most violent necessity can vindicate."

See Appendix, E.

[1] MS. *Elder Papers*.

The following verses are extracted from a poem, published at Philadelphia, by a partisan of the Paxton men, entitled,

"THE CLOVEN FOOT DISCOVERED.

"Go on, good Christians, never spare
To give your Indians Clothes to wear;
Send 'em good Beef, and Pork, and Bread,
Guns, Powder, Flints, and Store of Lead,
To Shoot your Neighbours through the Head;
Devoutly then, make Affirmation,
You're Friends to George and British Nation;
Encourage ev'ry friendly Savage,
To murder, burn, destroy, and ravage;
Fathers and Mothers here maintain,
Whose Sons add Numbers to the slain;
Of Scotch and Irish let them kill
As many Thousands as they will,
That you may lord it o'er the Land,
And have the whole and sole command."

tors harangued them on their violated rights; self-constituted preachers urged the duty of destroying the heathen, forgetting that the Moravian Indians were Christians, and their exasperated hearers were soon ripe for any rash attempt. They resolved to assemble and march in arms to Philadelphia. On a former occasion, they had sent thither a wagon laden with the mangled corpses of their friends and relatives, who had fallen by Indian butchery; but the hideous spectacle had failed of the intended effect, and the Assembly had still turned a deaf ear to their entreaties for more effective aid.[1] Appeals to sympathy had been thrown away, and they now resolved to try the efficacy of their rifles.

They mustered under their popular leaders, prominent among whom was Matthew Smith, who had led the murderers at Conestoga; and, towards the end of January, took the road to Philadelphia, in force variously estimated at from five hundred to fifteen hundred men. Their avowed purpose was to kill the Moravian Indians; but what vague designs they may have entertained to change the government, and eject the Quakers from a share in it, must remain a matter of uncertainty. Feeble

[1] This incident occurred during the French war, and is thus described by a Quaker eye-witness: "Some of the dead bodies were brought to Philadelphia in a wagon, in the time of the General Meeting of Friends there in December, with intent to animate the people to unite in preparations for war on the Indians. They were carried along the streets — many people following cursing the Indians, and also the Quakers, because they would not join in war for their destruction. The sight of the dead bodies, and the outcry of the people, were very afflicting and shocking." — Watson, *Annals of Phil.* 449 (Phil. 1830).

as they were in numbers, their enterprise was not so hopeless as might at first appear, for they counted on aid from the mob of the city, while a numerous party, comprising the members of the Presbyterian sect, were expected to give them secret support, or at least to stand neutral in the quarrel. The Quakers, who were their most determined enemies, could not take arms against them without glaring violation of the principles which they had so often and loudly professed; and even should they thus fly in the face of conscience, the warlike borderers would stand in little fear of such unpractised warriors. They pursued their march in high confidence, applauded by the inhabitants, and hourly increasing in numbers.

Startling rumors of the danger soon reached Philadelphia, spreading alarm among the citizens. The Quakers, especially, had reason to fear, both for themselves and for the Indians, of whom it was their pride to be esteemed the champions. These pacific sectaries found themselves in a new and embarrassing position, for hitherto they had been able to assert their principles at no great risk to person or property. The appalling tempest, which, during the French war, had desolated the rest of the province, had been unfelt near Philadelphia; and while the inhabitants to the westward had been slaughtered by hundreds, scarcely a Quaker had been hurt. Under these circumstances, the aversion of the sect to warlike measures had been a fruitful source of difficulty. It is true that, on several occasions, they had voted supplies for the public defence; but unwilling to place on record such a testimony of inconsistency, they had granted the money, not for the avowed purpose of raising and arming soldiers, but under the title of a gift to the crown.[1] They were now to be deprived of even this poor subterfuge, and subjected to the dilemma of suffering their friends to be slain and themselves to be plundered, or openly appealing to arms.

Their embarrassment was increased by the exaggerated ideas which prevailed among the ignorant and timorous respecting the size and strength of the borderers, their ferocity of temper, and their wonderful skill as marksmen. Quiet citizens, whose knowledge was confined to the narrow limits of their firesides and shops, listened horror-stricken to these reports; the prevalence of which is somewhat surprising, when it is considered that, at the present day, the district whence the dreaded rioters came may be reached from Philadelphia within a few hours.

Tidings of the massacre in Lancaster jail had arrived at Philadelphia on the twenty-ninth of December, and with them came the rumor that numerous armed mobs were already on their march to the city. Terror and confusion were universal; and, as the place was defenceless, no other expedient suggested itself than the pitiful one of removing the objects of popular resentment beyond reach of danger. Boats were sent to Province Island, and the Indians ordered to embark and proceed with

[1] See Gordon, *Hist. Penn.* Chaps. XII.–XVIII.

all haste down the river; but, the rumor proving groundless, a messenger was despatched to recall the fugitives.[1] The assurance that, for a time at least, the city was safe, restored some measure of tranquillity; but, as intelligence of an alarming kind came in daily from the country, Governor Penn sent to General Gage an earnest request for a detachment of regulars to repel the rioters;[2] and, in the interval, means to avert the threatened danger were eagerly sought. A proposal was laid before the Assembly to embark the Indians and send them to England;[3] but the scheme was judged inexpedient, and another, of equal weakness, adopted in its place. It was determined to send the refugees to New York, and place them under the protection of the Indian Superintendent, Sir William Johnson; a plan as hastily executed as timidly conceived.[4] At midnight, on the fourth of January, no measures having been taken to gain the consent of either the government of New York or Johnson himself, the Indians were ordered to leave the island and proceed to the city; where they arrived a little before daybreak, passing in

[1] Loskiel, Part II. 218.

[2] MS. Letter — *Penn to Gage*, Dec. 31.

[3] *Votes of Assembly*, V. 293.

[4] Extract from a MS. Letter — *Governor Penn to Governor Colden:* —

"Philadelphia, 5th January, 1764.

"Satisfied of the advantages arising from this measure, I have sent them thro' Jersey and your Government to Sir W. Johnson, & desire you will favour them with your protection and countenance, & give them the proper passes for their journey to Sir William's Seat.

"I have recommended it, in the most pressing terms, to the Assembly, to form a Bill that shall enable me to apprehend these seditious and barbarous Murderers, & to quell the like insurrections for the future."

mournful procession, thinly clad and shivering with cold, through the silent streets. The Moravian Brethren supplied them with food; and Fox, the commissary, with great humanity, distributed blankets among them. Before they could resume their progress, the city was astir; and as they passed the suburbs, they were pelted and hooted at by the mob. Captain Robertson's Highlanders, who had just arrived from Lancaster, were ordered to escort them. These soldiers, who had their own reasons for hating Indians, treated them at first with no less insolence and rudeness than the populace; but at length, overcome by the meekness and patience of the sufferers, they changed their conduct, and assumed a tone of sympathy and kindness.[1]

Thus escorted, the refugees pursued their dreary progress through the country, greeted on all sides by the threats and curses of the people. When they reached Trenton, they were received by Apty, the commissary at that place, under whose charge they continued their journey towards Amboy, where several small vessels had been provided to carry them to New York. Arriving at Amboy, however, Apty, to his great surprise, received a letter from Governor Colden of New York, forbidding him to bring the Indians within the limits of that province. A second letter, from General Gage to Captain Robertson, conveyed orders to prevent their advance; and a third, to the owners of the vessels, threatened heavy penalties if they should

[1] Loskiel, Part II. 220. Heckewelder, *Narrative*, 81.

bring the Indians to the city.[1] The charges of treachery against the Moravian Indians, the burden their presence would occasion, and the danger of popular disturbance, were the chief causes which induced the government of New York to adopt this course; a course that might have been foreseen from the beginning.[2]

Thus disappointed in their hopes of escape, the hapless Indians remained several days lodged in the barracks at Amboy, where they passed much of their time in religious services. A message, however, soon came from the Governor of New Jersey, requiring them to leave that province; and they were compelled reluctantly to retrace their steps to Philadelphia. A detachment of a hundred and seventy soldiers had arrived, sent by General Gage in compliance with the request of Governor Penn; and under the protection of these troops, the exiles began their backward journey. On the twenty-fourth of January, they reached Philadelphia, where they were lodged at the bar-

[1] Extract from a MS. Letter — *Thomas Apty to Governor Penn:* —
"Sir: —

"Agreeable to your Honour's orders, I passed on through the Province of New Jersey, in order to take the Indians under my care into New York; but no sooner was I ready to move from Amboy with the Indians under my care, than I was greatly surpriz'd & embarrass'd with express orders from the Governor of New York sent to Amboy, strictly forbidding the bringing of these poor Indians into his Province, & charging all his ferrymen not to let them pass."

[2] *Letters to Governor Penn from General Gage, Governor Franklin of New Jersey, and Governor Colden of New York.* See *Votes of Assembly,* V. 300–302. The plan was afterwards revived, at the height of the alarm caused by the march of the rioters on Philadelphia; and Penn wrote to Johnson, on the seventh of February, begging an asylum for the Indians. Johnson acquiesced, and wrote to Lieutenant-Governor Colden in favor of the measure, which, however, was never carried into effect. Johnson's letters express much sympathy with the sufferers.

racks within the city; the soldiers, forgetful of former prejudice, no longer refusing them entrance.

The return of the Indians, banishing the hope of repose with which the citizens had flattered themselves, and the tidings of danger coming in quick succession from the country, made it apparent that no time must be lost; and the Assembly, laying aside their scruples, unanimously passed a bill providing means for the public defence. The pacific city displayed a scene of unwonted bustle. All who held property, or regarded the public order, might, it should seem, have felt a deep interest in the issue; yet a numerous and highly respectable class stood idle spectators, or showed at best but a lukewarm zeal. These were the Presbyterians, who had naturally felt a strong sympathy with their suffering brethren of the frontier. To this they added a deep bitterness against the Quakers, greatly increased by a charge, most uncharitably brought by the latter against the whole Presbyterian sect, of conniving at and abetting the murders at Conestoga and Lancaster. They regarded the Paxton men as victims of Quaker neglect and injustice, and showed a strong disposition to palliate, or excuse altogether, the violence of which they had been guilty. Many of them, indeed, were secretly inclined to favor the designs of the advancing rioters; hoping that by their means the public grievances would be redressed, the Quaker faction put down, and the social and political balance of the state restored.[1]

[1] For indications of the state of feeling among the Presbyterians, see the numerous partisan pamphlets of the day. See also Appendix, E.

Whatever may have been the sentiments of the Presbyterians and of the city mob, the rest of the inhabitants bestirred themselves for defence with all the alacrity of fright. The Quakers were especially conspicuous for their zeal. Nothing more was heard of the duty of non-resistance. The city was ransacked for arms, and the Assembly passed a vote, extending the English riot act to the province, the Quaker members heartily concurring in the measure. Franklin, whose energy and practical talents made his services invaluable, was the moving spirit of the day; and under his auspices the citizens were formed into military companies, six of which were of infantry, one of artillery, and two of horse. Besides this force, several thousands of the inhabitants, including many Quakers, held themselves ready to appear in arms at a moment's notice.[1]

These preparations were yet incomplete, when, on the fourth of February, couriers came in with the announcement that the Paxton men, horse and foot, were already within a short distance of the city. Proclamation was made through the streets, and the people were called to arms. A mob of citizen soldiers repaired in great excitement to the barracks, where the Indians were lodged, under protection of the handful of regulars. Here the crowd remained all night, drenched with the rain, and in a dismal condition.[2]

On the following day, Sunday, a barricade was

[1] Gordon, *Hist. Penn.* 406. *Penn. Gaz.* No. 1833.
[2] *Haz. Pa. Reg.* XII. 10.

thrown up across the great square enclosed by the barracks; and eight cannon, to which four more were afterwards added, were planted to sweep the adjacent streets. These pieces were discharged, to convey to the rioters an idea of the reception prepared for them; but whatever effect the explosion may have produced on the ears for which it was intended, the new and appalling sounds struck the Indians in the barracks with speechless terror.[1] While the city assumed this martial attitude, its rulers thought proper to adopt the safer though less glorious course of conciliation; and a deputation of clergymen was sent out to meet the rioters, and pacify them by reason and Scripture. Towards night, as all remained quiet and nothing was heard from the enemy, the turmoil began to subside, the citizen soldiers dispersed, the regulars withdrew into quarters, and the city recovered something of the ordinary repose of a Sabbath evening.

Through the early part of the night, the quiet was undisturbed; but at about two o'clock in the morning, the clang of bells and the rolling of drums startled the people from their slumbers, and countless voices from the street echoed the alarm. Immediately, in obedience to the previous day's orders, lighted candles were placed in every window, till the streets seemed illuminated for a festival. The citizen soldiers, with more zeal than order, mustered under their officers. The governor, dreading an irruption of the mob, repaired to the house of Franklin; and the city was filled with the jangling

[1] Loskiel, Part II. 223.

of bells, and the no less vehement clamor of tongues. A great multitude gathered before the barracks, where it was supposed the attack would be made; and among them was seen many a Quaker, with musket in hand. Some of the more consistent of the sect, unwilling to take arms with their less scrupulous brethren, went into the barracks to console and reassure the Indians; who, however, showed much more composure than their comforters, and sat waiting the result with invincible calmness. Several hours of suspense and excitement passed, when it was recollected, that, though the other ferries of the Schuylkill had been secured, a crossing place, known as the Swedes' Ford, had been left open; and a party at once set out to correct this unlucky oversight.[1] Scarcely were they gone, when a cry rose among the crowd before the barracks, and a general exclamation was heard that the Paxton Boys were coming. In fact, a band of horsemen was seen advancing up Second Street. The people crowded to get out of the way; the troops fell into such order as they could; a cannon was pointed full at the horsemen, and the gunner was about to apply the match, when a man ran out from the crowd, and covered the touchhole with his hat. The cry of a false alarm was heard, and it was soon apparent to all that the supposed Paxton Boys were a troop of German butchers and carters, who had come to aid in defence of the city, and had nearly paid dear for their patriotic zeal.[2]

[1] *Historical Account of the Late Disturbances*, 4.

[2] *Haz. Pa. Reg.* XII. 11. *Memoirs of a Life passed chiefly in Pennsyl*

The tumult of this alarm was hardly over, when a fresh commotion was raised by the return of the men who had gone to secure the Swedes' Ford, and who reported that they had been too late; that the rioters had crossed the river, and were already at Germantown. Those who had crossed proved to be the van of the Paxton men, two hundred in number, and commanded by Matthew Smith; who, learning what welcome was prepared for them, thought it prudent to remain quietly at Germantown, instead of marching forward to certain destruction. In the afternoon, many of the inhabitants gathered courage, and went out to visit them. They found nothing very extraordinary in the aspect of the rioters, who, in the words of a writer of the day, were "a set of fellows in blanket coats and moccasons, like our Indian traders or back country wagoners, all armed with rifles and tomahawks, and some with pistols stuck in their belts."[1] They received their visitors with a courtesy which might doubtless be ascribed, in great measure, to their knowledge of the warlike prepa-

vania, 39. Heckewelder, *Narrative,* 85. Loskiel, Part II. 223. Sparks, *Writings of Franklin,* VII. 293.

The best remaining account of these riots will be found under the first authority cited above. It consists of a long letter, written in a very animated strain, by a Quaker to his friend, containing a detailed account of what passed in the city from the first alarm of the rioters to the conclusion of the affair. The writer, though a Quaker, is free from the prejudices of his sect, nor does he hesitate to notice the inconsistency of his brethren appearing in arms. See Appendix, E.

The scene before the barracks, and the narrow escape of the German butchers, was made the subject of several poems and farces, written by members of the Presbyterian faction, to turn their opponents into ridicule; for which, indeed, the subject offered tempting facilities.

[1] *Haz. Pa. Reg.* XII. 11.

rations within the city; and the report made by the adventurers, on their return, greatly tended to allay the general excitement.

The alarm, however, was again raised on the following day; and the cry to arms once more resounded through the city of peace. The citizen soldiers mustered with exemplary despatch; but their ardor was quenched by a storm of rain, which drove them all under shelter. A neighboring Quaker meeting-house happened to be open, and a company of the volunteers betook themselves in haste to this convenient asylum. Forthwith, the place was bristling with bayonets; and the walls, which had listened so often to angry denunciations against war, now echoed the clang of weapons, — an unspeakable scandal to the elders of the sect, and an occasion of pitiless satire to the Presbyterians.[1]

This alarm proving groundless, like all the others, the governor and council proceeded to the execution of a design which they had formed the day before. They had resolved, in pursuance of their timid policy, to open negotiations with the rioters, and persuade them, if possible, to depart peacefully. Many of the citizens protested against the plan, and the soldiers volunteered to attack the Paxton men; but none were so vehement as the Quakers, who held that fire and steel were the only welcome that should be accorded to such violators of the public peace, and audacious blasphemers of the

[1] *Haz Pa. Reg.* XII. 12.

society of Friends.[1] The plan was nevertheless sustained; and Franklin, with three other citizens of character and influence, set out for Germantown. The rioters received them with marks of respect; and, after a long conference, the leaders of the mob were so far wrought upon as to give over their hostile designs, the futility of which was now sufficiently apparent.[2] An assurance was given, on the part of the government, that their complaints should have a hearing; and safety was guarantied to those of their number who should enter the city as their representatives and advocates. For this purpose, Matthew Smith and James Gibson were appointed by the general voice; and two papers, a "Declaration" and a "Remonstrance," were drawn up, addressed to the governor and Assembly. With this assurance that their cause should be represented, the rioters signified their willingness to return home, glad to escape so easily from an affair which had begun to threaten worse consequences.

Towards evening, the commissioners, returning to the city, reported the success of their negotiations. Upon this, the citizen soldiers were convened in front of the court house, and addressed by a member of the council. He thanked them for their zeal, and assured them there was no farther occasion for their services; since the Paxton men,

[1] This statement is made in "The Quaker Unmasked," and other Presbyterian pamphlets of the day; and the Quakers, in their elaborate replies to these publications, do not attempt to deny the fact.

[2] Sparks, *Writings of Franklin*, VII. 293.

though falsely represented as enemies of govern ment, were in fact its friends, entertaining no worse design than that of gaining relief to their sufferings, without injury to the city or its inhabitants. The people, ill satisfied with what they heard, returned in no placid temper to their homes.[1] On the morrow, the good effect of the treaty was apparent in a general reopening of schools, shops, and warehouses, and a return to the usual activity of business, which had been wholly suspended for some days. The security was not of long duration. Before noon, an uproar more tumultuous than ever, a cry to arms, and a general exclamation that the Paxton Boys had broken the treaty and were enter ing the town, startled the indignant citizens. The streets were filled in an instant with a rabble of armed merchants and shopmen, who for once were fully bent on slaughter, and resolved to put an end to the long-protracted evil. Quiet was again restored; when it was found that the alarm was caused by about thirty of the frontiersmen, who, with singular audacity, were riding into the city on a visit of curiosity. As their deportment was inoffensive, it was thought unwise to molest them. Several of these visitors had openly boasted of the part they had taken in the Conestoga murders, and a large reward had been offered for their apprehension; yet such was the state of factions in the city, and such the dread of the frontiersmen, that no man dared lay hand on the criminals. The

[1] Barton, *Memoirs of Rittenhouse*, 148. Rupp, *Hist. York and Lancaster Counties*, 362.

party proceeded to the barracks, where they requested to see the Indians, declaring that they could point out several who had been in the battle against Colonel Bouquet, or engaged in other acts of open hostility. The request was granted, but no discovery made. Upon this, it was rumored abroad that the Quakers had removed the guilty individuals to screen them from just punishment; an accusation which, for a time, excited much ill blood between the rival factions.

The thirty frontiersmen withdrew from the city, and soon followed the example of their companions, who had begun to move homeward, leaving their leaders, Smith and Gibson, to adjust their differences with the government. Their departure gave great relief to the people of the neighborhood, to whom they had, at times, conducted themselves after a fashion somewhat uncivil and barbarous; uttering hideous outcries, in imitation of the war whoop; knocking down peaceable citizens, and pretending to scalp them; thrusting their guns in at windows, and committing unheard-of ravages among hen-roosts and hog-pens.[1]

Though the city was now safe from all external danger, contentions sprang up within its precincts, which, though by no means as perilous, were not less clamorous and angry than those menaced from an irruption of the rioters.[2] The rival factions

[1] David Rittenhouse, in one of his letters, speaks with great horror of the enormities committed by the Paxton Boys, and enumerates various particulars of their conduct. See Barton, *Mem. of Rittenhouse*, 148.

[2] "Whether the Paxton men were 'more sinned against than sinning, was a question which was agitated with so much ardor and acrimony,

turned savagely upon each other; while the more philosophic citizens stood laughing by, and ridiculed them both. The Presbyterians grew furious the Quakers dogged and spiteful. Pamphlets, farces, dialogues, and poems came forth in quick succession. These sometimes exhibited a few traces of wit, and even of reasoning; but abuse was the favorite weapon, and it is difficult to say which of the combatants handled it with the greater freedom and dexterity.[1] The Quakers

that even the schoolboys became warmly engaged in the contest. For my own part, though of the religious sect which had been long warring with the Quakers, I was entirely on the side of humanity and public duty, (or in this do I beg the question?) and perfectly recollect my indignation at the sentiments of one of the ushers who was on the opposite side. His name was Davis, and he was really a kind, good-natured man; yet from the dominion of his religious or political prejudices, he had been led to apologize for, if not to approve of an outrage, which was a disgrace to a civilized people. He had been among the riflemen on their coming into the city, and, talking with them upon the subject of the Lancaster massacre, and particularly of the killing of Will Sock, the most distinguished of the victims, related with an air of approbation, this rodomontade of the real or pretended murderer. 'I,' said he, 'am the man who killed Will Sock — this is the arm that stabbed him to the heart, and I glory in it.'" — *Memoir of a Life chiefly passed in Pennsylvania*, 40.

[1] "Persons who were intimate now scarcely speak; or, if they happen to meet and converse, presently get to quarrelling. In short, harmony and love seem to be banished from amongst us."

The above is an extract from the letter so often referred to. A fragment of the "Paxtoniad," one of the poems of the day, is given in the Appendix. Few of the party pamphlets are worth quoting, but the titles of some of them will give an idea of their character: The Quaker Unmasked — A Looking-Glass for Presbyterians — A Battle of Squirt — Plain Truth — Plain Truth found to be Plain Falsehood — The Author of Plain Truth Stripped Stark Naked — Clothes for a Stark Naked Author — The Squabble, a Pastoral Eclogue — etc., etc.

The pamphlet called Plain Truth drew down the especial indignation of the Quakers, and the following extract from one of their replies to it may serve as a fair specimen of the temper of the combatants: "But how came you to give your piece the Title of Plain Truth; if you had called it downright Lies, it would have agreed better with the Contents

accused the Presbyterians of conniving at the act of murderers, of perverting Scripture for their defence, and of aiding the rioters with counsel and money in their audacious attempt against the public peace. The Presbyterians, on their part, with about equal justice, charged the Quakers with leaguing themselves with the common enemy and exciting them to war. They held up to scorn those accommodating principles which denied the aid of arms to suffering fellow-countrymen, but justified their use at the first call of self-interest. The Quaker warrior, in his sober garb of ostentatious simplicity, his prim person adorned with military trappings, and his hands grasping a musket which threatened more peril to himself than to his enemy, was a subject of ridicule too tempting to be overlooked.

While this paper warfare was raging in the city, the representatives of the frontiersmen, Smith and Gibson, had laid before the Assembly the memorial, entitled the Remonstrance; and to this a second paper, styled a Declaration, was soon afterwards added.[1] Various grievances were specified, for which redress was demanded. It was urged that

the Title therefore is a deception, and the contents manifestly false: in short, I have carefully examined it, and find in it no less than 17 Positive Lies, and 10 false Insinuations contained in 15 pages, Monstrous, and from what has been said must conclude that when you wrote it, Truth was banished entirely from you, and that you wrote it with a truly Pious Lying P———n Spirit, which appears in almost every Line!"

The peaceful society of Friends found among its ranks more than one such champion as the ingenious writer of the above. Two collections of these pamphlets have been examined, one preserved in the City Library of Philadelphia, and the other in that of the New York Historical Society

[1] See Appendix, E.

those counties where the Quaker interest prevailed sent to the Assembly more than their due share of representatives. The memorialists bitterly complained of a law, then before the Assembly, by which those charged with murdering Indians were to be brought to trial, not in the district where the act was committed, but in one of the three eastern counties. They represented the Moravian converts as enemies in disguise, and denounced the policy which yielded them protection and support while the sick and wounded of the frontiers were cruelly abandoned to their misery. They begged that a suitable reward might be offered for scalps, since the want of such encouragement had "damped the spirits of many brave men." Angry invectives against the Quakers succeeded. To the "villany, infatuation, and influence of a certain faction, that have got the political reins in their hands, and tamely tyrannize over the other good subjects of the province," were to be ascribed, urged the memorialists, the intolerable evils which afflicted the people. The Quakers, they insisted, had held private treaties with the Indians, encouraged them to hostile acts, and excused their cruelties on the charitable plea that this was their method of making war.

The memorials were laid before a committee, who recommended that a public conference should be held with Smith and Gibson, to consider the grounds of complaint. To this the governor, in view of the illegal position assumed by the frontiersmen, would not give his consent; an assertion of dignity that would have done him more honor had he made it when the rioters were in arms before the city, at which time he had shown an abundant alacrity to negotiate. It was intimated to Smith and Gibson that they might leave Philadelphia; and the Assembly soon after became involved in its inevitable quarrels with the governor, relative to the granting of supplies for the service of the ensuing campaign. The supply bill passed, as mentioned in a former chapter; and the consequent military preparations, together with a threatened renewal of the war on the part of the enemy, engrossed the minds of the frontier people, and caused the excitements of the winter to be forgotten. No action on the two memorials was ever taken by the Assembly; and the memorable Paxton riots had no other definite result than that of exposing the weakness and distraction of the provincial government, and demonstrating the folly and absurdity of all principles of non-resistance.

Yet to the student of human nature these events supply abundant food for reflection. In the frontiersman, goaded by the madness of his misery to deeds akin to those by which he suffered, and half believing that, in the perpetration of these atrocities, he was but the minister of divine vengeance; in the Quaker, absorbed by one narrow philanthropy, and closing his ears to the outcries of his wretched countrymen; in the Presbyterian, urged by party spirit and sectarian zeal to countenance the crimes of rioters and murderers, — in each and all of these lies an embodied satire, which may find its application in every age of the world, and every condition of society.

The Moravian Indians, the occasion — and, at least, as regards most of them, the innocent occasion — of the tumult, remained for a full year in the barracks of Philadelphia. There they endured frightful sufferings from the small-pox, which destroyed more than a third of their number. After the conclusion of peace, they were permitted to depart; and, having thanked the governor for his protection and care, they withdrew to the banks of the Susquehanna, where, under the direction of the missionaries, they once more formed a prosperous settlement.[1]

[1] Loskiel, Part II. 231.

CHAPTER XXVI.

1764.

BRADSTREET'S ARMY ON THE LAKES.

The campaign of 1763, a year of disaster to the English colonies, was throughout of a defensive nature, and no important blow had been struck against the enemy. With the opening of the fol lowing spring, preparations were made to renew the war on a more decisive plan. Before the com mencement of hostilities, Sir William Johnson and his deputy, George Croghan, severally addressed to the lords of trade memorials, setting forth the character, temper, and resources of the Indian tribes, and suggesting the course of conduct which they judged it expedient to pursue. They represented that, before the conquest of Canada, all the tribes, jeal ous of French encroachment, had looked to the English to befriend and protect them; but that now one general feeling of distrust and hatred filled them all. They added that the neglect and injustice of the British government, the outrages of ruffian borderers and debauched traders, and the insolence of English soldiers, had aggravated this feeling, and given double effect to the restless machinations of the defeated French; who, to revenge themselves on their conquerors, were constantly stirring up the Indians to war. A race so brave and tenacious of liberty, so wild and erratic in their habits, dwelling in a country so savage and inaccessible, could not be exterminated or reduced to subjection without an immoderate expenditure of men, money, and time. The true policy of the British government was therefore to conciliate; to soothe their jealous pride, galled by injuries and insults; to gratify them by presents, and treat them with a respect and attention to which their haughty spirit would not fail to respond. We ought, they said, to make the Indians our friends; and, by a just, consistent, and straightforward course, seek to gain their esteem, and wean them from their partiality to the French. To remove the constant irritation which arose from the intrusion of the white inhabitants on their territory, Croghan urged the expediency of purchasing a large tract of land to the westward of the English settlements; thus confining the tribes to remoter hunting-grounds. For a moderate sum the Indians would part with as much land as might be required. A little more, laid out in annual presents, would keep them in good temper; and by judicious management all hostile collision might be prevented, till, by the extension of the settlements, it should become expedient to make yet another purchase.[1]

This plan was afterwards carried into execution by the British government. Founded as it is upon

[1] MS. *Johnson Papers.*

the supposition that the Indian tribes must gradually dwindle and waste away, it might well have awakened the utmost fears of that unhappy people. Yet none but an enthusiast or fanatic could condemn it as iniquitous. To reclaim the Indians from their savage state has again and again been attempted, and each attempt has failed. Their intractable, unchanging character leaves no other alternative than their gradual extinction, or the abandonment of the western world to eternal barbarism; and of this and other similar plans, whether the offspring of British or American legislation, it may alike be said that sentimental philanthropy will find it easier to cavil at than to amend them.

Now, turning from the Indians, let us observe the temper of those whose present business it was to cudgel them into good behavior; that is to say, the British officers, of high and low degree. They seem to have been in a mood of universal discontent, not in the least surprising when one considers that they were forced to wage, with crippled resources, an arduous, profitless, and inglorious war; while perverse and jealous legislatures added gall to their bitterness, and taxed their patience to its utmost endurance. The impossible requirements of the commander-in-chief were sometimes joined to their other vexations. Sir Jeffrey Amherst, who had, as we have seen, but a slight opinion of Indians, and possibly of everybody else except a British nobleman and a British soldier, expected much of his officers; and was at times unreasonable in his anticipations of a prompt "vengeance on the barbarians." Thus he had no sooner heard of the loss of Michillimackinac, Miami, and other western outposts, than he sent orders to Gladwyn to re-establish them at once. Gladwyn, who had scarcely force enough to maintain himself at Detroit, thereupon writes to his friend Bouquet: "The last I received from the General is of the second July, in which I am ordered to establish the outposts immediately. At the time I received these orders, I knew it was impossible to comply with any part of them: the event shows I was right. I am heartily wearied of my command, and I have signified the same to Colonel Amherst (Sir Jeffrey's adjutant). I hope I shall be relieved soon; if not, I intend to quit the service, for I would not choose to be any longer exposed to the villany and treachery of the settle ment and Indians."

Two or three weeks before the above was written George Croghan, Sir William Johnson's deputy, who had long lived on the frontier, and was as well versed in Indian affairs as the commander-in-chief was ignorant of them, wrote to Colonel Bouquet: — "Seven tribes in Canada have offered their services to act with the King's troops; but the General seems determined to neither accept of Indians' services, nor provincials'. . . . I have resigned out of the service, and will start for England about the beginning of December. Sir Jeffrey Amherst would not give his consent; so I made my resignation in writing, and gave my reasons for so doing. Had I continued, I could be of no more service than I have been these eighteen months past; which was none at all, as no regard was had to any intelligence I sent, no more than to my opinion." Croghan, who could not be spared, was induced, on Gage's accession to the command, to withdraw his resignation and retain his post.

Next, we have a series of complaints from Lieutenant Blane of Fort Ligonier; who congratulates Bouquet on his recent victory at Bushy Run, and adds: "I have now to beg that I may not be left any longer in this forlorn way, for I can assure you the fatigue I have gone through begins to get the better of me. I must therefore beg that you will appoint me, by the return of the convoy, a proper garrison. . . . My present situation is fifty times worse than ever." And again, on the seventeenth of September: "I must beg leave to recommend to your particular attention the sick soldiers here; as there is neither surgeon nor medicine, it would really be charity to order them up. I must also beg leave to ask what you intend to do with the poor starved militia, who have neither shirts, shoes, nor any thing else. I am sorry you can do nothing for the poor inhabitants. . . . I really get heartily tired of this post." He endured it some two months more, and then breaks out again on the twenty-fourth of November: "I intend going home by the first opportunity, being pretty much tired of a service that's so little worth any man's time; and the more so, as I cannot but think I have been particularly unlucky in it."

Now follow the letters, written in French, of the gallant Swiss, Captain Ecuyer, always lively and entertaining even in his discontent. He writes to Bouquet from Bedford, on the thirteenth of November. Like other officers on the frontier, he complains of the settlers, who, notwithstanding their fear of the enemy, always did their best to shelter deserters; and he gives a list of eighteen soldiers who had deserted within five days:[1] "I have been twenty-two years in service, and I never in my life saw any thing equal to it, — a gang of mutineers, bandits, cut-throats, especially the grenadiers. I have been obliged, after all the patience imaginable, to have two of them whipped on the spot, without court-martial. One wanted to kill the sergeant and the other wanted to kill me. . . . For God's sake, let me go and raise cabbages. You can do it if you will, and I shall thank you eternally for it. Don't refuse, I beg you. Besides, my health is not very good; and I don't know if I can go up again to Fort Pitt with this convoy."

Bouquet himself was no better satisfied than his correspondents. On the twentieth of June, 1764, he wrote to Gage, Amherst's successor: "I flatter myself that you will do me the favor to have me

[1] "The three companies of Royal Americans were reduced when I met them at Lancaster to 55 men, having lost 38 by desertion in my short absence. I look upon Sir Jeffrey Amherst's Orders forbidding me to continue to discharge as usual the men whose time of service was expired, and keeping us for seven years in the Woods, — as the occasion of this unprecedented desertion. The encouragement given everywhere in this Country to deserters, screened almost by every person, must in time ruin the Army, unless the Laws against Harbourers are better enforced by the American (*provincial*) government." — *Bouquet to Gage*, 20 June, 1764

relieved from this command, the burden and fatigues of which I begin to feel my strength very unequal to."

Gage knew better than to relieve him, and Bouquet was forced to resign himself to another year of bush-fighting. The plan of the summer's campaign had been settled; and he was to be the most important, if not the most conspicuous, actor in it. It had been resolved to march two armies from different points into the heart of the Indian country. The first, under Bouquet, was to advance from Fort Pitt into the midst of the Delaware and Shawanoe settlements of the valley of the Ohio. The other, under Colonel Bradstreet, was to pass up the lakes, and force the tribes of Detroit, and the regions beyond, to unconditional submission.

The name of Bradstreet was already well known in America. At a dark and ill-omened period of the French war, he had crossed Lake Ontario with a force of three thousand provincials, and captured Fort Frontenac, a formidable stronghold of the French, commanding the outlet of the lake. He had distinguished himself, moreover, by his gallant conduct in a skirmish with the French and Indians on the River Oswego. These exploits had gained for him a reputation beyond his merits. He was a man of more activity than judgment, self-willed, vain, and eager for notoriety; qualities which became sufficiently apparent before the end of the campaign.[1]

[1] In the correspondence of General Wolfe, recently published in *Tait's Magazine*, this distinguished officer speaks in high terms of Bradstreet's

Several of the northern provinces furnished troops for the expedition; but these levies did not arrive until after the appointed time; and, as the service promised neither honor nor advantage, they were of very indifferent quality, looking, according to an officer of the expedition, more like candidates for a hospital than like men fit for the arduous duty before them. The rendezvous of the troops was at Albany, and thence they took their departure about the end of June. Adopting the usual military route to the westward, they passed up the Mohawk, crossed the Oneida Lake, and descended the Onondaga. The boats and bateaux, crowded with men, passed between the war-worn defences of Oswego, which guarded the mouth of the river on either hand, and, issuing forth upon Lake Ontario, steered in long procession over its restless waters. A storm threw the flotilla into confusion; and several days elapsed before the ramparts of Fort Niagara rose in sight, breaking the tedious monotony of the forest-covered shores. The troops landed beneath its walls. The surrounding plains were soon dotted with the white tents of the little army, whose strength, far inferior to the original design, did not exceed twelve hundred men.

military character. His remarks, however, have reference solely to the capture of Fort Frontenac; and he seems to have derived his impressions from the public prints, as he had no personal knowledge of Bradstreet. The view expressed above is derived from the letters of Bradstreet himself, from the correspondence of General Gage and Sir William Johnson, and from a MS. paper containing numerous details of his conduct during the campaign of 1764, and drawn up by the officers who served under him.

This paper is in the possession of Mrs. W. L. Stone.

A striking spectacle greeted them on their landing. Hundreds of Indian cabins were clustered along the skirts of the forest, and a countless multitude of savages, in all the picturesque variety of their barbaric costume, were roaming over the fields, or lounging about the shores of the lake. Towards the close of the previous winter, Sir William Johnson had despatched Indian messengers to the tribes far and near, warning them of the impending blow; and urging all who were friendly to the English, or disposed to make peace while there was yet time, to meet him at Niagara, and listen to his words. Throughout the winter, the sufferings of the Indians had been great and general. The suspension of the fur-trade; the consequent want of ammunition, clothing, and other articles of necessity; the failure of expected aid from the French; and, above all, the knowledge that some of their own people had taken up arms for the English, combined to quench their thirst for war. Johnson's messengers had therefore been received with unexpected favor, and many had complied with his invitation. Some came to protest their friendship for the English; others hoped, by an early submission, to atone for past misconduct. Some came as spies; while others, again, were lured by the hope of receiving presents, and especially a draught of English milk, that is to say, a dram of whiskey.

The trader, Alexander Henry, the same who so narrowly escaped the massacre at Michillimackinac, was with a party of Ojibwas at the Sault Ste.

Marie, when a canoe, filled with warriors, arrived, bringing the message of Sir William Johnson. A council was called; and the principal messenger, offering a belt of wampum, spoke as follows: "My friends and brothers, I am come with this belt from our great father, Sir William Johnson. He desired me to come to you, as his ambassador, and tell you that he is making a great feast at Fort Niagara; that his kettles are all ready, and his fires lighted. He invites you to partake of the feast, in common with your friends, the Six Nations, who have all made peace with the English. He advises you to seize this opportunity of doing the same, as you cannot otherwise fail of being destroyed; for the English are on their march with a great army, which will be joined by different nations of Indians. In a word, before the fall of the leaf they will be at Michillimackinac, and the Six Nations with them."

The Ojibwas had been debating whether they should go to Detroit, to the assistance of Pontiac, who had just sent them a message to that effect; but the speech of Johnson's messenger turned the current of their thoughts. Most of them were in favor of accepting the invitation; but, distrusting mere human wisdom in a crisis so important, they resolved, before taking a decisive step, to invoke the superior intelligence of the Great Turtle, the chief of all the spirits. A huge wigwam was erected, capable of containing the whole population of the little village. In the centre, a sort of tabernacle was constructed by driving posts into the ground, and closely covering them with hides. With the arrival of night, the propitious time for consulting their oracle, all the warriors assembled in the spacious wigwam, half lighted by the lurid glare of fires, and waited, in suspense and awe, the issue of the invocation. The medicine man, or magician, stripped almost naked, now entered the central tabernacle, which was barely large enough to receive him, and carefully closed the aperture. At once the whole structure began to shake with a violence which threatened its demolition; and a confusion of horrible sounds, shrieks, howls, yells, and moans of anguish, mingled with articulate words, sounded in hideous discord from within. This outrageous clamor, which announced to the horror-stricken spectators the presence of a host of evil spirits, ceased as suddenly as it had begun. A low, feeble sound, like the whine of a young puppy, was next heard within the recess; upon which the warriors raised a cry of joy, and hailed it as the voice of the Great Turtle — the spirit who never lied. The magician soon announced that the spirit was ready to answer any question which might be proposed. On this, the chief warrior stepped forward; and, having propitiated the Great Turtle by a present of tobacco thrust through a small hole in the tabernacle, inquired if the English were in reality preparing to attack the Indians, and if the troops were already come to Niagara. Once more the tabernacle was violently shaken, a loud yell was heard, and it was apparent to all that the spirit was gone. A pause of anxious expectation ensued; when, after the lapse of a quarter of an hour, the weak, puppy-like voice of the Great Turtle was again heard addressing the magician in a language unknown to the auditors. When the spirit ceased speaking, the magician interpreted his words. During the short interval of his departure, he had crossed Lake Huron, visited Niagara, and descended the St. Lawrence to Montreal. Few soldiers had as yet reached Niagara; but as he flew down the St. Lawrence, he had seen the water covered with boats, all filled with English warriors, coming to make war on the Indians. Having obtained this answer to his first question, the chief ventured to propose another; and inquired if he and his people, should they accept the invitation of Sir William Johnson, would be well received at Niagara. The answer was most satisfactory. "Sir William Johnson," said the spirit, "will fill your canoes with presents; with blankets, kettles, guns, gunpowder and shot; and large barrels of rum, such as the stoutest of the Indians will not be able to lift; and every man will return in safety to his family." This grateful response produced a general outburst of acclamations; and, with cries of joy, many voices were heard to exclaim, "I will go too! I will go too!"

[1] Henry, *Travels and Adventures,* 171.

The method of invoking the spirits, described above, is a favorite species of imposture among the medicine men of most Algonquin tribes, and had been observed and described a century and a half before the period of this history. Champlain, the founder of Canada, witnessed one of these ceremonies; and the Jesuit Le Jeune gives an account of a sorcerer, who,

They set out, accordingly, for Niagara; and thither also numerous bands of warriors were tending, urged by similar messages, and encouraged, it may be, by similar responses of their oracles. Crossing fresh-water oceans in their birch canoes, and threading the devious windings of solitary streams, they came flocking to the common centre of attraction. Such a concourse of savages has seldom been seen in America. Menomonies, Ottawas, Ojibwas, Mississaugas, from the north; Caughnawagas from Canada, even Wyandots from Detroit, together with a host of Iroquois, were congregated round Fort Niagara to the number of more than two thousand warriors; many of whom had brought with them their women and children.[1]

having invoked a spirit in this manner, treacherously killed him with a hatchet; the mysterious visitant having assumed a visible and tangible form, which exposed him to the incidents of mortality. During these invocations, the lodge or tabernacle was always observed to shake violently to and fro, in a manner so remarkable as exceedingly to perplex the observers. The variety of discordant sounds, uttered by the medicine man, need not surprise us more than those accurate imitations of the cries of various animals, to which Indian hunters are accustomed to train their strong and flexible voices.

1 MS. *Johnson Papers.*

The following extract from Henry's *Travels* will exhibit the feelings with which the Indians came to the conference at Niagara, besides illustrating a curious feature of their superstitions. Many tribes, including some widely differing in language and habits, regard the rattlesnake with superstitious veneration; looking upon him either as a manitou, or spirit, or as a creature endowed with mystic powers and attributes, giving him an influence over the fortunes of mankind. Henry accompanied his Indian companions to Niagara; and, on the way, he chanced to discover one of these snakes near their encampment: —

"The reptile was coiled, and its head raised considerably above its body. Had I advanced another step before my discovery, I must have trodden upon it.

"I no sooner saw the snake, than I hastened to the canoe, in order to procure my gun; but the Indians, observing what I was doing, inquired

Even the Sacs, the Foxes, and the Winnebagoes had sent their deputies; and the Osages, a tribe

the occasion, and, being informed, begged me to desist. At the same time, they followed me to the spot, with their pipes and tobacco-pouches in their hands. On returning, I found the snake still coiled.

"The Indians, on their part, surrounded it, all addressing it by turns, and calling it their *grandfather*, but yet keeping at some distance. During this part of the ceremony, they filled their pipes; and now each blew the smoke toward the snake, who, as it appeared to me, really received it with pleasure. In a word, after remaining coiled, and receiving incense, for the space of half an hour, it stretched itself along the ground, in visible good humor. Its length was between four and five feet. Having remained outstretched for some time, at last it moved slowly away, the Indians following it, and still addressing it by the title of grandfather, beseeching it to take care of their families during their absence, and to be pleased to open the heart of Sir William Johnson, so that he might *show them charity*, and fill their canoe with rum.

"One of the chiefs added a petition, that the snake would take no notice of the insult which had been offered him by the Englishman, who would even have put him to death, but for the interference of the Indians to whom it was hoped he would impute no part of the offence. They further requested, that he would remain, and not return among the English that is, go eastward.

"After the rattlesnake was gone, I learned that this was the first time that an individual of the species had been seen so far to the northward and westward of the River Des Français; a circumstance, moreover, from which my companions were disposed to infer, that this *manito* had come, or been sent, on purpose to meet them; that his errand had been no other than to stop them on their way; and that consequently it would be most advisable to return to the point of departure. I was so fortunate, however, as to prevail with them to embark; and at six o'clock in the evening we again encamped.

"Early the next morning we proceeded. We had a serene sky and very little wind, and the Indians therefore determined on steering across the lake, to an island which just appeared in the horizon; saving, by this course, a distance of thirty miles, which would be lost in keeping the shore. At nine o'clock A.M. we had a light breeze, to enjoy the benefit of which we hoisted sail. Soon after, the wind increased, and the Indians, beginning to be alarmed, frequently called on the rattlesnake to come to their assistance. By degrees the waves grew high; and at eleven o'clock it blew a hurricane, and we expected every moment to be swallowed up. From prayers, the Indians proceeded now to sacrifices, both alike offered to the god-rattlesnake, or *manito-kinibic*. One of the chiefs took a dog, and after tying its fore legs together, threw it overboard, at the same time calling on the snake to preserve us from being drowned, and

beyond the Mississippi, had their representative in this general meeting.

Though the assembled multitude consisted, for the most part, of the more pacific members of the tribes represented, yet their friendly disposition was by no means certain. Several straggling soldiers were shot at in the neighborhood, and it soon became apparent that the utmost precaution must be taken to avert a rupture. The troops were kept always on their guard; while the black muzzles of the cannon, thrust from the bastions of the fort, struck a wholesome awe into the savage throng below.

Although so many had attended the meeting, there were still numerous tribes, and portions of tribes, who maintained a rancorous, unwavering hostility. The Delawares and Shawanoes, however, against whom Bouquet, with the army of the south, was then in the act of advancing, sent a message to the effect, that, though they had no fear of the English, and though they regarded them as old women, and held them in contempt, yet, out of

desiring him to satisfy his hunger with the carcass of the dog. The snake was unpropitious, and the wind increased. Another chief sacrificed another dog, with the addition of some tobacco. In the prayer which accompanied these gifts, he besought the snake, as before, not to avenge upon the Indians the insult which he had received from myself, in the conception of a design to put him to death. He assured the snake that I was absolutely an Englishman, and of kin neither to him nor to them.

"At the conclusion of this speech, an Indian, who sat near me, observed, that if we were drowned it would be for my fault alone, and that I ought myself to be sacrificed, to appease the angry manito; nor was I without apprehensions, that, in case of extremity, this would be my fate; but, happily for me, the storm at length abated, and we reached the island safely." — Henry, *Travels*, 175.

pity for their sufferings, they were willing to treat of peace. To this insolent missive Johnson made no answer; and, indeed, those who sent it were, at this very time, renewing the bloody work of the preceding year along the borders of Pennsylvania and Virginia. The Senecas, that numerous and warlike people, to whose savage enmity were to be ascribed the massacre at the Devil's Hole, and other disasters of the last summer, had recently made a preliminary treaty with Sir William Johnson, and at the same time pledged themselves to appear at Niagara to ratify and complete it. They broke their promise; and it soon became known that they had leagued themselves with a large band of hostile Delawares, who had visited their country. Upon this, a messenger was sent to them, threatening that, unless they instantly came to Niagara, the English would march upon them and burn their villages. The menace had full effect; and a large body of these formidable warriors appeared at the English camp, bringing fourteen prisoners, besides several deserters and runaway slaves. A peace was concluded, on condition that they should never again attack the English, and that they should cede to the British crown a strip of land, between the Lakes Erie and Ontario, four miles in width, on both sides of the River, or Strait, of Niagara.[1] A treaty was next made with a deputation of Wyandots from Detroit, on condition of the delivery of

[1] *Articles of Peace concluded with the Senecas, at Fort Niagara*, July 18, 1764 MS.

prisoners and the preservation of friendship for the future.

Councils were next held, in turn, with each of the various tribes assembled around the fort, some of whom craved forgiveness for the hostile acts they had committed, and deprecated the vengeance of the English; while others alleged their innocence, urged their extreme wants and necessities, and begged that English traders might once more be allowed to visit them. The council-room in the fort was crowded from morning till night; and the wearisome formalities of such occasions, the speeches made and replied to, and the final shaking of hands, smoking of pipes, and serving out of whiskey, engrossed the time of the superintendent for many successive days.

Among the Indians present were a band of Ottawas from Michillimackinac, and remoter settlements, beyond Lake Michigan, and a band of Menomonies from Green Bay. The former, it will be remembered, had done good service to the English, by rescuing the survivors of the garrison of Michillimackinac from the clutches of the Ojibwas; and the latter had deserved no less at their hands, by the protection they had extended to Lieutenant Gorell, and the garrison at Green Bay. Conscious of their merits, they had come to Niagara in full confidence of a favorable reception. Nor were they disappointed; for Johnson met them with a cordial welcome, and greeted them as friends and brothers. They, on their part, were not wanting in expressions of pleasure; and one of their orators exclaimed, in the figurative language of his people, "When our brother came to meet us, the storms ceased, the lake became smooth, and the whole face of nature was changed."

They disowned all connection or privity with the designs of Pontiac. "Brother," said one of the Ottawa chiefs, "you must not imagine I am acquainted with the cause of the war. I only heard a little bird whistle an account of it, and, on going to Michillimackinac, I found your people killed; upon which I sent our priest to inquire into the matter. On the priest's return, he brought me no favorable account, but a war-hatchet from Pontiac, which I scarcely looked on, and immediately threw away."

Another of the Ottawas, a chief of the remoter band of Lake Michigan, spoke to a similar effect, as follows: "We are not of the same people as those residing about Michillimackinac; we only heard at a distance that the enemy were killing your soldiers, on which we covered our heads, and I resolved not to suffer my people to engage in the war. I gathered them together, and made them sit still. In the spring, on uncovering my head, I perceived that they had again begun a war, and that the sky was all cloudy in that quarter."

The superintendent thanked them for their fidelity to the English; reminded them that their true interest lay in the preservation of peace, and concluded with a gift of food and clothing, and a permission, denied to all the rest, to open a traffic with the traders, who had already begun to assemble at the fort. "And now, my brother," said a warrior, as the council was about to break up, "we beg that you will tell us where we can find some rum to comfort us; for it is long since we have tasted any, and we are very thirsty." This honest request was not refused. The liquor was distributed, and a more copious supply promised for the future; upon which the deputation departed, and repaired to their encampment, much pleased with their reception.[1]

Throughout these conferences, one point of policy was constantly adhered to. No general council was held. Separate treaties were made, in order to promote mutual jealousies and rivalries, and discourage the feeling of union, and of a common cause among the widely scattered tribes. Johnson at length completed his task, and, on the sixth of August, set sail for Oswego. The march of the army had hitherto been delayed by rumors of hostile designs on the part of the Indians, who, it was said, had formed a scheme for attacking Fort Niagara, as soon as the troops should have left the ground. Now, however, when the concourse was melting away, and the tribes departing for their distant homes, it was thought that the danger was past, and that the army might safely resume its progress. They advanced, accordingly, to Fort Schlosser, above the cataract, whither their boats and bateaux had been sent before them, craned up

[1] MS. *Johnson Papers.* MS. *Minutes of Conference with the chiefs and warriors of the Ottawas and Menomonies at Fort Niagara,* July 20, 1764. The extracts given above are copied verbatim from the original record.

the rocks at Lewiston, and dragged by oxen over the rough portage road. The troops had been joined by three hundred friendly Indians, and an equal number of Canadians. The appearance of the latter in arms would, it was thought, have great effect on the minds of the enemy, who had always looked upon them as friends and supporters. Of the Indian allies, the greater part were Iroquois, and the remainder, about a hundred in number, Ojibwas and Mississaugas; the former being the same who had recently arrived from the Sault Ste. Marie, bringing with them their prisoner, Alexander Henry. Henry was easily persuaded to accompany the expedition; and the command of the Ojibwas and Mississaugas was assigned to him—"To me," writes the adventurous trader, "whose best hope it had lately been to live by their forbearance." His long-continued sufferings and dangers hardly deserved to be rewarded by so great a misfortune as that of commanding a body of Indian warriors; an evil from which, however, he was soon to be relieved. The army had hardly begun its march, when nearly all his followers ran off, judging it wiser to return home with the arms and clothing given them for the expedition, than to make war against their own countrymen and relatives. Fourteen warriors still remained; but on the following night, when the army lay at Fort Schlosser, having contrived by some means to obtain liquor, they created such a commotion in the camp, by yelling and firing their guns, as to excite the utmost indignation of the commander. They received from him, in consequence, a reproof so harsh and ill judged, that most of them went home in disgust; and Henry found his Indian battalion suddenly dwindled to four or five vagabond hunters.[1] A large number of Iroquois still followed the army, the strength of which, farther increased by a re-enforcement of Highlanders, was now very considerable.

The troops left Fort Schlosser on the eighth. Their boats and bateaux pushed out into the Niagara, whose expanded waters reposed in a serenity soon to be exchanged for the wild roar and tumultuous struggle of the rapids and the cataract. They coasted along the southern shore of Lake Erie until the twelfth, when, in the neighborhood of Presqu' Isle, they were overtaken by a storm of rain, which forced them to drag their boats on shore, and pitch their tents in the dripping forest. Before the day closed, word was brought that strange Indians were near the camp. They soon made their appearance, proclaiming themselves to be chiefs and deputies of the Delawares and Shawanoes, empowered to beg for peace in the name of their respective tribes. Various opinions were entertained of the visitors. The Indian allies wished to kill them, and many of the officers believed them to be spies. There was no proof of their pretended character of deputies; and, for all that appeared to the contrary, they might be a mere straggling party of warriors. Their professions of an earnest desire for peace were contra-

[1] Henry, *Travels*, 183.

dicted by the fact that they brought with them but one small belt of wampum; a pledge no less indispensable in a treaty with these tribes than seals and signatures in a convention of European sovereigns.[1] Bradstreet knew, or ought to have known, the character of the treacherous enemy with whom he had to deal. He knew that the Shawanoes and Delawares had shown, throughout the war, a ferocious and relentless hostility; that they had sent an insolent message to Niagara; and, finally, that in his own instructions he was enjoined to deal sternly with them, and not be duped by pretended overtures. Yet, in spite of the suspicious character of the self-styled deputies, in spite of the sullen wrath of his Indian allies, and the murmured dissent of his officers, he listened to their proposals, and entered into a preliminary treaty. He pledged himself to refrain from attacking the Delawares and Shawanoes, on condition that within twenty-five days the deputies should again meet him at Sandusky, in order to yield up their prisoners, and conclude a definite treaty of peace.[2] It afterwards appeared — and this, indeed, might have been suspected at the time — that the sole object of

[1] Every article in a treaty must be confirmed by a belt of wampum; otherwise it is void. Mante, the historian of the French war, asserts that they brought four belts. But this is contradicted in contemporary letters, including several of General Gage and Sir William Johnson. Mante accompanied Bradstreet's expedition with the rank of major; and he is a zealous advocate of his commander, whom he seeks to defend, at the expense both of Colonel Bouquet and General Gage.

[2] *Preliminary Treaty between Colonel Bradstreet and the Deputies of the Delawares and Shawanoes, concluded at L'Ance aux Feuilles, on Lake Erie,* August 12, 1764, MS.

the overtures was to retard the action of the army until the season should be too far advanced to prosecute the campaign. At this very moment, the Delaware and Shawanoe war-parties were murdering and scalping along the frontiers; and the work of havoc continued for weeks, until it was checked at length by the operations of Colonel Bouquet.

Bradstreet was not satisfied with the promise he had made to abandon his own hostile designs. He consummated his folly and presumption by despatching a messenger to his superior officer, Colonel Bouquet, informing him that the Delawares and Shawanoes had been reduced to submission without his aid, and that he might withdraw his troops, as there was no need of his advancing farther. Bouquet, astonished and indignant, paid no attention to this communication, but pursued his march as before.[1]

The course pursued by Bradstreet in this affair — a course which can only be ascribed to the vain ambition of finishing the war without the aid of others — drew upon him the severe censures of the commander-in-chief, who, on hearing of the treaty, at once annulled it.[2] Bradstreet has been accused

[1] MS. Letter — *Bouquet to Gage*, Sept. 3.

[2] Extract from a MS. Letter — *Gage to Bradstreet*, Sept. 2: —

"I again repeat that I annul and disavow the peace you have made."

The following extracts will express the opinions of Gage with respect to this affair.

MS. Letter — *Gage to Bradstreet*, Oct. 15: —

"They have negotiated with you on Lake Erie, and cut our throats upon the frontiers. With your letters of peace I received others, giving accounts of murders, and these acts continue to this time. Had you only

of having exceeded his orders, in promising to conclude a definite treaty with the Indians, a power which was vested in Sir William Johnson alone; but as upon this point his instructions were not explicit, he may be spared the full weight of this additional charge.[1]

Having, as he thought, accomplished not only a great part of his own task, but also the whole of that which had been assigned to Colonel Bouquet, Bradstreet resumed his progress westward, and in a few days reached Sandusky. He had been ordered to attack the Wyandots, Ottawas, and Miamis, dwelling near this place; but at his approach, these Indians, hastening to avert the

consulted Colonel Bouquet, before you agreed upon any thing with them (a deference he was certainly entitled to, instead of an order to stop his march), you would have been acquainted with the treachery of those people, and not have suffered yourself to be thus deceived, and you would have saved both Colonel Bouquet and myself from the dilemma you brought us into. You concluded a peace with people who were daily murdering us."

MS. Letter — *Gage to Johnson*, Sept. 4: —

"You will have received my letter of the 2d inst., enclosing you the unaccountable treaty betwixt Colonel Bradstreet and the Shawanese, Delawares, &c. On consideration of the treaty, it does not appear to me that the ten Indians therein mentioned were sent on an errand of peace. If they had, would they not have been at Niagara? or would the insolent and audacious message have been sent there in the lieu of offers of peace? Would not they have been better provided with belts on such an occasion? They give only one string of wampum. You will know this better, but it appears strange to me. They certainly came to watch the motions of the troops."

[1] MS. Letter — *Gage to Bradstreet*, Sept. 2: —

Bradstreet's instructions directed him to *offer peace* to such tribes as should make their submission. "*To offer peace,*" writes Gage, "I think can never be construed a power to *conclude and dictate the articles of peace,* and you certainly know that no such power could with propriety be lodged in any person but in Sir William Johnson, his majesty's sole agent and superintendent for Indian affairs."

danger, sent a deputation to meet him, promising that, if he would refrain from attacking them, they would follow him to Detroit, and there conclude a treaty. Bradstreet thought proper to trust this slippery promise; though, with little loss of time he might have reduced them, on the spot, to a much more effectual submission. He now bent his course for Detroit, leaving the Indians of Sandusky much delighted, and probably no less surprised, at the success of their embassy. Before his departure, however, he despatched Captain Morris, with several Canadians and friendly Indians, to the Illinois, in order to persuade the savages of that region to treat of peace with the English. The measure was in a high degree ill advised and rash, promising but doubtful advantage, and exposing the life of a valuable officer to imminent risk. The sequel of Morris's adventure will soon appear.

The English boats now entered the mouth of the Detroit, and on the twenty-sixth of August came within sight of the fort and adjacent settlements. The inhabitants of the Wyandot village on the right, who, it will be remembered, had recently made a treaty of peace at Niagara, ran down to the shore, shouting, whooping, and firing their guns, — a greeting more noisy than sincere, — while the cannon of the garrison echoed salutation from the opposite shore, and cheer on cheer, deep and heartfelt, pealed welcome from the crowded ramparts.

Well might Gladwyn's beleaguered soldiers rejoice at the approaching succor. They had been beset for more than fifteen months by their wily enemy; and though there were times when not an Indian could be seen, yet woe to the soldier who should wander into the forest in search of game, or stroll too far beyond range of the cannon. Throughout the preceding winter, they had been left in comparative quiet; but with the opening spring the Indians had resumed their pertinacious hostilities; not, however, with the same activity and vigor as during the preceding summer. The messages of Sir William Johnson, and the tidings of Bradstreet's intended expedition, had had great effect upon their minds, and some of them had begged abjectly for peace; but still the garrison were harassed by frequent alarms, and days and nights of watchfulness were their unvarying lot. Cut off for months together from all communication with their race; pent up in an irksome imprisonment; ill supplied with provisions, and with clothing worn threadbare, they hailed with delight the prospect of a return to the world from which they had been banished so long. The army had no sooner landed than the garrison was relieved, and fresh troops substituted in their place. Bradstreet's next care was to inquire into the conduct of the Canadian inhabitants of Detroit, and punish such of them as had given aid to the Indians. A few only were found guilty, the more culpable having fled to the Illinois on the approach of the army.

Pontiac too was gone. The great war-chief, his vengeance unslaked, and his purpose unshaken, had retired, as we have seen, to the banks of the Maumee, whence he sent a haughty defiance to the English commander. The Indian villages near Detroit were half emptied of their inhabitants, many of whom still followed the desperate fortunes of their indomitable leader. Those who remained were, for the most part, brought by famine and misery to a sincere desire for peace, and readily obeyed the summons of Bradstreet to meet him in council.

The council was held in the open air, on the morning of the seventh of September, with all the accompaniments of military display which could inspire awe and respect among the assembled savages. The tribes, or rather fragments of tribes, represented at this meeting, were the Ottawas, Ojibwas, Pottawattamies, Miamis, Sacs, and Wyandots. The Indians of Sandusky kept imperfectly the promise they had made, the Wyandots of that place alone sending a full deputation; while the other tribes were merely represented by the Ojibwa chief Wasson. This man, who was the principal chief of his tribe, and the most prominent orator on the present occasion, rose and opened the council.

"My brother," he said, addressing Bradstreet, "last year God forsook us. God has now opened our eyes, and we desire to be heard. It is God's will our hearts are altered. It was God's will you had such fine weather to come to us. It is God's will also there should be peace and tranquillity over the face of the earth and of the waters."

Having delivered this exordium, Wasson frankly confessed that the tribes which he represented were all justly chargeable with the war, and now deeply regretted their delinquency. It is common with Indians, when accused of acts of violence, to lay the blame upon the unbridled recklessness of their young warriors; and this excuse is often perfectly sound and valid; but since, in the case of a premeditated and long-continued war, it was glaringly inadmissible, they now reversed the usual course, and made scapegoats of the old chiefs and warriors, who, as they declared, had led the people astray by sinister counsel and bad example.[1]

Bradstreet would grant peace only on condition that they should become subjects of the King of England, and acknowledge that he held over their country a sovereignty as ample and complete as over any other part of his dominions. Nothing could be more impolitic and absurd than this demand. The smallest attempt at an invasion of their liberties has always been regarded by the Indians with extreme jealousy, and a prominent cause of the war had been an undue assumption of authority on the part of the English. This article of the treaty, could its purport have been fully understood, might have kindled afresh the quarrel which it sought to extinguish; but happily not a savage present was able to comprehend it. Subjection and sovereignty are ideas which never enter into the mind of an Indian, and therefore

[1] MS. *Minutes of Conference between Colonel Bradstreet and the Indians of Detroit,* Sept. 7, 1764. See also, Mante, 517

his language has no words to express them. Most of the western tribes, it is true, had been accustomed to call themselves children of the King of France; but the words were a mere compliment, conveying no sense of any political relation whatever. Yet it was solely by means of this harmless metaphor that the condition in question could be explained to the assembled chiefs. Thus interpreted, it met with a ready assent; since, in their eyes, it involved no concession beyond a mere unmeaning change of forms and words. They promised, in future, to call the English king father, instead of brother; unconscious of any obligation which so trifling a change could impose, and mentally reserving a full right to make war on him or his people, whenever it should suit their convenience. When Bradstreet returned from his expedition, he boasted that he had reduced the tribes of Detroit to terms of more complete submission than any other Indians had ever before yielded; but the truth was soon detected and exposed by those conversant with Indian affairs.[1]

At this council, Bradstreet was guilty of the bad policy and bad taste of speaking through the medium of a French interpreter; so that most of his own officers, as well as the Iroquois allies, who were strangers to the Algonquin language, remained in ignorance of all that passed. The latter were highly indignant, and refused to become parties to the treaty, or go through the usual ceremony of shaking hands with the chiefs of Detroit, insisting

[1] MS. Letter — *Johnson to the Board of Trade*, Oct 30

that they had not heard their speeches, and knew not whether they were friends or enemies. In another particular, also, Bradstreet gave great offence. From some unexplained impulse or motive, he cut to pieces, with a hatchet, a belt of wampum which was about to be used in the council; and all the Indians present, both friends and enemies, were alike incensed at this rude violation of the ancient pledge of faith, which, in their eyes, was invested with something of a sacred character.[1]

Having settled the affairs of Detroit, Bradstreet despatched Captain Howard, with a strong detachment, to take possession of Michillimackinac, which had remained unoccupied since its capture in the preceding summer. Howard effected his object without resistance, and, at the same time, sent parties of troops to reoccupy the deserted posts of Green Bay and Sault Ste. Marie. Thus, after the interval of more than a year, the flag of England was again displayed among the solitudes of the northern wilderness.[2]

While Bradstreet's army lay encamped on the fields near Detroit, Captain Morris, with a few Iroquois and Canadian attendants, was pursuing his adventurous embassy to the country of the Illinois. Morris, who has left us his portrait, prefixed to a little volume of prose and verse, was an officer of literary tastes, whose round English face

[1] MS. *Remarks on the Conduct of Colonel Bradstreet* — found among the *Johnson Papers*.

See, also, an extract of a letter from Sandusky, published in several newspapers of the day.

[2] MS. *Report of Captain Howard.*

did not indicate any especial degree of enterprise or resolution. He seems, however, to have had both; for, on a hint from the General, he had offered himself for the adventure, for which he was better fitted than most of his brother officers, inasmuch as he spoke French. He was dining, on the eve of his departure, in the tent of Bradstreet, when his host suddenly remarked, in the bluff way habitual to him, that he had a French fellow, a prisoner, whom he meant to hang; but that, if Morris would like him for an interpreter, he might have him. The prisoner in question was the Canadian Godefroy, who was presently led into the tent; and who, conscious of many misdemeanors, thought that his hour was come, and fell on his knees to beg his life. Bradstreet told him that he should be pardoned if he would promise to "go with this gentleman, and take good care of him," pointing to his guest. Godefroy promised; and, to the best of his power, he kept his word, for he imagined that Morris had saved his life.

Morris set out on the following afternoon with Godefroy, another Canadian, two servants, and a party of Indians, ascended the Maumee, and soon approached the camp of Pontiac; who, as already mentioned, had withdrawn to this river with his chosen warriors. The party disembarked from their canoes; and an Ottawa chief, who had joined them, lent them three horses. Morris and the Canadians mounted, and, preceded by their Indian attendants, displaying an English flag, advanced in state towards the camp, which was two leagues or more distant. As they drew near, they were met by a rabble of several hundred Indians, called by Morris "Pontiac's army." They surrounded him, beat his horse, and crowded between him and his followers, apparently trying to separate them. At the outskirts of the camp stood Pontiac himself, who met the ambassador with a scowling brow, and refused to offer his hand. Here, too, stood a man, in the uniform of a French officer, holding his gun with the butt resting on the ground, and assuming an air of great importance; while two Pawnee slaves stood close behind him. He proved to be a French drummer, calling himself St. Vincent, one of those renegades of civilization to be found in almost every Indian camp. He now took upon himself the office of a master of ceremonies; desired Morris to dismount, and seated himself at his side on a bearskin. Godefroy took his place near them; and the throng of savages, circle within circle, stood crowded around. "Presently, says Morris, "came Pontiac, and squatted himself, after his fashion, opposite to me." He opened the interview by observing that the English were liars, and demanding of the ambassador if he had come to lie to them, like the rest. "This Indian," pursues Morris, "has a more extensive power than ever was known among that people, for every chief used to command his own tribe; but eighteen nations, by French intrigue, had been brought to unite and choose this man for their commander."

Pontiac now produced a letter directed to him

self, and sent from New Orleans, though purporting to be written by the King of France. It contained, according to Morris, the grossest calumnies that the most ingenious malice could devise to incense the Indians against the English. The old falsehood was not forgotten: "Your French Father," said the writer, "is neither dead nor asleep; he is already on his way, with sixty great ships, to revenge himself on the English, and drive them out of America." Much excitement followed the reading of the letter, and Morris's situation became more than unpleasant; but St. Vincent befriended him, and hurried him off to his wigwam to keep him out of harm's way.

On the next day there was a grand council. Morris made a speech, in which he indiscreetly told the Indians that the King of France had given all the country to the King of England. Luckily, his auditors received the announcement with ridicule rather than anger. The chiefs, however, wished to kill him; but Pontiac interposed, on the ground that the life of an ambassador should be held sacred. "He made a speech," says Morris, "which does him honor, and shows that he was acquainted with the law of nations." He seemed in a mood more pacific than could have been expected, and said privately to Godefroy: "I will lead the nations to war no more. Let them be at peace if they choose; but I will never be a friend to the English. I shall be a wanderer in the woods; and, if they come there to seek me, I will shoot at them while I have an arrow left." Morris thinks that he said this in a fit of despair, and that, in fact, he was willing to come to terms.

The day following was an unlucky one. One of Morris's Indians, a Mohawk chief, ran off, having first stolen all he could lay hands on, and sold the ambassador's stock of rum, consisting of two barrels, to the Ottawas. A scene of frenzy ensued A young Indian ran up to Morris, and stabbed at him savagely; but Godefroy caught the assassin's hand, and saved his patron's life. Morris escaped from the camp, and lay hidden in a corn-field till the howling and screeching subsided, and the Indians slept themselves sober. When he returned, an Indian, called the Little Chief, gave him a volume of Shakespeare, — the spoil of some slaughtered officer, — and then begged for gunpowder.

Having first gained Pontiac's consent, Morris now resumed his journey to the Illinois. The river was extremely low, and it was with much ado that they pushed their canoe against the shallow current, or dragged it over stones and sandbars. On the fifth day, they met an Indian mounted on a handsome white horse, said to have belonged to General Braddock, and to have been captured at the defeat of his army, nine years before. On the morning of the seventh day, they reached the neighborhood of Fort Miami. This post, captured during the preceding year, had since remained without a garrison; and its only tenants were the Canadians, who had built their houses within its palisades, and a few Indians, who thought fit to make it their temporary abode. The meadows about the fort were dotted with the lodges of the Kickapoos, a large band of whom had recently arrived; but the great Miami village was on the opposite side of the stream, screened from sight by the forest which intervened.

The party landed a little below the fort; and, while his followers were making their way through the border of woods that skirted the river, Morris remained in the canoe, solacing himself by reading *Antony and Cleopatra* in the volume he had so oddly obtained. It was fortunate that he did so; for his attendants had scarcely reached the open meadow, which lay behind the woods, when they were encountered by a mob of savages, armed with spears, hatchets, and bows and arrows, and bent on killing the Englishman. Being, for the moment, unable to find him, the chiefs had time to address the excited rabble, and persuade them to postpone their intended vengeance. The ambassador, buffeted, threatened, and insulted, was conducted to the fort, where he was ordered to remain; though, at the same time, the Canadian inhabitants were forbidden to admit him into their houses. Morris soon discovered that this unexpected rough treatment was owing to the influence of a deputation of Delaware and Shawanoe chiefs, who had recently arrived, bringing fourteen war belts of wampum, and exciting the Miamis to renew their hostilities against the common enemy. Thus it was fully apparent that while the Delawares and Shawanoes were sending one deputation to treat of peace with Bradstreet on Lake Erie, they were sending another to rouse the tribes of the Illinois to war.[1] From Fort Miami, the deputation had proceeded westward, spreading the contagion among all the tribes between the Mississippi and the Ohio; declaring that they would never make peace with the English, but would fight them as long as the sun should shine, and calling on their brethren of the Illinois to follow their example.

They had been aware of the approach of Morris, and had urged the Miamis to put him to death when he arrived. Accordingly, he had not been long at the fort when two warriors, with tomahawks in their hands, entered, seized him by the arms, and dragged him towards the river. Godefroy stood by, pale and motionless. "*Eh bien, vous m'abandonnez donc!*" said Morris. "*Non, mon capitaine*," the Canadian answered, "*je ne vous abandonnerai jamais;*" and he followed, as the two savages dragged their captive into the water. Morris thought that they meant to drown and scalp him, but soon saw his mistake; for they led him through the stream, which was fordable, and thence towards the Miami village. As they drew near, they stopped, and began to strip him, but grew angry at the difficulty of the task; till, in rage and despair, he tore off his clothes himself. They then bound his arms behind him with his own sash,

1 "About the end of next month," said the deputies to the Miamis, "we shall send you the war-hatchet." "Doubtless," remarks Morris, "their design was to amuse General Bradstreet with fair language, to cut off his army at Sandusky when least expected, and then to send the hatchet to the nations."

and drove him before them to the village, where they made him sit on a bench. A whooping, screeching mob of savages was instantly about him, and a hundred voices clamored together in dispute as to what should be done with him. Godefroy stood by him with a courageous fidelity that redeemed his past rascalities. He urged a nephew of Pontiac, who was present, to speak for the prisoner. The young Indian made a bold harangue to the crowd; and Godefroy added that, if Morris were killed, the English would take revenge on those who were in their power at Detroit. A Miami chief, called the Swan, now declared for the Englishman, untied his arms, and gave him a pipe to smoke; whereupon another chief, called the White Cat, snatched it from him, seized him, and bound him fast by the neck to a post. Naked, helpless, and despairing, he saw the crowd gathering around to torture him. "I had not the smallest hope of life," he says, "and I remember that I conceived myself as if going to plunge into a gulf, vast, immeasurable; and that, a few moments after, the thought of torture occasioned a sort of torpor and insensibility. I looked at Godefroy, and, seeing him exceedingly distressed, I said what I could to encourage him; but he desired me not to speak. I supposed it gave offence to the savages, and therefore was silent; when Pacanne, chief of the Miami nation, and just out of his minority, having mounted a horse and crossed the river, rode up to me. When I heard him calling to those about me, and felt his hand behind my neck, I thought he was going to strangle me, out of pity; but he untied me, saying, as it was afterwards interpreted to me: 'I give that man his life. If you want English meat, go to Detroit, or to the lake, and you'll find enough. What business have you with this man's flesh, who is come to speak with us?' I fixed my eyes steadfastly on this young man, and endeavored by looks to express my gratitude."

An Indian now offered him a pipe, and he was then pushed with abuse and blows out of the village. He succeeded in crossing the river and regaining the fort, after receiving a sharp cut of a switch from a mounted Indian whom he met on the way.

He found the Canadians in the fort disposed to befriend him. Godefroy and the metamorphosed drummer, St. Vincent, were always on the watch to warn him of danger; and one l'Esperance gave him an asylum in his garret. He seems to have found some consolation in the compassion of two handsome young squaws, sisters, he was told, of his deliverer, Pacanne; but the two warriors who had stripped and bound him were constantly lurking about the fort, watching an opportunity to kill him; and the Kickapoos, whose lodges were pitched on the meadow, sent him a message to the effect that, if the Miamis did not put him to death, they themselves would do so, whenever he should pass their camp. He was still on the threshold of his journey, and his final point of destination was several hundred miles distant; yet, with great resolution, he determined to persevere, and, if possible, fulfil his mission. His Indian and Canadian attendants used every means to dissuade him, and in the evening held a council with the Miami chiefs, the result of which was most discouraging. Morris received message after message, threatening his life, should he persist in his design; and word was brought him that several of the Shawanoe deputies were returning to the fort, expressly to kill him. Under these circumstances, it would have been madness to persevere; and, abandoning his mission, he set out for Detroit. The Indian attendants, whom he had brought from Sandusky, after behaving with the utmost insolence, abandoned him in the woods; their ringleader being a Christian Huron, of the Mission of Lorette, whom Morris pronounces the greatest rascal he ever knew. With Godefroy and two or three others who remained with him, he reached Detroit on the seventeenth of September, half dead with famine and fatigue. He had expected to find Bradstreet; but that agile commander had decamped, and returned to Sandusky. Morris, too ill and exhausted to follow, sent him his journal, together with a letter, in which he denounced the Delaware and Shawanoe ambassadors, whom he regarded, and no doubt with justice, as the occasion of his misfortunes. The following is his amiable conclusion: —

"The villains have nipped our fairest hopes in the bud. I tremble for you at Sandusky; though I was greatly pleased to find you have one of the vessels with you, and artillery. I wish the chiefs were assembled on board the vessel, and that she had a hole in her bottom. Treachery should be paid with treachery; and it is a more than ordinary pleasure to deceive those who would deceive us."[1]

Bradstreet had retraced his course to Sandusky, to keep his engagement with the Delaware and Shawanoe deputies, and await the fulfilment of their worthless promise to surrender their prisoners, and conclude a definitive treaty of peace. His hopes were defeated. The appointed time expired, and not a chief was seen; though, a few days after, several warriors came to the camp, with a promise that, if Bradstreet would remain quiet, and refrain from attacking their villages, they would bring in the prisoners in the course of the following week. Bradstreet accepted their excuses; and, having removed his camp to the carrying-place of Sandusky, lay waiting in patient expectation. It was here that he received, for the

[1] MS. Letter — *Morris to Bradstreet*, 18 Sept. 1764.

The journal sent by Morris to Bradstreet is in the State Paper Office of London. This journal, and the record of an examination of Morris's Indian and Canadian attendants, made in Bradstreet's presence at Sandusky, were the authorities on which the account in the first edition of this work was based. Morris afterwards rewrote his journal, with many additions. Returning to England after the war, he lost his property by speculations, and resolved, for the sake of his children, to solicit a pension, on the score of his embassy to the Illinois. With this view it was that the journal was rewritten; but failing to find a suitable person to lay it before the King, he resolved to print it, together with several original poems and a translation of the fourth and fourteenth satires of Juvenal. The book appeared in 1791, under the title of *Miscellanies in Prose and Verse.* It is very scarce. I am indebted to the kindness of Mr. S. G. Drake for the opportunity of examining it.

The two journals and the evidence before Bradstreet's court of inquiry agree in essentials, but differ in some details. In this edition, I have followed chiefly the printed journal, borrowing some additional facts from the evidence taken before Bradstreet.

first time, a communication from General Gage, respecting the preliminary treaty, concluded several weeks before. Gage condemned his conduct in severe terms, and ordered him to break the engagements he had made, and advance at once upon the enemy, choosing for his first objects of attack the Indians living upon the plains of the Scioto. The fury of Bradstreet was great on receiving this message; and it was not diminished when the journal of Captain Morris was placed in his hands, fully proving how signally he had been duped. He was in no temper to obey the orders of the commander-in-chief; and, to justify himself for his inaction, he alleged the impossibility of reaching the Scioto plains at that advanced season. Two routes thither were open to his choice, one by the River Sandusky, and the other by Cayahoga Creek. The water in the Sandusky was sunk low with the drought, and the carrying-place at the head of Cayahoga Creek was a few miles longer than had been represented; yet the army were ready for the attempt, and these difficulties could not have deterred a vigorous commander. Under cover of such excuses, Bradstreet remained idle at Sandusky for several days, while sickness and discontent were rife in his camp. The soldiers complained of his capricious, peremptory temper, his harshness to his troops, and the unaccountable tenderness with which he treated the Sandusky Indians, some of whom had not yet made their submission; while he enraged his Iroquois allies by his frequent rebukes and curses.

At length, declaring that provisions were failing and the season growing late, he resolved to return home; and broke up his camp with such precipitancy that two soldiers, who had gone out in the morning to catch fish for his table, were inhumanly left behind;[1] the colonel remarking that they might stay and be damned. Soon after leaving Sandusky, he saw fit to encamp one evening on an open, exposed beach, on the south shore of Lake Erie, though there was in the neighborhood a large river, "wherein," say his critics, "a thousand boats could lie with safety." A storm came on: half his boats were dashed to pieces; and six pieces of cannon, with ammunition, provisions, arms, and baggage, were lost or abandoned. For three days the tempest raged unceasingly; and, when the angry lake began to resume its tranquillity, it was found that the remaining boats were insufficient to convey the troops. A body of Indians, together with a detachment of provincials, about a hundred

[1] "8th. His going away, leaving at Sandusky Two Jersey Soldiers, who were sent out by his Orders to Catch Fish for his Table & Five Principal Inds. who were Hunting, notwithstanding several spoke to him abt. it & begged to allow a Boat to stay an hour or two for them; his Answer was, they might stay there & be damned, not a Boat should stay one Minute for them." — *Remarks on the Conduct*, etc., MS.

Another article of these charges is as follows: "His harsh treatment at Setting off to the Inds. and their officers & leaving some of them behind at every encampment from his flighty and unsettled disposition, telling them sometimes he intended encamping, on which some of the briskest Inds. went to kill some Game, on their return found the Army moved on, so were obliged to march along shore without any necessarys, and with difficulty got to Detroit half starved. At other times on being asked by the Ind^{n} officers (when the Boats were crowded) how they and ye Inds. should get along, His answer always verry ill natured, such as swim and be damned, or let them stay and be damned, &c.; all which was understood by many & gave great uneasiness."

and fifty in all, were therefore ordered to make their way to Niagara along the pathless borders of the lake. They accordingly set out, and, after many days of hardship, reached their destination; though such had been their sufferings, from fatigue, cold, and hunger; from wading swamps, swimming creeks and rivers, and pushing their way through tangled thickets, that many of the provincials perished miserably in the woods. On the fourth of November, seventeen days after their departure from Sandusky, the main body of the little army arrived in safety at Niagara; and the whole, re-embarking on Lake Ontario, proceeded towards Oswego.[1] Fortune still seemed adverse; for a second tempest arose, and one of the schooners, crowded with troops, foundered in sight of Oswego, though most of the men were saved. The route to the settlements was now a short and easy one. On their arrival, the regulars went into quarters; while the troops levied for the campaign were sent home to their respective provinces.

This expedition, ill conducted as it was, produced some beneficial results. The Indians at Detroit had been brought to reason, and for the present, at least, would probably remain tranquil; while the re-establishment of the posts on the upper lakes must necessarily have great effect upon the natives of that region. At Sandusky, on the other hand, the work had been but half done. The tribes of that place felt no respect for the English; while those to the southward and

[1] Mante, 535.

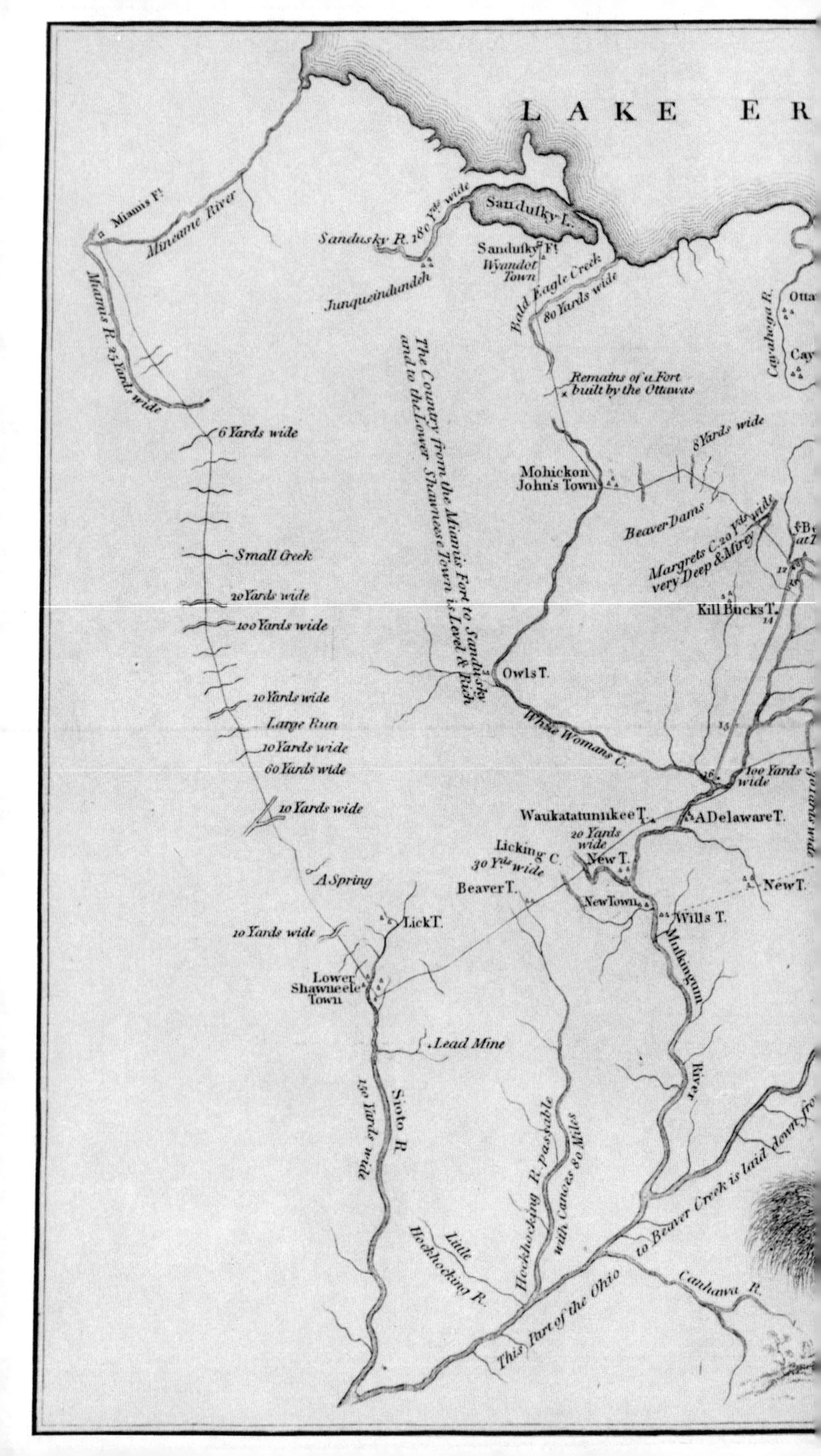
LAKE ER
Miamis Ft.
Mineame River
Miamis R. 25 Yards wide
Sandusky R. 180 Yds. wide
Sandusky L.
Sandusky Ft.
Wyandot Town
Junqueindundeh
Bald Eagle Creek
80 Yards wide
Cayahoga R.
The Country from the Miamis Fort to Sandusky and to the Lower Shawneese Town is Level & Rich
Remains of a Fort built by the Ottawas
6 Yards wide
8 Yards wide
Mohickon John's Town
Beaver Dams
Margrets C. 20 Yds. wide very Deep & Mirey
Small Creek
20 Yards wide
100 Yards wide
Kill Bucks T.
Owls T.
10 Yards wide
White Womans C.
Large Run
10 Yards wide
60 Yards wide
100 Yards wide
10 Yards wide
Waukatatunnkee T.
A Delaware T.
20 Yards wide
Licking C.
New T.
30 Yds. wide
A Spring
Beaver T.
New T.
New Town
Wills T.
10 Yards wide
Lick T.
Muskingum
Lower Shawneese Town
Lead Mine
River
Sioto R.
130 Yards wide
Hockhocking R. passable with Canoes 80 Miles
Little Hockhocking R.
to Beaver Creek is laid down from
This Part of the Ohio
Canhawa R.

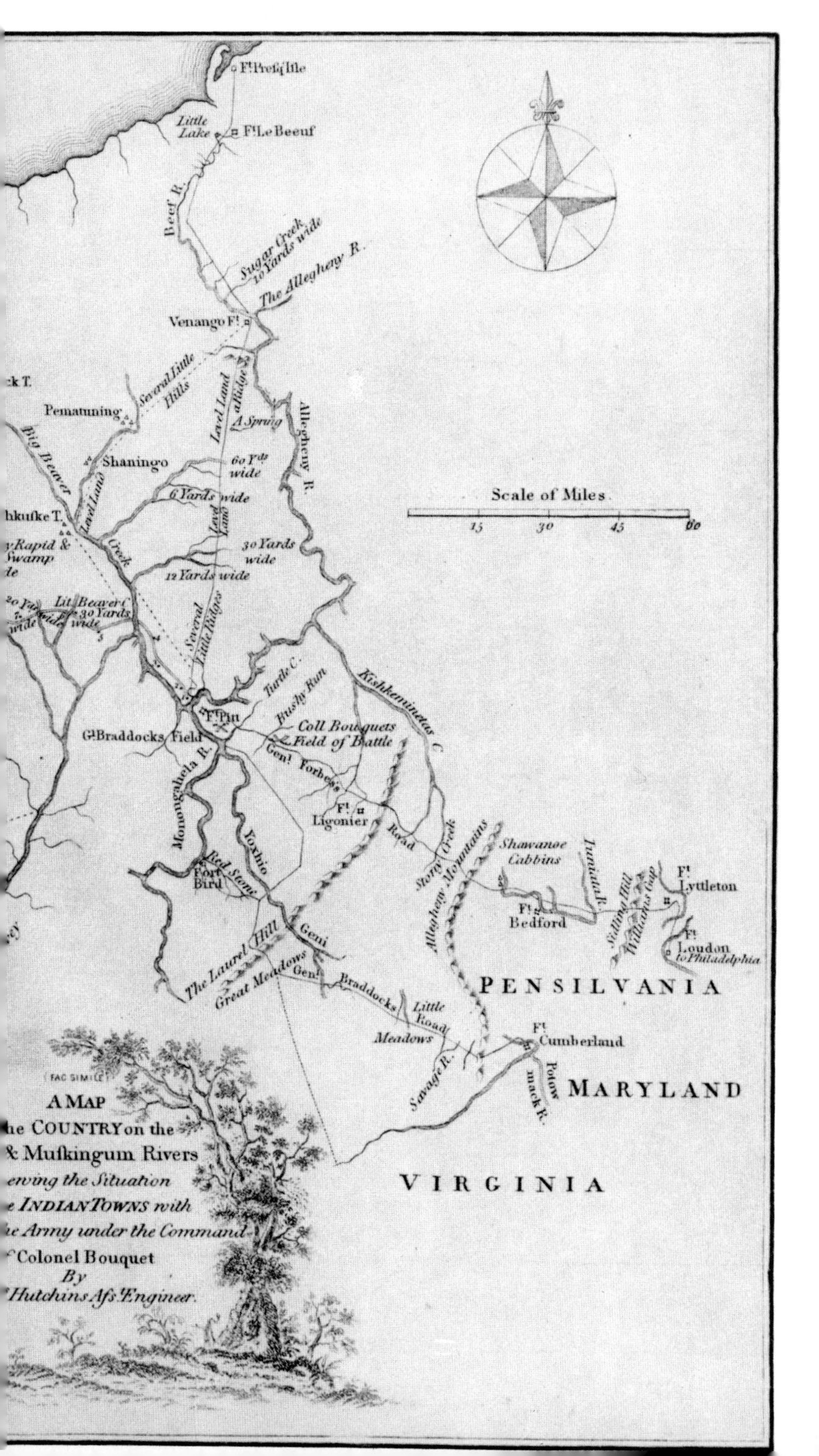
Ft. Presq Isle
Little Lake
Ft. Le Beeuf
Beef R.
Sugar Creek 10 Yards wide
The Allegheny R.
Venango Ft.
Several Little Hills
Level Land
a Ridge
Pematuning
A Spring
Allegheny R.
Big Beaver
Shaningo
60 Yds wide
6 Yards wide
Level Land
Scale of Miles
15
30
45
60
Rapid &
Swamp
Creek
30 Yards wide
12 Yards wide
Lit. Beaver C.
30 Yards wide
Several Little Ridges
Turtle C.
Bushy Run
Kishkeminetas C.
Ft. Pitt
Coll Bouquets Field of Battle
Gt. Braddocks Field
Genl. Forbes's
Monongahela R.
Ft. Ligonier
Road
Yoxhio
Stony Creek
Allegheny Mountains
Shawanoe Cabbins
Juniata R.
Ft. Lyttleton
Red Stone
Fort Bird
Ft. Bedford
Sideling Hill
Williams Gap
Ft. Loudon
to Philadelphia
The Laurel Hill
Genl.
Great Meadows
Genl.
Braddocks
Little
Road
Meadows
PENSILVANIA
Ft. Cumberland
Savage R.
Potow mack R.
MARYLAND
VIRGINIA
FAC SIMILE
A MAP
he COUNTRY on the
& Muskingum Rivers
ewing the Situation
e INDIAN TOWNS with
he Army under the Command
Colonel Bouquet
By
Hutchins Afs.t Engineer.

westward had been left in a state of turbulence, which promised an abundant harvest of future mischief.[1] In one particular, at least, Bradstreet had occasioned serious detriment to the English interest. The Iroquois allies, who had joined his army, were disgusted by his treatment of them, while they were roused to contempt by the imbecility of his conduct towards the enemy; and thus the efforts of Sir William Johnson to secure the attachment of these powerful tribes were in no small degree counteracted and neutralized.[2]

While Bradstreet's troops were advancing upon the lakes, or lying idle in their camp at Sandusky, another expedition was in progress at the southward, with abler conduct and a more auspicious result.

[1] MS. Letter — *Johnson to the Board of Trade*, December 26.

[2] The provincial officers, to whom the command of the Indian allies was assigned, drew up a paper containing complaints against Bradstreet, and particulars of his misconduct during the expedition. This curious document, from which a few extracts have been given, was found among the private papers of Sir William Johnson.

A curious discovery, in probable connection with Bradstreet's expedition, has lately been made public. At McMahon's Beach, on Lake Erie, eight or ten miles west of Cleveland, a considerable number of bayonets, bullets, musket-barrels, and fragments of boats, have from time to time been washed by storms from the sands, or dug up on the adjacent shore, as well as an English silver-hilted sword, several silver spoons, and a few old French and English coins. A mound full of bones and skulls, apparently of Europeans hastily buried, has also been found at the same place The probability is strong that these are the remains of Bradstreet's disaster. See a paper by Dr. J. P. Kirtland, in Whittlesey's *History of Cleveland*, 105.

CHAPTER XXVII.

1764.

BOUQUET FORCES THE DELAWARES AND SHAWANOES TO SUE FOR PEACE.

THE work of ravage had begun afresh upon the borders. The Indians had taken the precaution to remove all their settlements to the western side of the River Muskingum, trusting that the impervious forests, with their unnumbered streams, would prove a sufficient barrier against invasion. Having thus, as they thought, placed their women and children in safety, they had flung themselves upon the settlements with all the rage and ferocity of the previous season. So fierce and active were the war-parties on the borders, that the English governor of Pennsylvania had recourse to a measure which the frontier inhabitants had long demanded, and issued a proclamation, offering a high bounty for Indian scalps, whether of men or women; a barbarous expedient, fruitful of butcheries and murders, but incapable of producing any decisive result.[1]

[1] The following is an extract from the proclamation:—

"I do hereby declare and promise, that there shall be paid out of the moneys lately granted for his Majesty's use, to all and every person and

Early in the season, a soldier named David Owens, who, several years before, had deserted and joined the Indians, came to one of the outposts, accompanied by a young provincial recently taken prisoner on the Delaware, and bringing five scalps. While living among the Indians, Owens had formed a connection with one of their women, who had borne him several children. Growing tired, at length, of the forest life, he had become anxious to return to the settlements, but feared to do so without first having made some atonement for his former desertion. One night, he had been encamped on the Susquehanna, with four Shawanoe

persons not in the pay of this province, the following several and respective premiums and bounties for the prisoners and scalps of the enemy Indians that shall be taken or killed within the bounds of this province, as limited by the royal charter, or in pursuit from within the said bounds; that is to say, for every male Indian enemy above ten years old, who shall be taken prisoner, and delivered at any forts garrisoned by the troops in the pay of this province, or at any of the county towns, to the keeper of the common jails there, the sum of one hundred and fifty Spanish dollars, or pieces of eight. For every female Indian enemy, taken prisoner and brought in as aforesaid, and for every male Indian enemy of ten years old or under, taken prisoner and delivered as aforesaid, the sum of one hundred and thirty pieces of eight. For the scalp of every male Indian enemy above the age of ten years, produced as evidence of their being killed, the sum of one hundred and thirty-four pieces of eight. And for the scalp of every female Indian enemy above the age of ten years, produced as evidence of their being killed, the sum of fifty pieces of eight."

The action of such measures has recently been illustrated in the instance of New Mexico before its conquest by the Americans. The inhabitants of that country, too timorous to defend themselves against the Apaches and other tribes, who descended upon them in frequent forays from the neighboring mountains, took into pay a band of foreigners, chiefly American trappers, for whom the Apache lances had no such terrors, and, to stimulate their exertions, proclaimed a bounty on scalps. The success of the measure was judged admirable, until it was found that the unscrupulous confederates were in the habit of shooting down any Indian, whether friend or enemy, who came within range of their rifles, and that the government had been paying rewards for the scalps of its own allies and dependants.

warriors, a boy of the same tribe, his own wife and two children, and another Indian woman. The young provincial, who came with him to the settlements, was also of the party. In the middle of the night, Owens arose, and looking about him saw, by the dull glow of the camp-fire, that all were buried in deep sleep. Cautiously awakening the young provincial, he told him to leave the place, and lie quiet at a little distance, until he should call him. He next stealthily removed the weapons from beside the sleeping savages, and concealed them in the woods, reserving to himself two loaded rifles. Returning to the camp, he knelt on the ground between two of the yet unconscious warriors, and, pointing a rifle at the head of each, touched the triggers, and shot both dead at once. Startled by the reports, the survivors sprang to their feet in bewildered terror. The two remaining warriors bounded into the woods; but the women and children, benumbed with fright, had no power to escape, and one and all died shrieking under the hatchet of the miscreant. His devilish work complete, the wretch sat watching until daylight among the dead bodies of his children and comrades, undaunted by the awful gloom and solitude of the darkened forest. In the morning, he scalped his victims, with the exception of the two children, and, followed by the young white man, directed his steps towards the settlements, with the bloody trophies of his atrocity. His desertion was pardoned; he was employed as an interpreter, and ordered to accompany the troops on the intended expedition. His example is one of many in which the worst acts of Indian ferocity have been thrown into shade by the enormities of white barbarians.[1]

Bouquet was now urging on his preparations for his march into the valley of the Ohio. We have seen how, in the preceding summer, he had been embarrassed by what he calls "the unnatural obstinacy of the government of Pennsylvania." "It disables us," he had written to the equally indignant Amherst, "from crushing the savages on this side of the lakes, and may draw us into a lingering war, which might have been terminated by another blow. . . . I see that the whole burden of this war will rest upon us; and while the few regular troops you have left can keep the enemy at a distance, the Provinces will let them fight it out without interfering."[2]

Amherst, after vainly hoping that the Assembly of Pennsylvania would "exert themselves like men,"[3]

[1] Gordon, *Hist. Penn.* 625. Robison, *Narrative.*

Extract from a MS. Letter — *Sir W. Johnson to Governor Penn:* —

"Burnetsfield, June 18th, 1764.

"David Owens was a Corporal in Capt. McClean's Compy., and lay once in Garrison at my House. He deserted several times, as I am informed, & went to live among the Delaware & Shawanese, with whose language he was acquainted. His Father having been long a trader amongst them.

"The circumstances relating to his leaving the Indians have been told me by several Indians. That he went out a hunting with his Indian Wife and several of her relations, most of whom, with his Wife, he killed and scalped as they slept. As he was always much attached to Indians, I fancy he began to fear he was unsafe amongst them, & killed them rather to make his peace with the English, than from any dislike either to them or their principles."

[2] MS. Letter — *Bouquet to Amherst,* 15 Sept. 1763.

[3] "If the present situation of the poor families who have abandoned their settlements, and the danger that the whole province is threatened

had, equally in vain, sent Colonel James Robertson as a special messenger to the provincial commissioners. "I found all my pleading vain," the disappointed envoy had written, "and believe Cicero's would have been so. I never saw any men so determined in the right as these people are in this absurdly wrong resolve."[1] The resolve in question related to the seven hundred men whom the Assembly had voted to raise for protecting the gathering of the harvest, and whom the commissioners stiffly refused to place at the disposition of the military authorities.

It is apparent in all this that, at an early period of the war, a change had come over the spirit of the commander-in-chief, whose prejudices and pride had revolted, at the outset, against the asking of provincial aid to "chastise the savages," but who had soon been brought to reason by his own helplessness and the exigencies of the situation. In like manner, a change, though at the eleventh hour, had now come over the spirit of the Pennsylvania Assembly. The invasion of the Paxton borderers, during the past winter, had scared the Quaker faction into their senses. Their old quar-

with, can have no effect in opening the hearts of your Assembly to exert themselves *like men*, I am sure no arguments I could urge will be regarded." — *Amherst to Governor Hamilton*, 7 July, 1763.

"The situation of this country is deplorable, and the infatuation of their government in taking the most dilatory and ineffectual measures for their protection, highly blamable. They have not paid the least regard to the plan I proposed to them on my arrival here, and will lose this and York counties if the savages push their attacks." — *Bouquet to Amherst*, 13 July, 1763.

[1] MS. Letter — *Robertson to Amherst*, 19 July, 1763

rel with the governor and the proprietaries, their scruples about war, and their affection for Indians, were all postponed to the necessity of the hour. The Assembly voted to raise three hundred men to guard the frontiers, and a thousand to join Bouquet. Their commissioners went farther; for they promised to send to England for fifty couples of bloodhounds, to hunt Indian scalping-parties.[1]

In the preceding summer, half as many men would have sufficed; for, after the battle of Bushy Run, Bouquet wrote to Amherst from Fort Pitt, that, with a reinforcement of three hundred provin cial rangers, he could destroy all the Delaware towns, "and clear the country of that vermin between this fort and Lake Erie;"[2] but he added, with some bitterness, that the provinces would not even furnish escorts to convoys, so that his hands were completely tied.[3]

It was past midsummer before the thousand Pennsylvanians were ready to move; so that the

[1] "They have at my recommendation agreed to send to Great Britain for 50 Couples of Blood Hounds to be employed with Rangers on horse back against Indian scalping parties, which will I hope deter more effectually the Savages from that sort of war than our troops can possibly do." — *Bouquet to Amherst,* 7 June, 1764.

[2] MS. Letter — *Bouquet to Amherst,* 27 Aug. 1763.

[3] MS. Letter — *Bouquet to Amherst,* 24 Oct. 1763. In this letter, Bouquet enlarges, after a fashion which must have been singularly unpalatable to his commander, on the danger of employing regulars alone in forest warfare: "Without a certain number of woodsmen, I cannot think it advisable to employ regulars in the Woods against Savages, as they cannot procure any intelligence and are open to continual surprises, nor can they pursue to any distance their enemy when they have routed them; and should they have the misfortune to be defeated, the whole would be destroyed if above one day's march from a Fort. That is my opinion in wh. I hope to be deceived."

season for navigating the Ohio and its branches was lost. As for Virginia and Maryland, they would do absolutely nothing. On the fifth of August, Bouquet was at Carlisle, with his new levies and such regulars as he had, chiefly the veterans of Bushy Run. Before the tenth, two hundred of the Pennsylvanians had deserted, sheltered, as usual, by the country people. His force, even with full ranks, was too small; and he now took the responsibility of writing to Colonel Lewis, of the Virginia militia, to send him two hundred volunteers, to take the place of the deserters.[1] A body of Virginians accordingly joined him at Fort Pitt, to his great satisfaction, for he set a high value on these backwoods riflemen; but the responsibility he had assumed proved afterwards a source of extreme annoyance to him.

The little army soon reached Fort Loudon, then in a decayed and ruinous condition, like all the wooden forts built during the French war. Here Bouquet received the strange communication from Bradstreet, informing him that he might return home with his troops, as a treaty had been concluded with the Delawares and Shawanoes. Bouquet's disgust found vent in a letter to the commander-in-chief· "I received this moment advice from Colonel Bradstreet. . . . The terms he gives them (the Indians) are such as fill me with astonishment. . . . Had Colonel Bradstreet been as well informed as I am of the horrid perfidies of the Delawares and Shawanese, whose parties as late as the 22d instant

[1] MS. Letter — *Bouquet to Gage,* 10 Aug. 1764.

killed six men . . . he never could have compromised the honor of the nation by such disgraceful conditions, and that at a time when two armies, after long struggles, are in full motion to penetrate into the heart of the enemy's country. Permit me likewise humbly to represent to your Excellency that I have not deserved the affront laid upon me by this treaty of peace, concluded by a younger officer, in the department where you have done me the honor to appoint me to command, without referring the deputies of the savages to me at Fort Pitt, but telling them that he shall send and prevent my proceeding against them. I can therefore take no notice of his peace, but (*shall*) proceed forthwith to the Ohio, where I shall wait till I receive your orders."[1]

After waiting for more than a week for his wrath to cool, he wrote to Bradstreet in terms which, though restrained and temperate, plainly showed his indignation.[2] He had now reached Fort Bedford, where more Pennsylvanians ran off, with their arms and horses, and where he vainly waited the arrival of a large reinforcement of friendly Indians,

[1] MS. Letter — *Bouquet to Gage*, 27 Aug. 1764. He wrote to Governor Penn, as follows: —

"Fort Loudon, 27 Aug. 1764.

"Sir:

"I have the honor to transmit to you a letter from Colonel Bradstreet, who acquaints me that he has granted peace to all the Indians living between Lake Erie and the Ohio; but as no satisfaction is insisted on, I hope the General will not confirm it, and that I shall not be a witness to a transaction which would fix an indelible stain upon the Nation.

"I therefore take no notice of that pretended peace, & proceed forthwith on the expedition, fully determined to treat as enemies any Delawares or Shawanese I shall find in my way, till I receive contrary orders from the General."

[2] MS. Letter — *Bouquet to Bradstreet*, 5 Sept. 1764

who had been promised by Sir William Johnson, but who never arrived. On reaching Fort Ligonier, he had the satisfaction of forwarding two letters, which the commander-in-chief had significantly sent through his hands, to Bradstreet, containing a peremptory disavowal of the treaty.[1] Continuing to advance, he passed in safety the scene of his desperate fight of the last summer, and on the seventeenth of September arrived at Fort Pitt, with no other loss than that of a few men picked off from the flanks and rear by lurking Indian marksmen.[2]

The day before his arrival, ten Delaware chiefs and warriors appeared on the farther bank of the river, pretending to be deputies sent by their nation

[1] See p. 178, *note*.

[2] Captain Grant, who had commanded during the spring at Fort Pitt, had sent bad accounts of the disposition of the neighboring Indians; but added, "At this Post we defy all the Savages in the Woods. I wish they would dare appear before us. . . . Repairing Batteaux, ploughing, gardening, making Fences, and fetching home fire Wood goes on constantly every day, from sun rise to the setting of the same." — *Grant to Bouquet*, 2 April, 1764. A small boy, captured with his mother the summer before, escaped to the fort about this time, and reported that the Indians meant to plant their corn and provide for their families, after which they would come to the fort and burn it. The youthful informant also declared that none of them had more than a pound of powder left. Soon after, a man named Hicks appeared, professing to have escaped from the Indians, though he was strongly suspected of being a renegade and a spy, and was therefore cross-questioned severely. He confirmed what the boy had said as to the want of ammunition among the Indians, and added that they had sent for a supply to the French at the Illinois, but that the reception they received from the commandant had not satisfied them. General Gage sent the following not very judicial instructions with regard to Hicks: "He is a great villain. I am glad he is secured. I must desire you will have him tried by a general Court-Martial for a *Spy*. Let the proceedings of the Court prove him a *Spy* as strong as they can, and if he does turn out a *spy*, he must be hanged." — *Gage to Bouquet*, 14 May, 1764. The court, however, could find no proof.

to confer with the English commander. Three of them, after much hesitation, came over to the fort, where, being closely questioned, and found unable to give any good account of their mission, they were detained as spies; while their companions, greatly disconcerted, fled back to their villages. Bouquet, on his arrival, released one of the three captives, and sent him home with the following message to his people: —

"I have received an account, from Colonel Bradstreet, that your nations had begged for peace, which he had consented to grant, upon assurance that you had recalled all your warriors from our frontiers; and, in consequence of this, I would not have proceeded against your towns, if I had not heard that, in open violation of your engagements, you have since murdered several of our people.

"I was therefore determined to have attacked you, as a people whose promises can no more be relied on. But I will put it once more in your power to save yourselves and your families from total destruction, by giving us satisfaction for the hostilities committed against us. And, first, you are to leave the path open for my expresses from hence to Detroit; and as I am now to send two men with despatches to Colonel Bradstreet, who commands on the lakes, I desire to know whether you will send two of your people to bring them safe back with an answer. And if they receive any injury either in going or coming, or if the letters are taken from them, I will immediately put the Indians now in my power to death, and will show no mercy, for the future, to any of your nations that shall fall into my hands. I allow you ten days to have my letters delivered at Detroit, and ten days to bring me back an answer."[1]

The liberated spy faithfully discharged his mission; and the firm, decisive tone of the message had a profound effect upon the hostile warriors; clearly indicating, as it did, with what manner of man they had to deal. Many, who were before clamorous for battle, were now ready to sue for peace, as the only means to avert their ruin.

Before the army was ready to march, two Iroquois warriors came to the fort, pretending friendship, but anxious, in reality, to retard the expedition until the approaching winter should make it impossible to proceed. They represented the numbers of the enemy, and the extreme difficulty of penetrating so rough a country; and affirmed that, if the troops remained quiet, the hostile tribes, who were already collecting their prisoners, would soon arrive to make their submission. Bouquet turned a deaf ear to their advice, and sent them to inform the Delawares and Shawanoes that he was on his way to chastise them for their perfidy and cruelty, unless they should save themselves by an ample and speedy atonement.

Early in October, the troops left Fort Pitt, and began their westward march into a wilderness which no army had ever before sought to penetrate. Encumbered with their camp equipage, with droves of cattle and sheep for subsistence, and a long train

[1] *Account of Bouquet's Expedition*, 5.

of pack-horses laden with provisions, their progress was tedious and difficult, and seven or eight miles were the ordinary measure of a day's march. The woodsmen of Virginia, veteran hunters and Indian-fighters, were thrown far out in front and on either flank, scouring the forest to detect any sign of a lurking ambuscade. The pioneers toiled in the van, hewing their way through woods and thickets; while the army dragged its weary length behind them through the forest, like a serpent creeping through tall grass. The surrounding country, whenever a casual opening in the matted foliage gave a glimpse of its features, disclosed scenery of wild, primeval beauty. Sometimes the army defiled along the margin of the Ohio, by its broad eddying current and the bright landscape of its shores. Sometimes they descended into the thickest gloom of the woods, damp, still, and cool as the recesses of a cavern, where the black soil oozed beneath the tread, where the rough columns of the forest seemed to exude a clammy sweat, and the slimy mosses were trickling with moisture; while the carcasses of prostrate trees, green with the decay of a century, sank into pulp at the lightest pressure of the foot. More frequently, the forest was of a fresher growth; and the restless leaves of young maples and basswood shook down spots of sunlight on the marching columns. Sometimes they waded the clear current of a stream, with its vistas of arching foliage and sparkling water. There were intervals, but these were rare, when, escaping for a moment from the labyrinth of woods, they emerged into the light of an open meadow, rich with herbage, and girdled by a zone of forest; gladdened by the notes of birds, and enlivened, it may be, by grazing herds of deer. These spots, welcome to the forest traveller as an oasis to a wanderer in the desert, form the precursors of the prairies; which, growing wider and more frequent as one advances westward, expand at last into the boundless plains beyond the Mississippi.

On the tenth day after leaving Fort Pitt, the army reached the River Muskingum, and approached the objects of their march, the haunts of the barbarian warriors, who had turned whole districts into desolation. Their progress had met no interruption. A few skulking Indians had hovered about them, but, alarmed by their numbers, feared to venture an attack. The Indian cabins which they passed on their way were deserted by their tenants, who had joined their western brethren. When the troops crossed the Muskingum, they saw, a little below the fording-place, the abandoned wigwams of the village of Tuscaroras, recently the abode of more than a hundred families, who had fled in terror at the approach of the invaders.

Bouquet was in the heart of the enemy's country. Their villages, except some remoter settlements of the Shawanoes, all lay within a few days' march; and no other choice was left them than to sue for peace, or risk the desperate chances of battle against a commander who, a year before, with a third of his present force, had routed them at the fight of Bushy Run. The vigorous and active among them might, it is true, escape by flight; but, in doing so, they must abandon to the victors their dwellings, and their secret hordes of corn. They were confounded at the multitude of the invaders, exaggerated, doubtless, in the reports which reached their villages, and amazed that an army should force its way so deep into the forest fastnesses, which they had thought impregnable. They knew, on the other hand, that Colonel Bradstreet was still at Sandusky, in a position to assail them in the rear. Thus pressed on both sides, they saw that they must submit, and bend their stubborn pride to beg for peace; not alone with words, which cost nothing, and would have been worth nothing, but by the delivery of prisoners, and the surrender of chiefs and warriors as pledges of good faith. Bouquet had sent two soldiers from Fort Pitt with letters to Colonel Bradstreet; but these men had been detained, under specious pretexts, by the Delawares. They now appeared at his camp, sent back by their captors, with a message to the effect that, within a few days, the chiefs would arrive and hold a conference with him.

Bouquet continued his march down the valley of the Muskingum, until he reached a spot where the broad meadows, which bordered the river, would supply abundant grazing for the cattle and horses; while the terraces above, shaded by forest-trees, offered a convenient site for an encampment. Here he began to erect a small palisade work, as a depot for stores and baggage. Before the task was complete, a deputation of chiefs arrived, bringing word that their warriors were encamped, in great numbers, about eight miles from the spot, and desiring Bouquet to appoint the time and place for a council. He ordered them to meet him, on the next day, at a point near the margin of the river, a little below the camp; and thither a party of men was at once despatched, to erect a sort of rustic arbor of saplings and the boughs of trees, large enough to shelter the English officers and the Indian chiefs. With a host of warriors in the neighborhood, who would gladly break in upon them, could they hope that the attack would succeed, it behooved the English to use every precaution. A double guard was placed, and a stringent discipline enforced.

In the morning, the little army moved in battle order to the place of council. Here the principal officers assumed their seats under the canopy of branches, while the glittering array of the troops was drawn out on the meadow in front, in such a manner as to produce the most imposing effect on the minds of the Indians, in whose eyes the sight of fifteen hundred men under arms was a spectacle equally new and astounding. The perfect order and silence of the far-extended lines; the ridges of bayonets flashing in the sun; the fluttering tartans of the Highland regulars; the bright red uniform of the Royal Americans; the darker garb and duller trappings of the Pennsylvania troops, and the bands of Virginia backwoodsmen, who, in fringed hunting-frocks and Indian moccasons, stood leaning carelessly on their rifles,—all these combined to form a scene of military pomp and power not soon to be forgotten.

At the appointed hour, the deputation appeared. The most prominent among them were Kiashuta, chief of the band of Senecas who had deserted their ancient homes to form a colony on the Ohio; Custaloga, chief of the Delawares; and the head chief of the Shawanoes, whose name sets orthography at defiance. As they approached, painted and plumed in all their savage pomp, they looked neither to the right hand nor to the left, not deigning, under the eyes of their enemy, to cast even a glance at the military display around them. They seated themselves, with stern, impassive looks, and an air of sullen dignity; while their sombre brows betrayed the hatred still rankling in their hearts. After a few minutes had been consumed in the indispensable ceremony of smoking, Turtle Heart, a chief of the Delawares, and orator of the deputation, rose, bearing in his hand a bag containing the belts of wampum. Addressing himself to the English commander, he spoke as follows, delivering a belt for every clause of his speech: —

"Brother, I speak in behalf of the three nations whose chiefs are here present. With this belt I open your ears and your hearts, that you may listen to my words.

"Brother, this war was neither your fault nor ours. It was the work of the nations who live to the westward, and of our wild young men, who would have killed us if we had resisted them. We now put away all evil from our hearts; and we hope that your mind and ours will once more be united together.

"Brother, it is the will of the Great Spirit that there should be peace between us. We, on our side, now take fast hold of the chain of friendship; but, as we cannot hold it alone, we desire that you will take hold also, and we must look up to the Great Spirit, that he may make us strong, and not permit this chain to fall from our hands.

"Brother, these words come from our hearts, and not from our lips. You desire that we should deliver up your flesh and blood now captive among us; and, to show you that we are sincere, we now return you as many of them as we have at present been able to bring. [Here he delivered eighteen white prisoners, who had been brought by the deputation to the council.] You shall receive the rest as soon as we have time to collect them."[1]

In such figurative terms, not devoid of dignity, did the Indian orator sue for peace to his detested enemies. When he had concluded, the chiefs of every tribe rose in succession, to express concurrence in what he had said, each delivering a belt of wampum and a bundle of small sticks; the latter designed to indicate the number of English prisoners whom his followers retained, and whom he pledged himself to surrender. In an Indian coun-

[1] This speech is taken from the official journals of Colonel Bouquet, a copy of which is preserved in the archives of Pennsylvania, at Harrisburg, engrossed, if the writer's memory does not fail him, in one of the volumes of the *Provincial Records*. The published narrative, which has often been cited, is chiefly founded upon the authority of these documents, and the writer has used his materials with great skill and faithfulness, though occasionally it has been found advisable to have recourse to the original journals, to supply some omission or obscurity in the printed compilation.

cil, when one of the speakers has advanced a matter of weight and urgency, the other party defers his reply to the following day, that due time may be allowed for deliberation. Accordingly, in the present instance, the council adjourned to the next morning, each party retiring to its respective camp. But, when day dawned, the weather had changed. The valley of the Muskingum was filled with driving mist and rain, and the meeting was in consequence postponed. On the third day, the landscape brightened afresh, the troops marched once more to the place of council, and the Indian chiefs convened to hear the reply of their triumphant foe. It was not of a kind to please them. The opening words gave an earnest of what was to come; for Bouquet discarded the usual address of an Indian harangue: fathers, brothers, or children, — terms which imply a relation of friendship, or a desire to conciliate, — and adopted a sterner and more distant form.

"Sachems, war-chiefs, and warriors,[1] the excuses you have offered are frivolous and unavailing, and your conduct is without defence or apology. You could not have acted as you pretend to have done through fear of the western nations; for, had you stood faithful to us, you knew that we would have

[1] The sachem is the civil chief, who directs the counsels of the tribe, and governs in time of peace. His office, on certain conditions, is hereditary; while the war-chief, or military leader, acquires his authority solely by personal merit, and seldom transmits it to his offspring. Sometimes the civil and military functions are discharged by the same person, as in the instance of Pontiac himself.

The speech of Bouquet, as given above, is taken, with some omission and condensation, from the journals mentioned in the preceding note.

protected you against their anger; and as for your young men, it was your duty to punish them, if they did amiss. You have drawn down our just resentment by your violence and perfidy. Last summer, in cold blood, and in a time of profound peace, you robbed and murdered the traders, who had come among you at your own express desire. You attacked Fort Pitt, which was built by your consent; and you destroyed our outposts and garrisons, whenever treachery could place them in your power. You assailed our troops — the same who now stand before you — in the woods at Bushy Run; and, when we had routed and driven you off, you sent your scalping-parties to the frontier, and murdered many hundreds of our people. Last July, when the other nations came to ask for peace, at Niagara, you not only refused to attend, but sent an insolent message instead, in which you expressed a pretended contempt for the English; and, at the same time, told the surrounding nations that you would never lay down the hatchet. Afterwards, when Colonel Bradstreet came up Lake Erie, you sent a deputation of your chiefs, and concluded a treaty with him; but your engagements were no sooner made than broken; and, from that day to this, you have scalped and butchered us without ceasing. Nay, I am informed that, when you heard that this army was penetrating the woods, you mustered your warriors to attack us, and were only deterred from doing so when you found how greatly we outnumbered you. This is not the only instance of your bad faith;

for, since the beginning of the last war, you have made repeated treaties with us, and promised to give up your prisoners; but you have never kept these engagements, nor any others. We shall endure this no longer; and I am now come among you to force you to make atonement for the injuries you have done us. I have brought with me the relatives of those you have murdered. They are eager for vengeance, and nothing restrains them from taking it but my assurance that this army shall not leave your country until you have given them an ample satisfaction.

"Your allies, the Ottawas, Ojibwas, and Wyandots, have begged for peace; the Six Nations have leagued themselves with us; the great lakes and rivers around you are all in our possession, and your friends the French are in subjection to us, and can do no more to aid you. You are all in our power, and, if we choose, we can exterminate you from the earth; but the English are a merciful and generous people, averse to shed the blood even of their greatest enemies; and if it were possible that you could convince us that you sincerely repent of your past perfidy, and that we could depend on your good behavior for the future, you might yet hope for mercy and peace. If I find that you faithfully execute the conditions which I shall prescribe, I will not treat you with the severity you deserve.

"I give you twelve days from this date to deliver into my hands all the prisoners in your possession, without exception: Englishmen, Frenchmen, women, and children; whether adopted into your tribes, married, or living among you under any denomination or pretence whatsoever. And you are to furnish these prisoners with clothing, provisions, and horses, to carry them to Fort Pitt. When you have fully complied with these conditions, you shall then know on what terms you may obtain the peace you sue for."

This speech, with the stern voice and countenance of the speaker, told with chilling effect upon the awe-stricken hearers. It quelled their native haughtiness, and sunk them to the depths of humiliation. Their speeches in reply were dull and insipid, void of that savage eloquence, which, springing from a wild spirit of independence, has so often distinguished the forest orators. Judging the temper of their enemies by their own insatiable thirst for vengeance, they hastened, with all the alacrity of terror, to fulfil the prescribed conditions, and avert the threatened ruin. They dispersed to their different villages, to collect and bring in the prisoners; while Bouquet, on his part, knowing that his best security for their good faith was to keep up the alarm which his decisive measures had created, determined to march yet nearer to their settlements. Still following the course of the Muskingum, he descended to a spot near its confluence with its main branch, which might be regarded as a central point with respect to the surrounding Indian villages. Here, with the exception of the distant Shawanoe settlements, they were all within reach of his hand, and he could readily chastise the first attempt at deceit or evasion. The principal chiefs of each tribe had been forced to accompany him as hostages.[1]

For the space of a day, hundreds of axes were busy at their work. The trees were felled, the ground cleared, and, with marvellous rapidity, a town sprang up in the heart of the wilderness, martial in aspect and rigorous in discipline; with storehouses, hospitals, and works of defence, rude sylvan cabins mingled with white tents, and the forest rearing its sombre rampart around the whole. On one side of this singular encampment was a range of buildings, designed to receive the expected prisoners; and matrons, brought for this purpose with the army, were appointed to take charge of the women and children among them. At the opposite side, a canopy of branches, sustained on the upright trunks of young trees, formed a rude council-hall, in keeping with the savage assembly for whose reception it was designed.

And now, issuing from the forest, came warriors,

[1] The following is from a letter of Bouquet dated *Camp near Tuscarawas, 96 miles west of Fort Pitt*, 21st Oct. 1764: "They came accordingly on the 15th and met me here, to where I had moved the camp. Time does not permit me to send you all the messages which have passed since, and the conferences I have had with them, as we are going to march. I shall for the present inform you that they have behaved with the utmost submission, and have agreed to deliver into my hands all their prisoners, who appear to be very numerous, on the 1st of November, and, as I will not leave any thing undone, they have not only consented that I should march to their towns, but have given me four of their men to conduct the Army. This is the only point hitherto settled with them. Their excessive fear having nearly made them run away once more, that circumstance and the Treaty of Colonel Bradstreet, of which they produce the original, added to the total want of government among them, render the execution of my orders very intricate."

conducting troops of prisoners, or leading captive children, — wild young barbarians, born perhaps among themselves, and scarcely to be distinguished from their own. Yet, seeing the sullen reluctance which the Indians soon betrayed in this ungrateful task, Bouquet thought it expedient to stimulate their efforts by sending detachments of soldiers to each of the villages, still retaining the chiefs in pledge for their safety. About this time, a Canadian officer, named Hertel, with a party of Caughnawaga Indians, arrived with a letter from Colonel Bradstreet, dated at Sandusky. The writer declared that he was unable to remain longer in the Indian country, and was on the point of retiring down Lake Erie with his army; a movement which, at the least, was of doubtful necessity, and which might have involved the most disastrous consequences. Had the tidings been received but a few days sooner, the whole effect of Bouquet's measures would probably have been destroyed, the Indians encouraged to resistance, and the war brought to the arbitration of a battle, which must needs have been a fierce and bloody one. But, happily for both parties, Bouquet now had his enemies firmly in his grasp, and the boldest warrior dared not violate the truce.

The messengers who brought the letter of Bradstreet brought also the tidings that peace was made with the northern Indians; but stated, at the same time, that these tribes had murdered many of their captives, and given up but few of the remainder, so that no small number were still within their power. The conduct of Bradstreet in this matter was the more disgraceful, since he had been encamped for weeks almost within gunshot of the Wyandot villages at Sandusky, where most of the prisoners were detained. Bouquet, on his part, though separated from this place by a journey of many days, resolved to take upon himself the duty which his brother officer had strangely neglected. He sent an embassy to Sandusky, demanding that the prisoners should be surrendered. This measure was in a great degree successful. He despatched messengers soon after to the principal Shawanoe village, on the Scioto, distant about eighty miles from his camp, to rouse the inhabitants to a greater activity than they seemed inclined to display. This was a fortunate step; for the Shawanoes of the Scioto, who had been guilty of atrocious cruelties during the war, had conceived the idea that they were excluded from the general amnesty, and marked out for destruction. This notion had been propagated, and perhaps suggested, by the French traders in their villages; and so thorough was the conviction of the Shawanoes, that they came to the desperate purpose of murdering their prisoners, and marching, with all the warriors they could muster, to attack the English. This plan was no sooner formed than the French traders opened their stores of bullets and gunpowder, and dealt them out freely to the Indians. Bouquet's messengers came in time to prevent the catastrophe, and relieve the terrors of the Shawanoes, by the assurance that peace would be granted to them on the same conditions as to the rest. Thus encouraged, they abandoned their design, and set out with lighter hearts for the English camp, bringing with them a portion of their prisoners. When about half-way on their journey, they were met by an Indian runner, who told them that a soldier had been killed in the woods, and their tribe charged with the crime. On hearing this, their fear revived, and with it their former purpose. Having collected their prisoners in a meadow, they surrounded the miserable wretches, armed with guns, war-clubs, and bows and arrows, and prepared to put them to death. But another runner arrived before the butchery began, and, assuring them that what they had heard was false, prevailed on them once more to proceed. They pursued their journey without farther interruption, and, coming in safety to the camp, delivered the prisoners whom they had brought.

These by no means included all of their captives, for nearly a hundred were left behind, because they belonged to warriors who had gone to the Illinois to procure arms and ammunition from the French; and there is no authority in an Indian community powerful enough to deprive the meanest warrior of his property, even in circumstances of the greatest public exigency. This was clearly understood by the English commander, and he therefore received the submission of the Shawanoes, at the same time compelling them to deliver hostages for the future surrender of the remaining prisoners.

Band after band of captives had been daily arriving, until upwards of two hundred were now collected in the camp; including, as far as could be ascertained, all who had been in the hands of the Indians, excepting those belonging to the absent warriors of the Shawanoes. Up to this time, Bouquet had maintained a stern and rigorous demeanor; repressing his natural clemency and humanity, refusing all friendly intercourse with the Indians, and telling them that he should treat them as enemies until they had fully complied with all the required conditions. In this, he displayed his knowledge of their character; for, like all warlike savages, they are extremely prone to interpret lenity and moderation into timidity and indecision; and he who, from good-nature or mistaken philanthropy, is betrayed into yielding a point which he has before insisted on, may have deep cause to rue it. As their own dealings with their enemies are not leavened with such humanizing ingredients, they can seldom comprehend them; and to win over an Indian foe by kindness should only be attempted by one who has already proved clearly that he is able and ready to subdue him by force.

But now, when every condition was satisfied, such inexorable rigor was no longer demanded; and, having convoked the chiefs in the sylvan council-house, Bouquet signified his willingness to receive their offers of peace.

"Brother," began the Indian orator, "with this belt of wampum I dispel the black cloud that has hung so long over our heads, that the sunshine of peace may once more descend to warm and gladden us. I wipe the tears from your eyes, and condole with you on the loss of your brethren who have perished in this war. I gather their bones together, and cover them deep in the earth, that the sight of them may no longer bring sorrow to your hearts ; and I scatter dry leaves over the spot that it may depart for ever from memory.

"The path of peace, which once ran between your dwellings and mine, has of late been choked with thorns and briers, so that no one could pass that way; and we have both almost forgotten that such a path had ever been. I now clear away all such obstructions, and make a broad, smooth road, so that you and I may freely visit each other, as our fathers used to do. I kindle a great council fire, whose smoke shall rise to heaven, in view of all the nations; while you and I sit together and smoke the peace-pipe at its blaze." [1]

[1] An Indian council, on solemn occasions, is always opened with preliminary forms, sufficiently wearisome and tedious, but made indispensable by immemorial custom ; for this people are as much bound by their conventional usages as the most artificial children of civilization. The forms are varied to some extent, according to the imagination and taste of the speaker; but in all essential respects they are closely similar, through out the tribes of Algonquin and Iroquois lineage. They run somewhat as follows, each sentence being pronounced with great solemnity, and confirmed by the delivery of a wampum belt: Brothers, with this belt I open your ears that you may hear — I remove grief and sorrow from your hearts — I draw from your feet the thorns which have pierced them as you journeyed thither — I clean the seats of the council-house, that you may sit at ease — I wash your head and body, that your spirits may be refreshed — I condole with you on the loss of the friends who have died since we last met — I wipe out any blood which may have been spilt between us. This ceremony, which, by the delivery of so many belts of wampum, entailed no small expense, was never used except on the most important occasions ; and at the councils with Colonel Bouquet the angry warriors seem wholly to have dispensed with it.

In this strain, the orator of each tribe, in turn, expressed the purpose of his people to lay down their arms, and live for the future in friendship with the English. Every deputation received a separate audience, and the successive conferences were thus extended through several days. To each and all, Bouquet made a similar reply, in words to the following effect: —

"By your full compliance with the conditions which I imposed, you have satisfied me of your sincerity, and I now receive you once more as brethren. The King, my master, has commissioned me, not to make treaties for him, but to fight his battles; and though I now offer you peace, it is not in my power to settle its precise terms and conditions. For this, I refer you to Sir William Johnson, his Majesty's agent and superintendent

An Indian orator is provided with a stock of metaphors, which he always makes use of for the expression of certain ideas. Thus, to make war is to raise the hatchet; to make peace is to take hold of the chain of friendship; to deliberate is to kindle the council-fire; to cover the bones of the dead is to make reparation and gain forgiveness for the act of killing them. A state of war and disaster is typified by a black cloud; a state of peace, by bright sunshine, or by an open path between the two nations.

The orator seldom speaks without careful premeditation of what he is about to say; and his memory is refreshed by the belts of wampum, which he delivers after every clause in his harangue, as a pledge of the sincerity and truth of his words. These belts are carefully preserved by the hearers, as a substitute for written records; a use for which they are the better adapted, as they are often worked with hieroglyphics expressing the meaning they are designed to preserve. Thus, at a treaty of peace, the principal belt often bears the figures of an Indian and a white man holding a chain between them.

For the nature and uses of wampum, see note, *ante*, p. 186, *note*.

Though a good memory is an essential qualification of an Indian orator, it would be unjust not to observe that striking outbursts of spontaneous eloquence have sometimes proceeded from their lips.

for Indian affairs, who will settle with you the articles of peace, and determine every thing in relation to trade. Two things, however, I shall insist on. And, first, you are to give hostages, as security that you will preserve good faith, and send, without delay, a deputation of your chiefs to Sir William Johnson. In the next place, these chiefs are to be fully empowered to treat in behalf of your nation; and you will bind yourselves to adhere strictly to every thing they shall agree upon in your behalf."

These demands were readily complied with. Hostages were given, and chiefs appointed for the embassy; and now, for the first time, Bouquet, to the great relief of the Indians, — for they doubted his intentions, — extended to them the hand of friendship, which he had so long withheld. A prominent chief of the Delawares, too proud to sue for peace, had refused to attend the council; on which Bouquet ordered him to be deposed, and a successor, of a less obdurate spirit, installed in his place. The Shawanoes were the last of the tribes admitted to a hearing; and the demeanor of their orator clearly evinced the haughty reluctance with which he stooped to ask peace of his mortal enemies.

"When you came among us," such were his concluding words, "you came with a hatchet raised to strike us. We now take it from your hand, and throw it up to the Great Spirit, that he may do with it what shall seem good in his sight. We hope that you, who are warriors, will take hold of the chain of friendship which we now extend to you. We, who are also warriors, will take hold as you do; and we will think no more of war, in pity for our women, children, and old men."[1]

On this occasion, the Shawanoe chiefs, expressing a hope for a renewal of the friendship which in former years had subsisted between their people and the English, displayed the dilapidated parchments of several treaties made between their ancestors and the descendants of William Penn, — documents, some of which had been preserved among them for more than half a century, with the scrupulous respect they are prone to exhibit for such ancestral records. They were told that, since they had not delivered all their prisoners, they could scarcely expect to meet the same indulgence which had been extended to their brethren; but that, nevertheless, in full belief of their sincerity, the English would grant them peace, on condition of their promising to surrender the remaining cap-

[1] The Shawanoe speaker, in expressing his intention of disarming his enemy by laying aside his own designs of war, makes use of an unusual metaphor. To *bury the hatchet* is the figure in common use on such occasions, but he adopts a form of speech which he regards as more significant and emphatic, — that of throwing it up to the Great Spirit. Unwilling to confess that he yields through fear of the enemy, he professes to wish for peace merely for the sake of his women and children.

At the great council at Lancaster, in 1762, a chief of the Oneidas, anxious to express, in the strongest terms, the firmness of the peace which had been concluded, had recourse to the following singular figure: "In the country of the Oneidas there is a great pine-tree, so huge and old that half its branches are dead with time. I tear it up by the roots, and, looking down into the hole, I see a dark stream of water, flowing with a strong current, deep under ground. Into this stream I fling the hatchet, and the current sweeps it away, no man knows whither. Then I plant the tree again where it stood before, and thus this war will be ended for ever"

tives early in the following spring, and giving up six of their chiefs as hostages. These conditions were agreed to; and it may be added that, at the appointed time, all the prisoners who had been left in their hands, to the number of a hundred, were brought in to Fort Pitt, and delivered up to the commanding officer.[1]

From the hard formalities and rigid self-control of an Indian council-house, where the struggles of fear, rage, and hatred were deep buried beneath a surface of iron immobility, we turn to scenes of a widely different nature; an exhibition of mingled and contrasted passions, more worthy the pen of the dramatist than that of the historian; who, restricted to the meagre outline of recorded authority, can reflect but a feeble image of the truth. In the ranks of the Pennsylvania troops, and among the Virginia riflemen, were the fathers, brothers, and husbands of those whose rescue from captivity was a chief object of the march. Ignorant what had befallen them, and doubtful whether they were yet among the living, these men had joined the

[1] A party of the Virginia volunteers had been allowed by Bouquet to go to the remoter Shawanoe towns, in the hope of rescuing captive relatives. They returned to Fort Pitt at midwinter, bringing nine prisoners, all children or old women. The whole party was frost-bitten, and had endured the extremity of suffering on the way. They must have perished but for a Shawanoe chief, named Benewisica, to whose care Bouquet had confided them, and who remained with them both going and returning, hunting for them to keep them from famishing. — *Capt. Murray to Bouquet*, 31 Jan. 1765.

Besides the authorities before mentioned in relation to these transactions, the correspondence of Bouquet with the commander-in-chief, throughout the expedition, together with letters from some of the officers who accompanied him, have been examined. For General Gage's summary of the results of the campaign, see Appendix, F.

army, in the feverish hope of winning them back to home and civilization. Perhaps those whom they sought had perished by the slow torments of the stake; perhaps by the more merciful hatchet; or perhaps they still dragged out a wretched life in the midst of a savage horde. There were instances in which whole families had been carried off at once. The old, the sick, or the despairing, had been tomahawked, as useless encumbrances; while the rest, pitilessly forced asunder, were scattered through every quarter of the wilderness. It was a strange and moving sight, when troop after troop of prisoners arrived in succession – the meeting of husbands with wives, and fathers with children, the reunion of broken families, long separated in a disastrous captivity; and, on the other hand, the agonies of those who learned tidings of death and horror, or groaned under the torture of protracted suspense. Women, frantic between hope and fear, were rushing hither and thither, in search of those whose tender limbs had, perhaps, long since fattened the cubs of the she-wolf; or were pausing, in an agony of doubt, before some sunburnt young savage, who, startled at the haggard apparition, shrank from his forgotten parent, and clung to the tawny breast of his adopted mother. Others were divided between delight and anguish: on the one hand, the joy of an unexpected recognition; and, on the other, the misery of realized fears, or the more intolerable pangs of doubts not yet resolved. Of all the spectators of this tragic drama, few were obdurate enough to stand unmoved. The roughest soldiers felt the contagious sympathy, and softened into unwonted tenderness.

Among the children brought in for surrender, there were some, who, captured several years before, as early, perhaps, as the French war, had lost every recollection of friends and home. Terrified by the novel sights around them, the flash and glitter of arms, and the strange complexion of the pale-faced warriors, they screamed and struggled lustily when consigned to the hands of their relatives. There were young women, too, who had become the partners of Indian husbands; and who now, with all their hybrid offspring, were led reluctantly into the presence of fathers or brothers whose images were almost blotted from their memory. They stood agitated and bewildered; the revival of old affections, and the rush of dormant memories, painfully contending with more recent attachments, and the shame of their real or fancied disgrace; while their Indian lords looked on, scarcely less moved than they, yet hardening themselves with savage stoicism, and standing in the midst of their enemies, imperturbable as statues of bronze These women were compelled to return with their children to the settlements; yet they all did so with reluctance, and several afterwards made their escape, eagerly hastening back to their warrior husbands, and the toils and vicissitudes of an Indian wigwam.[1]

[1] *Penn. Hist. Coll.* 267. *Haz. Pa. Reg.* IV. 390. M'Culloch, *Narrative.* M'Culloch was one of the prisoners surrendered to Bouquet. His narrative first appeared in a pamphlet form, and has since been repub-

Day after day brought renewals of these scenes, deepening in interest as they drew towards their close. A few individual incidents have been recorded. A young Virginian, robbed of his wife but a few months before, had volunteered in the expedition with the faint hope of recovering her; and, after long suspense, had recognized her among a troop of prisoners, bearing in her arms a child born during her captivity. But the joy of the meeting was bitterly alloyed by the loss of a former child, not two years old, captured with the mother, but soon taken from her, and carried, she could not tell whither. Days passed on; they could learn no tidings of its fate, and the mother, harrowed with terrible imaginations, was almost driven to despair; when, at length, she discovered her child in the arms of an Indian warrior, and snatched it with an irrepressible cry of transport.

When the army, on its homeward march, reached the town of Carlisle, those who had been unable to follow the expedition came thither in numbers, to inquire for the friends they had lost. Among the rest was an old woman, whose daughter had been carried off nine years before. In the crowd of female captives, she discovered one in whose wild and swarthy features she discerned the altered

lished in the *Incidents of Border Warfare*, and other similar collections. The autobiography of Mary Jemison, a woman captured by the Senecas during the French war, and twice married among them, contains an instance of attachment to Indian life similar to those mentioned above. After the conclusion of hostilities, learning that she was to be given up to the whites in accordance with a treaty, she escaped into the woods with her half-breed children, and remained hidden, in great dismay and agitation, until the search was over. She lived to an advanced age, but never lost her attachment to the Indian life.

lineaments of her child; but the girl, who had almost forgotten her native tongue, returned no sign of recognition to her eager words, and the old woman bitterly complained that the daughter, whom she had so often sung to sleep on her knee, had forgotten her in her old age. Bouquet suggested an expedient which proves him a man of feeling and perception. "Sing the song that you used to sing to her when a child." The old woman obeyed; and a sudden start, a look of bewilderment, and a passionate flood of tears, removed every doubt, and restored the long-lost daughter to her mother's arms.[1]

The tender affections by no means form a salient feature in the Indian character. They hold them in contempt, and scorn every manifestation of them, yet, on this occasion, they would not be repressed, and the human heart betrayed itself, though throbbing under a breastplate of ice. None of the ordinary signs of emotion, neither tears, words, nor looks, declared how greatly they were moved. It was by their kindness and solicitude, by their attention to the wants of the captives, by their offers of furs, garments, the choicest articles of food, and every thing which in their eyes seemed luxury, that they displayed their sorrow at parting from their adopted relatives and friends.[2] Some

[1] *Ordinances of the Borough of Carlisle, Appendix. Penn. Hist. Coll.* 267.

[2] The author of *The Expedition against the Ohio Indians* speaks of the Indians "shedding torrents of tears." This is either a flourish of rhetoric, or is meant to apply solely to the squaws. A warrior, who, under the circumstances, should have displayed such emotion, would have been disgraced for ever.

among them went much farther, and asked permission to follow the army on its homeward march, that they might hunt for the captives, and supply them with better food than the military stores could furnish. A young Seneca warrior had become deeply enamoured of a Virginian girl. At great risk of his life, he accompanied the troops far within the limits of the settlements; and, at every night's encampment, approaching the quarters of the captives as closely as the sentinels would permit, he sat watching, with patient vigilance, to catch a glimpse of his lost mistress.

The Indian women, whom no idea of honor compels to wear an iron mask, were far from emulating the frigid demeanor of their lords. All day they ran wailing through the camp; and, when night came, the hills and woods resounded with their dreary lamentations.[1]

The word *prisoner*, as applied to captives taken by the Indians, is a misnomer, and conveys a wholly false impression of their situation and treatment. When the vengeance of the conquerors is sated; when they have shot, stabbed, burned, or beaten

[1] The outcries of the squaws, on such occasions, would put to shame an Irish death-howl. The writer was once attached to a large band of Indians, who, being on the march, arrived, a little after nightfall, at a spot where, not long before, a party of their young men had been killed by the enemy. The women instantly raised a most astounding clamor, some two hundred voices joining in a discord as wild and dismal as the shrieking of the damned in the *Inferno;* while some of the chief mourners gashed their bodies and limbs with knives, uttering meanwhile most piteous lamentations. A few days later, returning to the same encampment after darkness had closed in, a strange and startling effect was produced by the prolonged wailings of several women, who were pacing the neighboring hills, lamenting the death of a child, killed by the bite of a rattlesnake.

to death, enough to satisfy the shades of their departed relatives, they usually treat those who survive their wrath with moderation and humanity; often adopting them to supply the place of lost brothers, husbands, or children, whose names are given to the successors thus substituted in their place. By a formal ceremony, the white blood is washed from their veins; and they are regarded thenceforth as members of the tribe, faring equally with the rest in prosperity or adversity, in famine or abundance. When children are adopted in this manner by Indian women, they nurture them with the same tenderness and indulgence which they extend, in a remarkable degree, to their own offspring; and such young women as will not marry an Indian husband are treated with a singular forbearance, in which superstition, natural temperament, and a sense of right and justice may all claim a share.[1] The captive, unless he excites suspicion by his conduct, or exhibits peculiar contumacy, is left with no other restraint than his own free will. The warrior who captured him, or to whom he was assigned in the division of the spoil, sometimes claims, it is true, a certain right of property in him, to the exclusion of others; but this claim is soon forgotten, and is seldom exercised to the inconvenience of the captive, who has no other prison than the earth, the air, and the forest.[2] Five hun-

[1] This and what precedes is meant to apply only to tribes east of the Mississippi. Some of the western and south-western tribes treat prisoners merely as slaves, and habitually violate female captives.

[2] The captives among the Shawanoes of the Scioto had most of them been recently taken; and only a small part had gone through the cere-

dred miles of wilderness, beset with difficulty and danger, are the sole bars to his escape, should he desire to effect it; but, strange as it may appear, this wish is apt to expire in his heart, and he often remains to the end of his life a contented denizen of the woods.

Among the captives brought in for delivery were some bound fast to prevent their escape; and many others, who, amid the general tumult of joy and sorrow, sat sullen and scowling, angry that they were forced to abandon the wild license of the forest for the irksome restraints of society.[1] Thus to look back with a fond longing to inhospitable deserts, where men, beasts, and Nature herself, seem arrayed in arms, and where ease, security, and all that civilization reckons among the goods of life, are alike cut off, may appear to argue some strange perversity or moral malformation. Yet such has been the experience of many a sound and healthful mind. To him who has once tasted the reckless independence, the haughty self-reliance, the sense of irresponsible freedom, which the forest life engenders, civilization thenceforth seems flat and stale. Its pleasures are insipid, its pursuits wearisome, its conventionalities, duties, and mutual dependence alike tedious and disgusting. The entrapped wanderer grows fierce and restless, and pants for breathing-room. His path, it is true,

mony of adoption. Hence it was that the warriors, in their desperation, formed the design of putting them to death, fearing that, in the attack which they meditated, the captives would naturally take part with their countrymen.

[1] *Account of Bouquet's Expedition*, 29

was choked with difficulties, but his body and soul were hardened to meet them; it was beset with dangers, but these were the very spice of his life, gladdening his heart with exulting self-confidence, and sending the blood through his veins with a livelier current. The wilderness, rough, harsh, and inexorable, has charms more potent in their seductive influence than all the lures of luxury and sloth. And often he on whom it has cast its magic finds no heart to dissolve the spell, and remains a wanderer and an Ishmaelite to the hour of his death.[1]

There is a chord, in the breasts of most men, prompt to answer loudly or faintly, as the case may

[1] Colden, after describing the Indian wars of 1699, 1700, concludes in the following words: —

"I shall finish this Part by observing that notwithstanding the French Commissioners took all the Pains possible to carry Home the French that were Prisoners with the Five Nations, and they had full Liberty from the Indians, few of them could be persuaded to return. It may be thought that this was occasioned from the Hardships they had endured in their own Country, under a tyrannical Government and a barren Soil. But this certainly was not the Reason, for the English had as much Difficulty to persuade the People that had been taken Prisoners by the French Indians to leave the Indian Manner of living, though no People enjoy more Liberty, and live in greater Plenty than the common Inhabitants of New York do. No Arguments, no Intreaties, nor Tears of their Friends and Relations, could persuade many of them to leave their new Indian Friends and Acquaintance. Several of them that were by the Caressings of their Relations persuaded to come Home, in a little Time grew tired of our Manner of living, and ran away to the Indians, and ended their Days with them. On the other Hand, Indian Children have been carefully educated among the English, clothed and taught; yet, I think, there is not one Instance that any of these, after they had Liberty to go among their own People, and were come to Age, would remain with the English, but returned to their own Nations, and became as fond of the Indian Manner of Life as those that knew nothing of a civilized Manner of living. What I now tell of Christian Prisoners among Indians relates not only to what happened at the Conclusion of this War, but has been found true on many other Occasions." — Colden, 203.

be, to such rude appeals. But there is influence of another sort, strongest with minds of the finest texture, yet sometimes holding a controlling power over those who neither acknowledge nor suspect its workings. There are few so imbruted by vice, so perverted by art and luxury, as to dwell in the closest presence of Nature, deaf to her voice of melody and power, untouched by the ennobling influences which mould and penetrate the heart that has not hardened itself against them. Into the spirit of such an one the mountain wind breathes its own freshness, and the midsummer tempest, as it rends the forest, pours its own fierce energy. His thoughts flow with the placid stream of the broad, deep river, or dance in light with the sparkling current of the mountain brook. No passing mood or fancy of his mind but has its image and its echo in the wild world around him. There is softness in the mellow air, the warm sunshine, and the budding leaves of spring; and in the forest flower, which, more delicate than the pampered offspring of gardens, lifts its tender head through the refuse and decay of the wilderness. But it is the grand and heroic in the hearts of men which finds its worthiest symbol and noblest inspiration amid these desert realms, — in the mountain, rearing its savage head through clouds and sleet, or basking its majestic strength in the radiance of the sinking sun; in the interminable forest, the thunder booming over its lonely waste, the whirlwind tearing through its inmost depths, or the sun at length setting in gorgeous majesty beyond its waves of verdure. To the sick, the wearied, or the sated spirit, nature opens a theatre of boundless life, and holds forth a cup brimming with redundant pleasure. In the other joys of existence, fear is balanced against hope, and satiety against delight; but here one may fearlessly drink, gaining, with every draught, new vigor and a heightened zest, and finding no dregs of bitterness at the bottom.

Having accomplished its work, the army left the Muskingum, and, retracing its former course, arrived at Fort Pitt on the twenty-eighth of November. The recovered captives were sent to their respective homes in Pennsylvania or Virginia; and the provincial troops disbanded, not without warm praises for the hardihood and steadiness with which they had met the difficulties of the campaign. The happy issue of the expedition spread joy throughout the country. At the next session of the Pennsylvania Assembly, one of its first acts was to pass a vote of thanks to Colonel Bouquet, expressing in earnest terms its sense of his services and personal merits, and conveying its acknowledgments for the regard which he had constantly shown to the civil rights of the inhabitants.[1] The Assembly of Virginia passed a similar vote; and both houses concurred in recommending Bouquet to the King for promotion.

Nevertheless, his position was far from being an easy or a pleasant one. It may be remembered that the desertion of his newly levied soldiers had forced him to ask Colonel Lewis to raise for him

[1] See Appendix, F.

one or two companies of Virginian volunteers Virginia, which had profited by the campaign, though contributing nothing to it, refused to pay these troops; and its agents tried to throw the burden upon Bouquet in person. The Assembly of Pennsylvania, with a justice and a generosity which went far to redeem the past, came to his relief and assumed the debt, though not till he had suffered the most serious annoyance. Certain recent military regulations contributed at the same time to increase his vexation and his difficulties. He had asked in vain, the year before, to be relieved from his command. He now asked again, and the request was granted; on which he wrote to Gage: "The disgust I have conceived from the ill-nature and ingratitude of those individuals (*the Virginian officials*) makes me accept with great satisfaction your obliging offer to discharge me of this department, in which I never desire to serve again, nor, indeed, to be commanding officer in any other, since the new regulations you were pleased to communicate to me; being sensible of my inability to carry on the service upon the terms prescribed."[1]

He was preparing to return to Europe, when he received the announcement of his promotion to the rank of Brigadier General. He was taken completely by surprise; for he had supposed that the rigid prescriptions of the service had closed the path of advancement against him, as a foreigner, "I had, to-day," he wrote to Gage, "the honor of your Excellency's letter of the fifteenth instant.

[1] MS. Letter – *Bouquet to Gage*, 4 March, 1765.

The unexpected honor, which his Majesty has condescended to confer upon me, fills my heart with the utmost gratitude. Permit me, sir, to express my sincere acknowledgments of my great obligation to you. . . . The flattering prospect of preferment, open to the other foreign officers by the removal of that dreadful barrier, gives me the highest satisfaction, being convinced that his Majesty has no subjects more devoted to his service."[1]

Among the letters of congratulation which he received from officers serving under him is the following, from Captain George Etherington, of the first battalion of the Royal American regiment, who commanded at Michillimackinac when it was captured: —

"Lancaster, Pa., 19 April, 1765.

"Sir:

Though I almost despair of this reaching you before you sail for Europe, yet I cannot deny myself the pleasure of giving you joy on your promotion, and can with truth tell you that it gives great joy to all the gentlemen of the battalion, for two reasons: first, on your account; and, secondly, on our own, as by that means we may hope for the pleasure of continuing under your command.

"You can hardly imagine how this place rings with the news of your promotion, for the townsmen and boors (*i.e.*, *German farmers*) stop us in the streets to ask if it is true that the King has made Colonel Bouquet a general; and, when they are told it is true, they march off with great joy;

[1] MS. Letter — *Bouquet to Gage* 17 April, 1765.

so you see the old proverb wrong for once, which says, he that prospers is envied; for sure I am that all the people here are more pleased with the news of your promotion than they would be if the government would take off the stamp duty. . .

"GEO. ETHERINGTON.

"BRIGADIER GENERAL HENRY BOUQUET."

"And," concludes Dr. William Smith, the chronicler of the campaign, "as he is rendered as dear by his private virtues to those who have the honor of his more intimate acquaintance, as he is by his military services to the public, it is hoped he may long continue among us, where his experienced abilities will enable him, and his love of the English constitution entitle him, to fill any future trust to which his Majesty may be pleased to call him." This hope was not destined to fulfilment. Bouquet was assigned to the command of the southern military department; and, within three years after his return from the Muskingum, he was attacked with a fever at Pensacola, which closed the career of a gallant soldier and a generous man.

The Delawares and Shawanoes, mindful of their engagement and of the hostages which they had given to keep it, sent their deputies, within the appointed time, to Sir William Johnson, who concluded a treaty with them; stipulating, among the other terms, that they should grant free passage through their country to English troops and travellers; that they should make full restitution for the goods taken from the traders at the breaking out of the war; and that they should aid their triumphant enemies in the difficult task which yet remained to be accomplished, — that of taking possession of the Illinois, and occupying its posts and settlements with British troops.[1]

[1] MS. *Johnson Papers.*

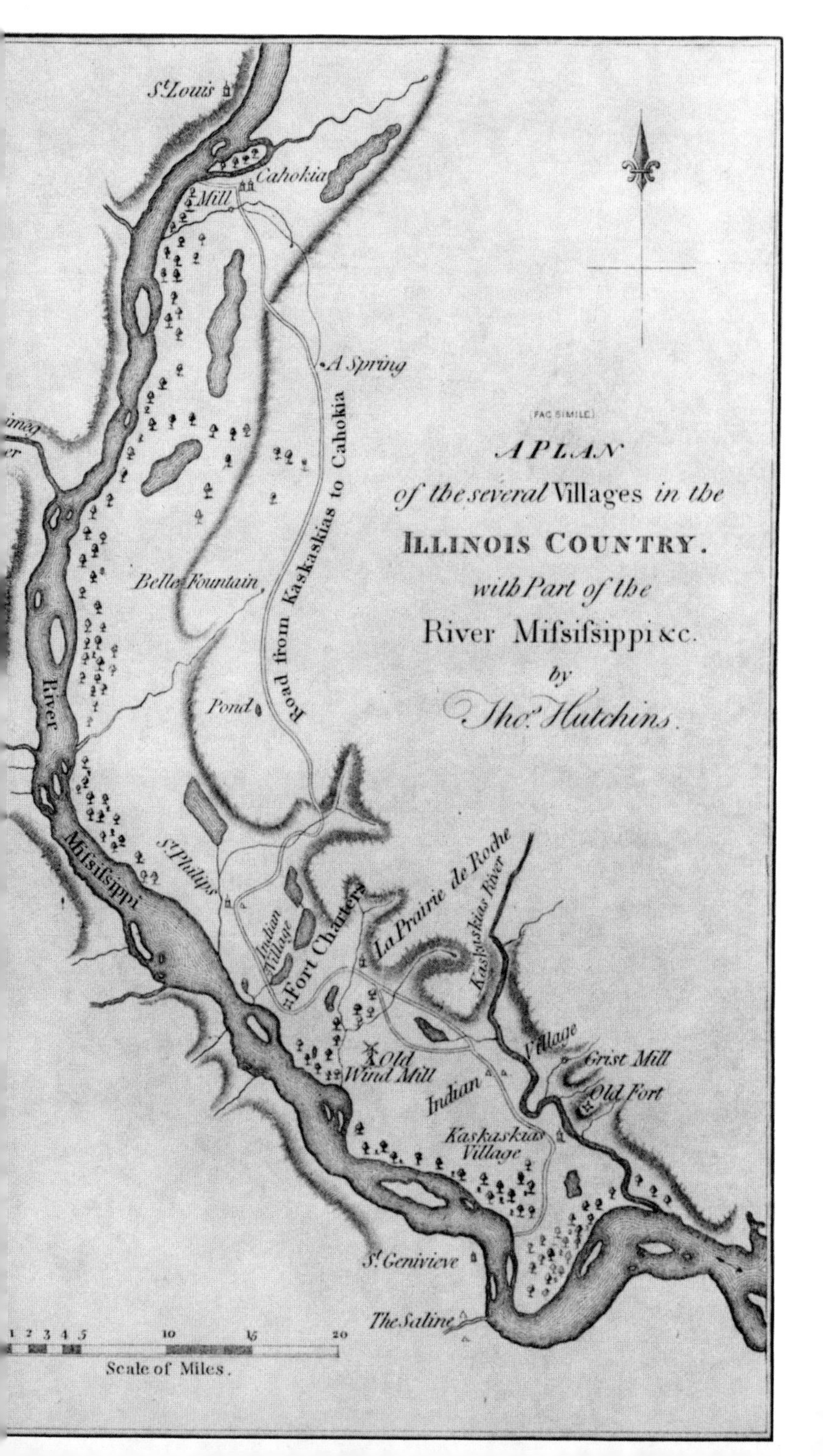
St. Louis
Cahokia
Mill
A Spring
Road from Kaskaskias to Cahokia
(FAC SIMILE)
A PLAN
of the several Villages in the
ILLINOIS COUNTRY.
with Part of the
River Mifsifsippi &c.
by
Thos. Hutchins.
Belle Fountain
Pond
River
Mifsifsippi
St. Philips
Indian Village
Fort Chartres
La Prairie de Roche
Kaskaskias River
Old Wind Mill
Indian Village
Grist Mill
Old Fort
Kaskaskias Village
St. Genivieve
The Saline
1 2 3 4 5 10 15 20
Scale of Miles.

CHAPTER XXVIII.

1764.

THE ILLINOIS.

We turn to a region of which, as yet, we have caught but transient glimpses; a region which to our forefathers seemed remote and strange, as to us the mountain strongholds of the Apaches, or the wastes of farthest Oregon. The country of the Illinois was chiefly embraced within the boundaries of the state which now retains the name. Thitherward, from the east, the west, and the north, three mighty rivers rolled their tributary waters; while countless smaller streams — small only in comparison — traversed the land with a watery network, impregnating the warm soil with exuberant fecundity. From the eastward, the Ohio — La Belle Rivière — pursued its windings for more than a thousand miles. The Mississippi descended from the distant north; while from its fountains in the west, three thousand miles away, the Missouri poured its torrent towards the same common centre. Born among mountains, trackless even now, except by the adventurous footstep of the trapper, — nurtured amid the howling of beasts and the war cries of savages, never silent in that wilderness,—it holds its angry course through sun-scorched deserts, among towers and palaces, the architecture of no human hand, among lodges of barbarian hordes, and herds of bison blackening the prairie to the horizon. Fierce, reckless, headstrong, exulting in its tumultuous force, it plays a thousand freaks of wanton power; bearing away forests from its shores, and planting them, with roots uppermost, in its quicksands; sweeping off islands, and rebuilding them; frothing and raging in foam and whirlpool, and, again, gliding with dwindled current along its sandy channel. At length, dark with uncurbed fury, it pours its muddy tide into the reluctant Mississippi. That majestic river, drawing life from the pure fountains of the north, wandering among emerald prairies and wood-crowned bluffs, loses all its earlier charm with this unhallowed union. At first, it shrinks as with repugnance; and along the same channel the two streams flow side by side, with unmingled waters. But the disturbing power prevails at length; and the united torrent bears onward in its might, boiling up from the bottom, whirling in many a vortex, flooding its shores with a malign deluge fraught with pestilence and fever, and burying forests in its depths, to insnare the heedless voyager. Mightiest among rivers, it is the connecting link of adverse climates and contrasted races; and, while at its northern source the fur-clad Indian shivers in the cold, where it mingles with the ocean, the growth of the tropics springs along its banks, and the panting negro cools his limbs in its refreshing waters.

To these great rivers and their tributary streams the country of the Illinois owed its wealth, its grassy prairies, and the stately woods that flourished on its deep, rich soil. This prolific land teemed with life. It was a hunter's paradise Deer grazed on its meadows. The elk trooped in herds, like squadrons of cavalry. In the still morning, one might hear the clatter of their antlers for half a mile over the dewy prairie. Countless bison roamed the plains, filing in grave procession to drink at the rivers, plunging and snorting among the rapids and quicksands, rolling their huge bulk on the grass, rushing upon each other in hot encounter, like champions under shield The wildcat glared from the thicket; the racoon thrust his furry countenance from the hollow tree, and the opossum swung, head downwards, from the overhanging bough.

With the opening spring, when the forests are budding into leaf, and the prairies gemmed with flowers; when a warm, faint haze rests upon the landscape,—then heart and senses are inthralled with luxurious beauty. The shrubs and wild fruit-trees, flushed with pale red blossoms, and the small clustering flowers of grape-vines, which choke the gigantic trees with Laocoön writhings, fill the forest with their rich perfume. A few days later, and a cloud of verdure overshadows the land; while birds innumerable sing beneath its canopy, and brighten its shades with their glancing hues.

Yet this western paradise is not free from the primal curse. The beneficent sun, which kindles into life so many forms of loveliness and beauty, fails not to engender venom and death from the rank slime of pestilential swamp and marsh. In some stagnant pool, buried in the jungle-like depths of the forest, where the hot and lifeless water reeks with exhalations, the water-snake basks by the margin, or winds his checkered length of loathsome beauty across the sleepy surface. From beneath the rotten carcass of some fallen tree, the moccason thrusts out his broad flat head, ready to dart on the intruder. On the dry, sun-scorched prairie, the rattlesnake, a more generous enemy, reposes in his spiral coil. He scorns to shun the eye of day, as if conscious of the honor accorded to his name by the warlike race, who, jointly with him, claim lordship over the land.[1] But some intrusive footstep awakes him

[1] The superstitious veneration which the Indians entertain for the rattlesnake has been before alluded to. The Cherokees christened him by a name which, being interpreted, signifies *the bright old inhabitants,* a title of affectionate admiration of which his less partial acquaintance would hardly judge him worthy.

"Between the heads of the northern branch of the Lower Cheerake River, and the heads of that of Tuckaschchee, winding round in a long course by the late Fort Loudon, and afterwards into the Mississippi, there is, both in the nature and circumstances, a great phenomenon. Between two high mountains, nearly covered with old mossy rocks, lofty cedars and pines, in the valleys of which the beams of the sun reflect a powerful heat, there are, as the natives affirm, some bright old inhabitants, or rattlesnakes, of a more enormous size than is mentioned in history. They are so large and unwieldy, that they take a circle almost as wide as their length, to crawl round in their shortest orbit; but bountiful nature compensates the heavy motion of their bodies; for, as they say, no living creature moves within the reach of their sight, but they can draw it to them; which is agreeable to what we observe through the

from his slumbers. His neck is arched; the white fangs gleam in his distended jaws; his small eyes dart rays of unutterable fierceness; and his rattles, invisible with their quick vibration, ring the sharp warning which no man will dare to contemn.

The land thus prodigal of good and evil, so remote from the sea, so primitive in its aspect, might well be deemed an undiscovered region, ignorant of European arts; yet it may boast a colonization as old as that of many a spot to which are accorded the scanty honors of an American antiquity. The earliest settlement of Pennsylvania was made in 1681; the first occupation of the Illinois took place in the previous year. La Salle may be called the father of the colony. That remarkable man entered the country with a handful of followers, bent on his grand scheme of Mississippi discovery. A legion of enemies rose in his path; but neither delay, disappointment, sickness, famine, open force, nor secret conspiracy, could bend his soul of iron. Disasters accumulated upon him. He flung them off, and still pressed forward to his object. His victorious energy bore all before it; but the success on which he had staked his life served only to entail fresh calamity and an untimely death; and his best reward is, that his name stands forth in history an imperishable monument of heroic constancy. When on his

whole system of animated beings. Nature endues them with proper capacities to sustain life: as they cannot support themselves by their speed or cunning, to spring from an ambuscade, it is needful they should have the bewitching craft of their eyes and forked tongues."—Adair 237.

way to the Mississippi, in the year 1680, La Salle built a fort in the country of the Illinois; and, on his return from the mouth of the great river, some of his followers remained, and established themselves near the spot. Heroes of another stamp took up the work which the daring Norman had begun. Jesuit missionaries, among the best and purest of their order, burning with zeal for the salvation of souls, and the gaining of an immortal crown, here toiled and suffered, with a self-sacrificing devotion which extorts a tribute of admiration even from sectarian bigotry. While the colder apostles of Protestantism labored upon the outskirts of heathendom, these champions of the cross, the forlorn hope of the army of Rome, pierced to the heart of its dark and dreary domain, confronting death at every step, and well repaid for all, could they but sprinkle a few drops of water on the forehead of a dying child, or hang a gilded crucifix round the neck of some warrior, pleased with the glittering trinket. With the beginning of the eighteenth century, the black robe of the Jesuit was known in every village of the Illinois. Defying the wiles of Satan and the malice of his emissaries, the Indian sorcerers; exposed to the rage of the elements, and every casualty of forest life, they followed their wandering proselytes to war and to the chase; now wading through morasses, now dragging canoes over rapids and sand-bars; now scorched with heat on the sweltering prairie, and now shivering houseless in the blasts of January. At Kaskaskia and

Cahokia they established missions, and built frail churches from the bark of trees, fit emblems of their own transient and futile labors. Morning and evening, the savage worshippers sang praises to the Virgin, and knelt in supplication before the shrine of St. Joseph.[1]

Soldiers and fur-traders followed where these pioneers of the church had led the way. Forts were built here and there throughout the country, and the cabins of settlers clustered about the mission-houses. The new colonists, emigrants from Canada or disbanded soldiers of French regiments, bore a close resemblance to the settlers of Detroit, or the primitive people of Acadia; whose simple life poetry has chosen as an appropriate theme, but who, nevertheless, are best contemplated from a distance. The Creole of the Illinois, contented, light-hearted, and thriftless, by no means fulfilled the injunction to increase and multiply; and the colony languished in spite of the fertile soil. The people labored long enough to gain a bare subsistence for each passing day, and spent the rest of their time in dancing and merry-making, smoking, gossiping, and hunting. Their native gayety was irrepressible, and they found means to stimulate it with wine made from the fruit of the wild grapevines. Thus they passed their days, at peace with themselves, hand and glove with their Indian neighbors, and ignorant of all the world beside. Money was scarcely known among them. Skins and furs

[1] For an account of Jesuit labors in the Illinois, see the letters of Father Marest, in *Lett. Edif.* IV.

were the prevailing currency, and in every village a great portion of the land was held in common. The military commandant, whose station was at Fort Chartres, on the Mississippi, ruled the colony with a sway absolute as that of the Pacha of Egypt, and judged civil and criminal cases without right of appeal. Yet his power was exercised in a patriarchal spirit, and he usually commanded the respect and confidence of the people. Many years later, when, after the War of the Revolution, the Illinois came under the jurisdiction of the United States, the perplexed inhabitants, totally at a loss to understand the complicated machinery of republicanism, begged to be delivered from the intolerable burden of self-government, and to be once more subjected to a military commandant.[1]

The Creole is as unchanging in his nature and habits as the Indian himself. Even at this day, one may see, along the banks of the Mississippi, the same low-browed cottages, with their broad eaves and picturesque verandas, which, a century ago, were clustered around the mission-house at Kaskaskia; and, entering, one finds the inmate the same lively, story-telling, and pipe-smoking being that his ancestor was before him. Yet, with all his genial traits, the rough world deals hardly

1 The principal authorities for the above account of the Illinois colony are Hutchins, *Topographical Description*, 37. Volney, *View of the United States*, 370. Pitman, *Present State of the European Settlements on the Mississippi, passim*. Law, *Address before the Historical Society of Vincennes*, 14. Brown, *Hist. Illinois*, 208. *Journal of Captain Harry Gordon*, in Appendix to Pownall's *Topographical Description*. Nicollet, *Report on the Hydrographical Basin of the Mississippi*, 75.

with him. He lives a mere drone in the busy hive of an American population. The living tide encroaches on his rest, as the muddy torrent of the great river chafes away the farm and homestead of his fathers. Yet he contrives to be happy, though looking back regretfully to the better days of old.

At the date of this history, the population of the colony, exclusive of negroes, who, in that simple community, were treated rather as humble friends than as slaves, did not exceed two thousand souls, distributed in several small settlements. There were about eighty houses at Kaskaskia, forty or fifty at Cahokia, a few at Vincennes and Fort Chartres, and a few more scattered in small clusters upon the various streams. The agricultural portion of the colonists were, as we have described them, marked with many weaknesses, and many amiable virtues; but their morals were not improved by a large admixture of fur-traders,—reckless, harebrained adventurers, who, happily for the peace of their relatives, were absent on their wandering vocation during the greater part of the year.[1]

[1] Lieutenant Alexander Fraser visited the Illinois in 1765, as we shall see hereafter. He met extreme ill-treatment, and naturally takes a prejudiced view of the people. The following is from his MS. account of the country:—

"The Illinois Indians are about 650 able to bear arms. Nothing can equal their passion for drunkenness, but that of the French inhabitants, who are for the greatest part drunk every day, while they can get drink to buy in the Colony. They import more of this Article from New Orleans than they do of any other, and they never fail to meet a speedy and good market for it. They have a great many Negroes, who are obliged to labour very hard to support their Masters in their extravagant debauch

Swarms of vagabond Indians infested the settlements; and, to people of any other character, they would have proved an intolerable annoyance. But the easy-tempered Creoles made friends and comrades of them; ate, drank, smoked, and often married with them. They were a debauched and drunken rabble, the remnants of that branch of the Algonquin stock known among the French as the Illinois, a people once numerous and powerful, but now miserably enfeebled, and corrupted by foreign wars, domestic dissensions, and their own licentious manners. They comprised the broken fragments of five tribes, — the Kaskaskias, Cahokias, Peorias, Mitchigamias, and Tamaronas. Some of their villages were in the close vicinity of the Creole settlements. On a hot summer morning, they might be seen lounging about the trading-house, basking in the sun, begging for a dram of

eries; any one who has had any dealings with them must plainly see that they are for the most part transported Convicts, or people who have fled for some crimes; those who have not done it themselves are the offspring of such as those I just mentioned, inheriting their Forefathers' vices. They are cruel and treacherous to each other, and consequently so to Strangers; they are dishonest in every kind of business and lay themselves out to overreach Strangers, which they often do by a lcw cunning, peculiar to themselves; and their artful flatteries, with extravagant Entertainments (in which they affect the greatest hospitality) generally favor their schemes."

Of the traders, he says, "They are in general most unconscious (*unconscionable*) Rascals, whose interest it was to debauch from us such Indians as they found well disposed towards us, and to foment and increace the animosity of such as they found otherwise. To this we should alone impute our late war with the Indians."

He sets down the number of white inhabitants at about seven hundred able to bear arms, though he says that it is impossible to form a just estimate, as they are continually going and coming to and from the Indian nations

whiskey, or chaffering with the hard-featured trader for beads, tobacco, gunpowder, and red paint.

About the Wabash and its branches, to the eastward of the Illinois, dwelt tribes of similar lineage, but more warlike in character, and less corrupt in manners. These were the Miamis, in their three divisions, their near kindred, the Piankishaws, and a portion of the Kickapoos. There was another settlement of the Miamis upon the River Maumee, still farther to the east; and it was here that Bradstreet's ambassador, Captain Morris, had met so rough a welcome. The strength of these combined tribes was very considerable; and, one and all, they looked with wrath and abhorrence on the threatened advent of the English.

CHAPTER XXIX.

1763–1765.

PONTIAC RALLIES THE WESTERN TRIBES.

When, by the treaty of Paris, in 1763, France ceded to England her territories east of the Mississippi, the Illinois was of course included in the cession. Scarcely were the articles signed, when France, as if eager to rob herself, at one stroke, of all her western domain, threw away upon Spain the vast and indefinite regions beyond the Mississippi, destined at a later day to return to her hands, and finally to swell the growing empire of the United States. This transfer to Spain was for some time kept secret; but orders were immediately sent to the officers commanding at the French posts within the territory ceded to England, to evacuate the country whenever British troops should appear to occupy it. These orders reached the Illinois towards the close of 1763. Some time, however, must necessarily elapse before the English could take possession; for the Indian war was then at its height, and the country was protected from access by a broad barrier of savage tribes, in the hottest ferment of hostility.

The colonists, hating the English with a more than national hatred, deeply imbittered by years of disastrous war, received the news of the treaty with disgust and execration. Many of them left the country, loath to dwell under the shadow of the British flag. Of these, some crossed the Missis sippi to the little hamlet of St. Genevieve, on the western bank; others followed the commandant, Neyon de Villiers, to New Orleans; while others, taking with them all their possessions, even to the frames and clapboarding of their houses, passed the river a little above Cahokia, and established themselves at a beautiful spot on the opposite shore, where a settlement was just then on the point of commencement. Here a line of richly wooded bluffs rose with easy ascent from the margin of the water; while from their summits extended a wide plateau of fertile prairie, bordered by a framework of forest. In the shadow of the trees, which fringed the edge of the declivity, stood a newly built storehouse, with a few slight cabins and works of defence, belonging to a company of fur-traders. At their head was Pierre Laclede, who had left New Orleans with his followers in August, 1763; and, after toiling for three months against the impetuous stream of the Mississippi, had reached the Illinois in November, and selected the spot alluded to as the site of his first establishment. To this he gave the name of St. Louis.[1] Side by side with Laclede, in his adventurous en-

[1] Nicollet, *Historical Sketch of St. Louis.* See *Report on the Hydrographical Basin of the Upper Mississippi River,* 75.

terprise, was a young man, slight in person, but endowed with a vigor and elasticity of frame which could resist heat or cold, fatigue, hunger, or the wasting hand of time. Not all the magic of a dream, nor the enchantments of an Arabian tale, could outmatch the waking realities which were to rise upon the vision of Pierre Chouteau. Where, in his youth, he had climbed the woody bluff, and looked abroad on prairies dotted with bison, he saw, with the dim eye of his old age, the land darkened for many a furlong with the clustered roofs of the western metropolis. For the silence of the wilderness, he heard the clang and turmoil of human labor, the din of congregated thousands; and where the great river rolled down through the forest, in lonely grandeur, he saw the waters lashed into foam beneath the prows of panting steamboats, flocking to the broad levee.[1]

[1] Laclede, the founder of St. Louis, died before he had brought his grand fur-trading enterprise to a conclusion; but his young assistant lived to realize schemes still more bold and comprehensive; and to every trader, trapper, and voyageur, from the frontier of the United States to the Rocky Mountains, and from the British Possessions to the borders of New Mexico, the name of Pierre Chouteau is familiar as his own. I visited this venerable man in the spring of 1846, at his country seat, in a rural spot surrounded by woods, within a few miles of St. Louis. The building, in the picturesque architecture peculiar to the French dwellings of the Mississippi Valley, with its broad eaves and light verandas, and the surrounding negro houses filled with gay and contented inmates, was in singular harmony with the character of the patriarchal owner, who prided himself on his fidelity to the old French usages. Though in extreme old age, he still retained the vivacity of his nation. His memory, especially of the events of his youth, was clear and vivid; and he delighted to look back to the farthest extremity of the long vista of his life, and recall the acts and incidents of his earliest years. Of Pontiac, whom he had often seen, he had a clear recollection; and I am indebted to this interesting interview for several particulars regarding the chief and his coadjutors.

In the summer of 1764, the military commandant, Neyon, had abandoned the country in disgust, and gone down to New Orleans, followed by many of the inhabitants; a circumstance already mentioned. St. Ange de Bellerive remained behind to succeed him. St. Ange was a veteran Canadian officer, the same who, more than forty years before, had escorted Father Charlevoix through the country, and who is spoken of with high commendation by the Jesuit traveller and historian. He took command of about forty men, the remnant of the garrison of Fort Chartres; which, remote as it was, was then esteemed one of the best constructed military works in America. Its ramparts of stone, garnished with twenty cannon, scowled across the encroaching Mississippi, destined, before many years, to ingulf curtain and bastion in its ravenous abyss.

St. Ange's position was by no means an enviable one. He had a critical part to play. On the one hand, he had been advised of the cession to the English, and ordered to yield up the country whenever they should arrive to claim it. On the other, he was beset by embassies from Pontiac, from the Shawanoes, and from the Miamis, and plagued day and night by an importunate mob of Illinois Indians, demanding arms, ammunition, and assistance against the common enemy. Perhaps, in his secret heart, St. Ange would have rejoiced to see the scalps of all the Englishmen in the backwoods fluttering in the wind over the Illinois wigwams; but his situation forbade him to comply with the solicitations of his intrusive petitioners, and it is to be hoped that some sense of honor and humanity enforced the dictates of prudence. Accordingly, he cajoled them with flatteries and promises, and from time to time distributed a few presents to stay their importunity, still praying daily that the English might appear and relieve him from his uneasy dilemma.[1]

While Laclede was founding St. Louis, while the discontented settlers of the Illinois were deserting their homes, and while St. Ange was laboring to pacify his Indian neighbors, all the tribes from the Maumee to the Mississippi were in a turmoil of excitement. Pontiac was among them, furious as a wild beast at bay. By the double campaign of 1764, his best hopes had been crushed to the earth; but he stood unshaken amidst the ruin, and still struggled with desperate energy to retrieve his broken cause. On the side of the northern lakes, the movements of Bradstreet had put down the insurrection of the tribes, and wrested back the military posts which cunning and treachery had placed within their grasp. In the south, Bouquet had forced to abject submission the warlike Delawares and Shawanoes, the warriors on whose courage and obstinacy Pontiac had grounded his strongest confidence. On every hand defeat and disaster were closing around him. One sanctuary alone remained, the country of the Illinois. Here the flag of France still floated on the banks of the Mississippi, and here no English foot had dared to penetrate. He

[1] MS. Letter — *St. Ange to D'Abbadie,* Sept. 9.

resolved to invoke all his resources, and bend all his energies to defend this last citadel.[1]

He was not left to contend unaided. The fur trading French, living at the settlements on the Mississippi, scattered about the forts of Ouatanon, Vincennes, and Miami, or domesticated among the Indians of the Rivers Illinois and Wabash, dreaded the English as dangerous competitors in their vocation, and were eager to bar them from the country. They lavished abuse and calumny on the objects of their jealousy, and spared no falsehood which ingenious malice and self-interest could suggest. They gave out that the English were bent on the ruin of the tribes, and to that end were stirring them up to mutual hostility. They insisted that, though the armies of France had been delayed so long, they

[1] By the following extract from an official paper, signed by Captain Grant, and forwarded from Detroit, it appears that Pontiac still retained, or professed to retain, his original designs against the garrison of Detroit. The paper has no date, but was apparently written in the autumn of 1764. By a note appended to it, we are told that the Baptiste Campau referred to was one of those who had acted as Pontiac's secretaries during the summer of 1763: —

"On Tuesday last Mr. Jadeau told me, in the presence of Col. Gladwin & Lieut. Hay of the 6th Regiment, that one Lesperance, a Frenchman, on his way to the Illinois, he saw a letter with the Ottawas, at the Miamee River, he is sure wrote by one Baptist Campau (a deserter from the settlement of Detroit), & signed by Pontiac, from the Illinois, setting forth that there were five hundred English coming to the Illinois, & that they, the Ottawas, must have patience; that he, Pontiac, was not to return until he had defeated the English, and then he would come with an army from the Illinois to take Detroit, which he desired they might publish to all the nations about. That powder & ball was in as great plenty as water. That the French Commissary La Cleff had sold above forty thousand weight of powder to the inhabitants, that the English if they came there might not have it.

"There was another letter on the subject sent to an inhabitant of Detroit, but he can't tell in whose hands it is"

were nevertheless on their way, and that the bayonets of the white-coated warriors would soon glitter among the forests of the Mississippi. Forged letters were sent to Pontiac, signed by the King of France, exhorting him to stand his ground but a few weeks longer, and all would then be well. To give the better coloring to their falsehoods, some of these incendiaries assumed the uniform of French officers, and palmed themselves off upon their credulous auditors as ambassadors from the king. Many of the principal traders distributed among the warriors supplies of arms and ammunition, in some instances given gratuitously, and in others sold on credit, with the understanding that payment should be made from the plunder of the English.[1]

[1] MS. *Gage Papers.* MS. *Johnson Papers.* Croghan, *Journal.* Hildreth, *Pioneer History*, 68. *Examination of Gershom Hicks*, see *Penn. Gaz.* No. 1846.

Johnson's letters to the Board of Trade, in the early part of 1765, contain constant references to the sinister conduct of the Illinois French. The commander-in-chief is still more bitter in his invectives, and seems to think that French officers of the crown were concerned in these practices, as well as the traders. If we may judge, however, from the correspondence of St. Ange and his subordinates, they may be acquitted of the charge of any active interference in the matter.

"Sept. 14. I had a private meeting with the Grand Sauteur, when he told me he was well disposed for peace last fall, but was then sent for to the Illinois, where he met with Pondiac; and that then their fathers, the French, told them, if they would be strong, and keep the English out of the possession of that country but this summer, that the King of France would send over an army next spring, to assist his children, the Indians." — Croghan, *Journal*, 1765.

The *Diary of the Siege of Detroit*, under date May 17, 1765, says that Pontiac's nephew came that day from the Illinois, with news that Pontiac had caused six Englishmen and several disaffected Indians to be burned; and that he had seven large war-belts to raise the western tribes for another attack on Detroit, to be made in June of that year, without French assistance.

Now that the insurrection in the east was quelled, and the Delawares and Shawanoes were beaten into submission, it was thought that the English would lose no time in taking full possession of the country, which, by the peace of 1763, had been transferred into their hands. Two principal routes would give access to the Illinois. Troops might advance from the south up the great natural highway of the Mississippi, or they might descend from the east by way of Fort Pitt and the Ohio. In either case, to meet and repel them was the determined purpose of Pontiac.

In the spring, or early summer, he had come to the Illinois and visited the commandant, Neyon, who was then still at his post. Neyon's greeting was inauspicious. He told his visitor that he hoped he had returned at last to his senses. Pontiac laid before him a large belt of wampum. "My Father," he said, "I come to invite you and all your allies to go with me to war against the English." Neyon asked if he had not received his message of the last autumn, in which he told him that the French and English were thenceforth one people; but Pontiac persisted, and still urged him to take up the hatchet. Neyon at length grew angry, kicked away the wampum-belt, and demanded if he could not hear what was said to him. Thus repulsed, Pontiac asked for a keg of rum. Which being given him, he caused to be carried to a neighboring Illinois village; and, with the help of this potent auxiliary, made the assembled warriors join him in the war-song.[1]

[1] *Diary of the Siege of Detroit*, under date June 9, 1764.

It does not appear that, on this occasion, he had any farther success in firing the hearts of the Illinois. He presently returned to his camp on the Maumee, where, by a succession of ill-tidings, he learned the humiliation of his allies, and the triumph of his enemies. Towards the close of autumn, he again left the Maumee; and, followed by four hundred warriors, journeyed westward, to visit in succession the different tribes, and gain their co-operation in his plans of final defence. Crossing over to the Wabash, he passed from village to village, among the Kickapoos, the Piankishaws, and the three tribes of the Miamis, rousing them by his imperious eloquence, and breathing into them his own fierce spirit of resistance. Thence, by rapid marches through forests and over prairies, he reached the banks of the Mississippi, and summoned the four tribes of the Illinois to a general meeting. But these degenerate savages, beaten by the surrounding tribes for many a generation past, had lost their warlike spirit; and, though abundantly noisy and boastful, showed no zeal for fight, and entered with no zest into the schemes of the Ottawa war-chief. Pontiac had his own way of dealing with such spirits. "If you hesitate," he exclaimed, frowning on the cowering assembly, "I will consume your tribes as the fire consumes the dry grass on the prairie." The doubts of the Illinois vanished like the mist, and with marvellous alacrity they declared their concurrence in the views of the orator. Having secured these allies, such as they were, Pontiac departed, and hastened to Fort Chartres. St. Ange, so long tormented with embassy after embassy, and mob after mob, thought that the crowning evil was come at last, when he saw the arch-demon Pontiac enter at the gate, with four hundred warriors at his back. Arrived at the council-house, Pontiac addressed the commandant in a tone of great courtesy: "Father, we have long wished to see you, to shake hands with you, and, whilst smoking the calumet of peace, to recall the battles in which we fought together against the misguided Indians and the English dogs. I love the French, and I have come hither with my warriors to avenge their wrongs."[1] Then followed a demand for arms, ammunition, and troops, to act in concert with the Indian warriors. St. Ange was forced to decline rendering the expected aid; but he sweetened his denial with soothing compliments, and added a few gifts, to remove any lingering bitterness. Pontiac would not be appeased. He angrily complained of such lukewarm friendship, where he had looked for ready sympathy and support. His warriors pitched their lodges about the fort, and threatening symptoms of an approaching rupture began to alarm the French.

In the mean time, Pontiac had caused his squaws to construct a belt of wampum of extraordinary size, six feet in length, and four inches wide. It was wrought from end to end with the symbols of the various tribes and villages, forty-seven in num-

[1] Nicollet, *Report on the Basin of the Upper Mississippi*, 81. M. Nicollet's account is given on the authority of documents and oral narratives derived from Chouteau, Menard, and other patriarchs of the Illinois.

ber, still leagued together in his alliance.[1] He consigned it to an embassy of chosen warriors, directing them to carry it down the Mississippi, displaying it, in turn, at every Indian village along its banks; and exhorting the inhabitants, in his name, to watch the movements of the English, and repel any attempt they might make to ascend the river. This done, they were to repair to New Orleans, and demand from the governor, M. D'Abbadie, the aid which St. Ange had refused. The bark canoes of the embassy put out from the shore, and whirled down the current like floating leaves in autumn.

Soon after their departure, tidings came to Fort Chartres, which caused a joyous excitement among the Indians, and relieved the French garrison from any danger of an immediate rupture. In our own day, the vast distance between the great city of New Orleans and the populous state of Illinois has dwindled into insignificance beneath the magic of science; but at the date of this history, three or four months were often consumed in the upward passage, and the settlers of the lonely forest colony were sometimes cut off from all communication with the world for half a year together. The above-mentioned tidings, interesting as they were, had occupied no less time in their passage. Their import was as follows: —

Very early in the preceding spring, an English officer, Major Loftus, having arrived at New Orleans with four hundred regulars, had attempted

[1] MS. Letter — *St. Ange to D'Abbadie,* Sept. 9.

to ascend the Mississippi, to take possession of Fort Chartres and its dependent posts. His troops were embarked in large and heavy boats. Their progress was slow; and they had reached a point not more than eighty leagues above New Orleans, when, one morning, their ears were greeted with the crack of rifles from the thickets of the western shore; and a soldier in the foremost boat fell, with a mortal wound. The troops, in dismay, sheered over towards the eastern shore; but, when fairly within gunshot, a score of rifles obscured the forest edge with smoke, and filled the nearest boat with dead and wounded men. On this, they steered for the middle of the river, where they remained for a time, exposed to a dropping fire from either bank, too distant to take effect.

The river was high, and the shores so flooded, that nothing but an Indian could hope to find foothold in the miry labyrinth. Loftus was terrified; the troops were discouraged, and a council of officers determined that to advance was impossible. Accordingly, with their best despatch, they steered back for New Orleans, where they arrived without farther accident; and where the French, in great glee at their discomfiture, spared no ridicule at their expense. They alleged, and with much appearance of truth, that the English had been repulsed by no more than thirty warriors. Loftus charged D'Abbadie with having occasioned his disaster by stirring up the Indians to attack him. The governor called Heaven to witness his innocence; and, in truth, there is not the smallest reason to believe him guilty of such villany.[1] Loftus, who had not yet recovered from his fears, conceived an idea that the Indians below New Orleans were preparing an ambuscade to attack him on his way back to his station at Pensacola; and he petitioned D'Abbadie to interfere in his behalf. The latter, with an ill-dissembled sneer, offered to give him and his troops an escort of French soldiers to protect them. Loftus rejected the humiliating proposal, and declared that he only wished for a French interpreter, to confer with any Indians whom he might meet by the way. The interpreter was furnished; and Loftus returned in safety to Pensacola, his detachment not a little reduced by the few whom the Indians had shot, and by numbers who, disgusted by his overbearing treatment, had deserted to the French.[2]

The futile attempt of Loftus to ascend the Mis sissippi was followed, a few months after, by another equally abortive. Captain Pittman came to New Orleans with the design of proceeding to the Illinois, but was deterred by the reports which reached

[1] D'Abbadie's correspondence with St. Ange goes far to exonerate him; and there is a letter addressed to him from General Gage, in which the latter thanks him very cordially for the efforts he had made in behalf of Major Loftus, aiding him to procure boats and guides, and make other preparations for ascending the river.

The correspondence alluded to forms part of a collection of papers preserved in the archives of the Department of the Marine and Colonies at Paris. These papers include the reports of various councils with the Indian tribes of the Illinois, and the whole official correspondence of the French officers in that region during the years 1763-5. They form the principal authorities for this part of the narrative, and throw great light on the character of the Indian war, from its commencement to its close.

[2] *London Mag.* XXXIII. 380. MS. *Detail de ce qui s'est passé à La Louisiane à l'occasion de la prise de possession des Illinois.*

him concerning the temper of the Indians. The latter, elated beyond measure by their success against Loftus, and excited, moreover, by the messages and war-belt of Pontiac, were in a state of angry commotion, which made the passage too hazardous to be attempted. Pittman bethought himself of assuming the disguise of a Frenchman, joining a party of Creole traders, and thus reaching his destination by stealth; but, weighing the risk of detection, he abandoned this design also, and returned to Mobile.[1] Between the Illinois and the settlements around New Orleans, the Mississippi extended its enormous length through solitudes of marsh and forest, broken here and there by a squalid Indian village; or, at vast intervals, by one or two military posts, erected by the French, and forming the resting-places of the voyager. After the failure of Pittman, more than a year elapsed before an English detachment could succeed in passing this great thoroughfare of the wilderness, and running the gauntlet of the savage tribes who guarded its shores. It was not till the second of December, 1765, that Major Farmar, at the head of a strong body of troops, arrived, after an uninterrupted voyage, at Fort Chartres, where the flag of his country had already supplanted the standard of France.[2]

To return to our immediate theme. The ambassadors, whom Pontiac had sent from Fort Chartres

[1] MS. *Correspondence of Pittman with M. D'Abbadie,* among the Paris Documents.

[2] MS. Letter — *Campbell to Gage,* Feb. 24, 1766.

in the autumn of 1764, faithfully acquitted themselves of their trust. They visited the Indian villages along the river banks, kindling the thirst for blood and massacre in the breasts of the inmates. They pushed their sanguinary mission even to the farthest tribes of Southern Louisiana, to whom the great name of Pontiac had long been known, and of late made familiar by repeated messages and embassies.[1] This portion of their task accomplished, they repaired to New Orleans, and demanded an audience of the governor.

New Orleans was then a town of about seven thousand white inhabitants, guarded from the river floods by a levee extending for fifty miles along the banks. The small brick houses, one story in height, were arranged with geometrical symmetry, like the squares of a chess-board. Each house had its yard and garden, and the town was enlivened with the verdure of trees and grass. In front, a public square, or parade ground, opened upon the river, enclosed on three sides by the dilapidated church of St. Louis, a prison, a convent, government buildings, and a range of barracks. The place was surrounded by a defence of palisades strong enough to repel an attack of Indians, or insurgent slaves.[2]

[1] By the correspondence between the French officers of Upper and Lower Louisiana, it appears that Pontiac's messengers, in several instances, had arrived in the vicinity of New Orleans, whither they had come, partly to beg for aid from the French, and partly to urge the Indians of the adjacent country to bar the mouth of the Mississippi against the English.

[2] Pittman, *European Settlements on the Mississippi*, 10. The author of this book is the officer mentioned in the text as having made an unsuccessful attempt to reach the Illinois

When Pontiac's ambassadors entered New Orleans, they found the town in a state of confusion It had long been known that the regions east of the Mississippi had been surrendered to England; a cession from which, however, New Orleans and its suburbs had been excepted by a special provision. But it was only within a few weeks that the dismayed inhabitants had learned that their mother country had transferred her remaining American possessions to the crown of Spain, whose government and people they cordially detested. With every day they might expect the arrival of a Spanish governor and garrison. The French officials, whose hour was drawing to its close, were making the best of their short-lived authority by every species of corruption and peculation; and the inhabitants were awaiting, in anger and repugnance, the approaching change, which was to place over their heads masters whom they hated. The governor, D'Abbadie, an ardent soldier and a zealous patriot, was so deeply chagrined at what he conceived to be the disgrace of his country, that his feeble health gave way, and he betrayed all the symptoms of a rapid decline.

Haggard with illness, and bowed down with shame, the dying governor received the Indian envoys in the council-hall of the province, where he was never again to assume his seat of office. Besides the French officials in attendance, several English officers, who chanced to be in the town, had been invited to the meeting, with the view of soothing the jealousy with which they regarded all intercourse between the French and the Indians. A Shawanoe chief, the orator of the embassy, displayed the great war-belt, and opened the council. "These red dogs," he said, alluding to the color of the British uniform, "have crowded upon us more and more; and when we ask them by what right they come, they tell us that you, our French fathers, have given them our lands. We know that they lie. These lands are neither yours nor theirs, and no man shall give or sell them without our consent. Fathers, we have always been your faithful children; and we now have come to ask that you will give us guns, powder, and lead, to aid us in this war."

D'Abbadie replied in a feeble voice, endeavoring to allay their vindictive jealousy of the English, and promising to give them all that should be necessary to supply their immediate wants. The council then adjourned until the following day; but, in the mean time, the wasted strength of the governor gave way beneath a renewed attack of his disorder; and, before the appointed hour arrived, he had breathed his last, hurried to a premature death by the anguish of mortified pride and patriotism. M. Aubry, his successor, presided in his place, and received the savage embassy. The orator, after the solemn custom of his people, addressed him in a speech of condolence, expressing his deep regret for D'Abbadie's untimely fate.[1]

[1] At all friendly meetings with Indians, it was customary for the latter, when the other party had sustained any signal loss, to commence by a formal speech of condolence, offering, at the same time, a black belt of wampum, in token of mourning. This practice may be particularly observed in the records of early councils with the Iroquois.

A chief of the Miamis then rose to speak, with a scowling brow, and words of bitterness and reproach. "Since we last sat on these seats, our ears have heard strange words. When the English told us that they had conquered you, we always thought that they lied; but now we have learned that they spoke the truth. We have learned that you, whom we have loved and served so well, have given the lands that we dwell upon to your enemies and ours. We have learned that the English have forbidden you to send traders to our villages to supply our wants; and that you, whom we thought so great and brave, have obeyed their commands like women, leaving us to starve and die in misery. We now tell you, once for all, that our lands are our own; and we tell you, moreover, that we can live without your aid, and hunt, and fish, and fight, as our fathers did before us. All that we ask of you is this: that you give us back the guns, the powder, the hatchets, and the knives which we have worn out in fighting your battles. As for you," he exclaimed, turning to the English officers, who were present as on the preceding day, — "as for you, our hearts burn with rage when we think of the ruin you have brought on us." Aubry returned but a weak answer to the cutting attack of the Indian speaker. He assured the ambassadors that the French still retained their former love for the Indians, that the English meant them no harm, and that, as all the world were now at peace, it behooved them also to take hold of the chain of friendship. A few presents were then distributed, but with no apparent effect. The features of the Indians still retained their sullen scowl; and on the morrow their canoes were ascending the Mississippi on their homeward voyage.[1]

[1] MS. *Report of Conference with the Shawanoe and Miami delegates from Pontiac, held at New Orleans*, March, 1765. Paris Documents

CHAPTER XXX.

1765.

RUIN OF THE INDIAN CAUSE.

THE repulse of Loftus, and rumors of the fierce temper of the Indians who guarded the Mississippi, convinced the commander-in-chief that to reach the Illinois by the southern route was an enterprise of no easy accomplishment. Yet, at the same time, he felt the strong necessity of a speedy military occupation of the country; since, while the *fleur de lis* floated over a single garrison in the ceded territory, it would be impossible to disabuse the Indians of the phantom hope of French assistance, to which they clung with infatuated tenacity. The embers of the Indian war would never be quenched until England had enforced all her claims over her defeated rival. Gage determined to despatch a force from the eastward, by way of Fort Pitt and the Ohio; a route now laid open by the late success of Bouquet, and the submission of the Delawares and Shawanoes.

To prepare a way for the passage of the troops, Sir William Johnson's deputy, George Croghan, was ordered to proceed in advance, to reason with the Indians as far as they were capable of reasoning; to soften their antipathy to the English, to expose the falsehoods of the French, and to distribute presents among the tribes by way of propitiation.[1] The mission was a critical one; but, so far as regarded the Indians, Croghan was well fitted to discharge it. He had been for years a trader among the western tribes, over whom he had gained much influence by a certain vigor of character, joined to a wary and sagacious policy, concealed beneath a bluff demeanor. Lieutenant Fraser, a young officer of education and intelligence, was associated with him. He spoke French, and, in other respects also, supplied qualifications in which his rugged colleague was wanting. They set out for Fort Pitt in February, 1765; and after traversing inhospitable mountains, and valleys clogged with snow, reached their destination at about the same time that Pontiac's ambassadors were entering New Orleans, to hold their council with the French.

A few days later, an incident occurred, which afterwards, through the carousals of many a winter evening, supplied an absorbing topic of anecdote and boast to the braggadocio heroes of the border. A train of pack-horses, bearing the gifts which Croghan was to bestow upon the Indians, followed him towards Fort Pitt, a few days' journey in the rear of his party. Under the same escort came several companies of traders, who, believing that the long suspended commerce with the Indians was

[1] MS. *Gage Papers.*

about to be reopened, were hastening to Fort Pitt with a great quantity of goods, eager to throw them into the market the moment the prohibition should be removed. There is reason to believe that Croghan had an interest in these goods, and that, under pretence of giving presents, he meant to open a clandestine trade.[1] The Paxton men, and their kindred spirits of the border, saw the proceeding with sinister eyes. In their view, the traders were about to make a barter of the blood of the people; to place in the hands of murdering savages the means of renewing the devastation to which the reeking frontier bore frightful witness. Once possessed with this idea, they troubled themselves with no more inquiries; and, having tried remonstrances in vain, they adopted a summary mode of doing themselves justice. At the head of the enterprise was a man whose name had been connected with more praiseworthy exploits, James Smith, already mentioned as leading a party of independent riflemen, for the defence of the borders, during the bloody autumn of 1763. He now mustered his old associates, made them resume their Indian disguise, and led them to their work with characteristic energy and address.

The government agents and traders were in the act of passing the verge of the frontiers. Their united trains amounted to seventy pack-horses,

[1] "The country people appear greatly incensed at the attempt they imagine has been made of opening a clandestine trade with the Savages under cover of presents; and, if it is not indiscreet in me, I would beg leave to ask whether Croghan had such extensive orders." — *Bouquet to Amherst,* 10 April, 1765, MS.

carrying goods to the value of more than four thousand pounds; while others, to the value of eleven thousand, were waiting transportation at Fort Loudon. Advancing deeper among the mountains, they began to descend the valley at the foot of Sidling Hill. The laden horses plodded knee-deep in snow. The mountains towered above the wayfarers in gray desolation; and the leafless forest, a mighty Æolian harp, howled dreary music to the wind of March. Suddenly, from behind snow-beplastered trunks and shaggy bushes of evergreen, uncouth apparitions started into view. Wild visages protruded, grotesquely horrible with vermilion and ochre, white lead and soot; stalwart limbs appeared, encased in buckskin; and rusty rifles thrust out their long muzzles. In front, and flank, and all around them, white puffs of smoke and sharp reports assailed the bewildered senses of the travellers, who were yet more confounded by the hum of bullets shot by unerring fingers within an inch of their ears. "Gentlemen," demanded the traders, in deprecating accents, "what would you have us do?" "Unpack your horses," roared a voice from the woods, "pile your goods in the road, and be off." The traders knew those with whom they had to deal. Hastening to obey the mandate, they departed with their utmost speed, happy that their scalps were not numbered with the booty. The spoilers appropriated to themselves such of the plunder as pleased them, made a bonfire of the rest, and went on their way rejoicing. The discomfited traders repaired to Fort Loudon, and laid their complaints before Lieutenant Grant, the commandant; who, inflamed with wrath and zealous for the cause of justice, despatched a party of soldiers, seized several innocent persons, and lodged them in the guard-house.[1] In high dudgeon at such an infraction of their liberties, the borderers sent messengers through the country, calling upon all good men to rise in arms. Three hundred obeyed the summons, and pitched their camp on a hill opposite Fort Loudon; a rare muster of desperadoes, yet observing a certain moderation in their wildest acts, and never at a loss for a plausible reason to justify any pranks which it might please them to exhibit. By some means, they contrived to waylay and capture a considerable number of the garrison, on which the commandant condescended to send them a flag of truce, and offer an exchange of prisoners. Their object thus accomplished, and their imprisoned comrades restored to them, the borderers dispersed for the present to their homes. Soon after, however, upon the occurrence of some fresh difficulty, the commandant, afraid or unable to apprehend the misdoers, endeavored to deprive them of the power of mischief by sending soldiers to their houses and carrying off their rifles. His triumph was short; for, as he rode out one afternoon, he fell into an ambuscade of countrymen, who, dispensing with all forms of respect, seized the incensed officer, and detained him in an uncom-

[1] Before me is a curious letter from Grant, in which he expatiates on his troubles in language which is far from giving a flattering impression of the literary accomplishments of officers of the 42d Highlanders, at that time.

fortable captivity until the rifles were restored. From this time forward, ruptures were repeatedly occurring between the troops and the frontiersmen; and the Pennsylvania border retained its turbulent character until the outbreak of the Revolutionary War.[1]

[1] The account of the seizure of the Indian goods is derived chiefly from the narrative of the ringleader, Smith, published in Drake's *Tragedies of the Wilderness*, and elsewhere. The correspondence of Gage and Johnson is filled with allusions to this affair, and the subsequent proceedings of the freebooters. Gage spares no invectives against what he calls the licentious conduct of the frontier people. In the narrative is inserted a ballad, or lyrical effusion, written by some partisan of the frontier faction, and evidently regarded by Smith as a signal triumph of the poetic art. He is careful to inform the reader that the author received his education in the great city of Dublin. The following melodious stanzas embody the chief action of the piece:—

"Astonished at the wild design,
Frontier inhabitants combin'd
With brave souls to stop their career;
Although some men apostatiz'd,
Who first the grand attempt advis'd,
The bold frontiers they bravely stood,
To act for their king and their country's good,
In joint league, and strangers to fear.

"On March the fifth, in sixty-five,
The Indian presents did arrive,
In long pomp and cavalcade,
Near Sidelong Hill, where in disguise
Some patriots did their train surprise,
And quick as lightning tumbled their loads,
And kindled them bonfires in the woods,
And mostly burnt their whole brigade."

The following is an extract from Johnson's letter to the Board of Trade, dated July 10, 1765:—

"I have great cause to think that Mr. Croghan will succeed in his enterprise, unless circumvented by the artifices of the French, or through the late licentious conduct of our own people. Although His Excellency General Gage has written to the Ministry on that subject, yet I think I should not be silent thereupon, as it may be productive of very serious consequences.

Whatever may have been Croghan's real attitude in this affair, the border robbers had wrought great injury to his mission; since the agency most potent to gain the affections of an Indian had been com pletely paralyzed in the destruction of the presents. Croghan found means, however, partially to repair his loss from the storehouse of Fort Pitt, where the rigor of the season and the great depth of the snow forced him to remain several weeks. This cause alone would have served to detain him; but he was yet farther retarded by the necessity of holding a meeting with the Delawares and Shawanoes, along whose southern borders he would be compelled to pass. An important object of the proposed meeting was to urge these tribes to fulfil the promise they had made, during the previous

"The frontier inhabitants of Pennsylvania, Maryland, and Virginia, after having attacked and destroyed the goods which were going to Fort Pitt (as in my last), did form themselves into parties, threatening to destroy all Indians they met, or all white people who dealt with them. They likewise marched to Fort Augusta, and from thence over the West branch of the Susquehanna, beyond the Bounds of the last purchase made by the Proprietaries, where they declare they will form a settlement, in defiance of Whites or Indians. They afterwards attacked a small party of His Majesty's troops upon the Road, but were happily obliged to retire with the loss of one or two men. However, from their conduct and threats since, there is reason to think they will not stop here. Neither is their licentiousness confined to the Provinces I have mentioned, the people of Carolina having cut off a party, coming down under a pass from Col. Lewis, of the particulars of which your Lordships have been doubtless informed.

"Your Lordships may easily conceive what effects this will have upon the Indians, who begin to be all acquainted therewith. I wish it may not have already gone too great a length to receive a timely check, or prevent the Indians' Resentment, who see themselves attacked, threatened and their property invaded, by a set of ignorant, misled Rioters, who defy Government itself, and this at a time when we have just treated with some, and are in treaty with other Nations."

autumn, to Colonel Bouquet, to yield up their remaining prisoners, and send deputies to treat of peace with Sir William Johnson; engagements which, when Croghan arrived at the fort, were as yet unfulfilled, though, as already mentioned, they were soon after complied with.

Immediately on his arrival, he had despatched messengers inviting the chiefs to a council; a summons which they obeyed with their usual reluctance and delay, dropping in, band after band, with such tardiness that a month was consumed before a sufficient number were assembled. Croghan then addressed them, showing the advantages of peace, and the peril which they would bring on their own heads by a renewal of the war; and urging them to stand true to their engagements, and send their deputies to Johnson as soon as the melting of the snows should leave the forest pathways open. Several replies, all of a pacific nature, were made by the principal chiefs; but the most remarkable personage who appeared at the council was the Delaware prophet mentioned in an early portion of the narrative, as having been strongly instrumental in urging the tribes to war by means of pretended or imaginary revelations from the Great Spirit.[1] He now delivered a speech by no means remarkable for eloquence, yet of most beneficial consequence; for he intimated that the Great Spirit had not only revoked his sanguinary mandates, but had commanded the Indians to lay down the hatchet, and

[1] See *ante*, Vol. I. p. 179.

smoke the pipe of peace.[1] In spite of this auspicious declaration, and in spite of the chastisement and humiliation of the previous autumn, Croghan was privately informed that a large party among the Indians still remained balanced between their anger and their fears; eager to take up the hatchet, yet dreading the consequences which the act might bring. Under this cloudy aspect of affairs, he was doubly gratified when a party of Shawanoe warriors arrived, bringing with them the prisoners whom they had promised Colonel Bouquet to surrender; and this faithful adherence to their word, contrary alike to Croghan's expectations, and to the prophecies of those best versed in Indian character, made it apparent that, whatever might be the sentiments of the turbulent among them, the more influential portion were determined on a pacific attitude.

These councils, and the previous delays, consumed so much time, that Croghan became fearful that the tribes of the Illinois might, meanwhile, commit themselves by some rash outbreak, which would increase the difficulty of reconciliation. In view of this danger, his colleague, Lieutenant Fraser, volunteered to proceed in advance, leaving Croghan to follow when he had settled affairs at Fort Pitt. Fraser departed, accordingly, with a few attendants. The rigor of the season had now begun to relent, and the ice-locked Ohio was flinging off its wintry fetters. Embarked in a birch

[1] MS. *Journal of the Transactions of George Croghan, Esq., deputy agent for Indian affairs, with different tribes of Indians, at Fort Pitt, from the 28th af February,* 1765, *to the* 12*th of May following.* In this journal the prophet's speech is given in full.

canoe, and aided by the current, Fraser floated prosperously downwards for a thousand miles, and landed safely in the country of the Illinois. Here he found the Indians in great destitution, and in a frame of mind which would have inclined them to peace but for the secret encouragement they received from the French. A change, however, soon took place. Boats arrived from New Orleans, loaded with a great quantity of goods, which the French, at that place, being about to abandon it, had sent in haste to the Illinois. The traders' shops at Kaskaskia were suddenly filled again. The Indians were delighted; and the French, with a view to a prompt market for their guns, hatchets, and gunpowder, redoubled their incitements to war. Fraser found himself in a hornet's nest. His life was in great danger; but Pontiac, who was then at Kaskaskia, several times interposed to save him. The French traders picked a quarrel with him, and instigated the Indians to kill him; for it was their interest that the war should go on. A party of them invited Pontiac to dinner; plied him with whiskey; and, having made him drunk, incited him to have Fraser and his servant seized. They were brought to the house where the debauch was going on; and here, among a crowd of drunken Indians, their lives hung by a hair. Fraser writes, "He (Pontiac) and his men fought all night about us. They said we would get off next day if they should not prevent our flight by killing us. This Pontiac would not do. All night they did nothing else but sing the death song; but my servant and

I, with the help of an Indian who was sober, defended ourselves till morning, when they thought proper to let us escape. When Pontiac was sober, he made me an apology for his behavior; and told me it was owing to bad counsel he had got that he had taken me; but that I need not fear being taken in that manner for the future."[1]

Fraser's situation was presently somewhat improved by a rumor that an English detachment was about to descend the Ohio. The French traders, before so busy with their falsehoods and calumnies, now held their peace, dreading the impending chastisement. They no longer gave arms and ammunition to the Indians; and when the latter questioned them concerning the fabrication of a French army advancing to the rescue, they treated the story as unfounded, or sought to evade the subject. St. Ange, too, and the other officers of the crown, confiding in the arrival of the English, assumed a more decisive tone; refusing to give the Indians presents, telling them that thenceforward they must trust to the English for supplies, reproving them for their designs against the latter, and advising them to remain at peace.[2]

Nevertheless, Fraser's position was neither safe nor pleasant. He could hear nothing of Croghan, and he was almost alone, having sent away all his men, except his servant, to save them from being abused and beaten by the Indians. He had dis-

[1] MS. Letter — *Fraser to Lieut. Col. Campbell,* 20 May, 1765.

[2] *Harangue faitte à la nation Illinoise et au Chef Pondiak par M. de St. Ange, Cap. Commandant au pais des Illinois pour S. M. T. C. au sujet de la guerre que Les Indiens font aux Anglois.*

cretionary orders to go down to Mobile and report to the English commandant there; and of these he was but too glad to avail himself. He descended the Mississippi in disguise, and safely reached New Orleans.[1]

Apparently, it was about this time that an incident took place, mentioned, with evident satisfaction, in a letter of the French commandant, Aubry. The English officers in the south, unable to send troops up the Mississippi, had employed a Frenchman, whom they had secured in their interest, to ascend the river with a boat-load of goods, which he was directed to distribute among the Indians, to remove their prejudice against the English and pave the way to reconciliation. Intelligence of this movement reached the ears of Pontiac, who, though much pleased with the approaching supplies, had no mind that they should be devoted to

1 MS. Letter — *Aubry to the Minister*, July, 1765. Aubry makes himself merry with the fears of Fraser; who, however, had the best grounds for his apprehensions, as is sufficiently clear from the above as well as from the minutes of a council held by him with Pontiac and other Indians at the Illinois, during the month of April. The minutes referred to are among the Paris Documents.

Pontiac's first reception of Fraser was not auspicious, as appears from the following. Extract from a Letter — *Fort Pitt*, July 24 (*Pa. Gaz. Nos.* 1912, 1913): —

"Pondiac immediately collected all the Indians under his influence to the Illinois, and ordered the French commanding officer there to deliver up these Englishmen [Fraser and his party] to him, as he had prepared a large kettle in which he was determined to boil them and all other Englishmen that came that way. . . . Pondiac told the French that he had been informed of Mr. Croghan's coming that way to treat with the Indians, and that he would keep his kettle boiling over a large fire to receive him likewise."

Pontiac soon after relented as we have seen. Another letter, dated New Orleans, June 19, adds: "He [Fraser] says Pondiac is a very clever fellow and had it not been for him he would never have got away alive."

serve the interests of his enemies. He descended to the river bank with a body of his warriors; and as La Garantais, the Frenchman, landed, he seized him and his men, flogged them severely, robbed them of their cargo, and distributed the goods with exemplary impartiality among his delighted followers.[1]

Notwithstanding this good fortune, Pontiac daily saw his followers dropping off from their allegiance; for even the boldest had lost heart. Had any thing been wanting to convince him of the hopelessness of his cause, the report of his ambassadors returning from New Orleans would have banished every doubt. No record of his interview with them remains; but it is easy to conceive with what chagrin he must have learned that the officer of France first in rank in all America had refused to aid him, and urged the timid counsels of peace. The vanity of those expectations, which had been the mainspring of his enterprise, now rose clear and palpable before him; and, with rage and bitterness, he saw the rotten foundation of his hopes sinking into dust, and the whole structure of his plot crumbling in ruins about him.

All was lost. His allies were falling off, his followers deserting him. To hold out longer would be destruction, and to fly was scarcely an easier task. In the south lay the Cherokees, hereditary enemies of his people. In the west were the Osages and Missouries, treacherous and uncertain friends, and the fierce and jealous Dahcotah. In

[1] MS. Letter—*Aubry to the Minister*, 10 July, 1765.

the east the forests would soon be filled with English traders, and beset with English troops; while in the north his own village of Detroit lay beneath the guns of the victorious garrison. He might, indeed, have found a partial refuge in the remoter wilderness of the upper lakes; but those dreary wastes would have doomed him to a life of unambitious exile. His resolution was taken. He determined to accept the peace which he knew would be proffered, to smoke the calumet with his triumphant enemies, and patiently await his hour of vengeance.[1]

The conferences at Fort Pitt concluded, Croghan left that place on the fifteenth of May, and embarked on the Ohio, accompanied by several Delaware and Shawanoe deputies, whom he had persuaded those newly reconciled tribes to send with him, for the furtherance of his mission. At the mouth of the Scioto, he was met by a band of Shawanoe warriors, who, in compliance with a message previously sent to them, delivered into his hands seven intriguing Frenchmen, who for some time past had lived in their villages. Thence he pursued his voyage smoothly and prosperously, until, on the eighth of June, he reached a spot a little below the mouth of the Wabash. Here he landed with his party; when suddenly the hideous war-whoop, the explosion of musketry, and the whistling of arrows greeted him from the covert of the neighboring thickets. His men fell thick about

[1] One of St. Ange's letters to Aubry contains views of the designs and motives of Pontiac similar to those expressed above.

him. Three Indians and two white men were shot dead on the spot; most of the remainder were wounded; and on the next instant the survivors found themselves prisoners in the hands of eighty yelling Kickapoos, who plundered them of all they had. No sooner, however, was their prey fairly within their clutches, than the cowardly assailants began to apologize for what they had done, saying it was all a mistake, and that the French had set them on by telling them that the Indians who accompanied Croghan were Cherokees, their mortal enemies; excuses utterly without foundation, for the Kickapoos had dogged the party for several days, and perfectly understood its character.[1]

It is superfluous to inquire into the causes of this attack. No man practically familiar with Indian character need be told the impossibility of foreseeing to what strange acts the wayward impulses of this murder-loving race may prompt them. Unstable as water, capricious as the winds, they seem in some of their moods like ungoverned children fired with the instincts of devils. In the present case, they knew that they hated the English, — knew that they wanted scalps; and thinking nothing of the consequences, they seized the first opportunity to gratify their rabid longing. This done, they thought it best to avert any probable effects of

[1] A few days before, a boy belonging to Croghan's party had been lost, as was supposed, in the woods. It proved afterwards that he had been seized by the Kickapoo warriors, and was still prisoner among them at the time of the attack. They must have learned from him the true character of Croghan and his companions. — *MS. Gage Papers.*

their misconduct by such falsehoods as might suggest themselves to their invention.

Still apologizing for what they had done, but by no means suffering their prisoners to escape, they proceeded up the Wabash, to the little French fort and settlement of Vincennes, where, to his great joy, Croghan found among the assembled Indians some of his former friends and acquaintance. They received him kindly, and sharply rebuked the Kickapoos, who, on their part, seemed much ashamed and crestfallen. From Vincennes the English were conducted, in a sort of honorable captivity, up the river to Ouatanon, where they arrived on the twenty-third, fifteen days after the attack, and where Croghan was fortunate enough to find a great number of his former Indian friends, who received him, to appearance at least, with much cordiality. He took up his quarters in the fort, where there was at this time no garrison, a mob of French traders and Indians being the only tenants of the place. For several days, his time was engrossed with receiving deputation after deputation from the various tribes and sub-tribes of the neighborhood, smoking pipes of peace, making and hearing speeches, and shaking hands with greasy warriors, who, one and all, were strong in their professions of good-will, promising not only to regard the English as their friends, but to aid them, if necessary, in taking possession of the Illinois.

While these amicable conferences were in progress, a miscreant Frenchman came from the Mississippi with a message from a chief of that region, urging the Indians of Ouatanon to burn the Englishman alive. Of this proposal the Indians signified their strong disapprobation, and assured the startled envoy that they would stand his friends, — professions the sincerity of which, happily for him, was confirmed by the strong guaranty of their fears.

The next arrival was that of Maisonville, a messenger from St. Ange, requesting Croghan to come to Fort Chartres, to adjust affairs in that quarter. The invitation was in accordance with Croghan's designs; and he left the fort on the following day, attended by Maisonville, and a concourse of the Ouatanon Indians, who, far from regarding him as their prisoner, were now studious to show him every mark of respect. He had advanced but a short distance into the forest when he met Pontiac himself, who was on his way to Ouatanon, followed by a numerous train of chiefs and warriors. He gave his hand to the English envoy, and both parties returned together to the fort. Its narrow precincts were now crowded with Indians, a perilous multitude, dark, malignant, inscrutable; and it behooved the Englishman to be wary, in his dealings with them, since a breath might kindle afresh the wildfire in their hearts.

At a meeting of the chiefs and warriors, Pontiac offered the calumet and belt of peace, and professed his concurrence with the chiefs of Ouatanon in the friendly sentiments which they expressed towards the English. The French, he added, had deceived him, telling him and his people that the English meant to enslave the Indians of the Illinois, and turn loose upon them their enemies the Cherokees. It was this which drove him to arms; and now that he knew the story to be false, he would no longer stand in the path of the English. Yet they must not imagine that, in taking possession of the French forts, they gained any right to the country; for the French had never bought the land, and lived upon it by sufferance only.

As this meeting with Pontiac and the Illinois chiefs made it needless for Croghan to advance farther on his western journey, he now bent his footsteps towards Detroit, and, followed by Pontiac and many of the principal chiefs, crossed over to Fort Miami, and thence descended the Maumee, holding conferences at the several villages which he passed on his way. On the seventeenth of August, he reached Detroit, where he found a great gathering of Indians, Ottawas, Pottawattamies, and Ojibwas; some encamped about the fort, and others along the banks of the River Rouge. They obeyed his summons to a meeting with alacrity, partly from a desire to win the good graces of a victorious enemy, and partly from the importunate craving for liquor and presents, which never slumbers in an Indian breast. Numerous meetings were held; and the old council-hall where Pontiac had essayed his scheme of abortive treachery was now crowded with repentant warriors, anxious, by every form of submission, to appease the conqueror. Their ill success, their fears of chastisement, and the miseries they had endured from the long suspension of the fur-trade, had banished from their minds every thought of hostility. They were glad, they said, that the dark clouds were now dispersing, and the sunshine of peace once more returning; and since all the nations to the sunrising had taken their great father the King of England by the hand, they also wished to do the same. They now saw clearly that the French were indeed conquered; and thenceforth they would listen no more to the whistling of evil birds, but lay down the war hatchet, and sit quiet on their mats. Among those who appeared to make or renew their submission was the Grand Sauteur, who had led the massacre at Michillimackinac, and who, a few years after expiated his evil deeds by a bloody death. He now pretended great regret for what he had done. "We red people," he said, "are a very jealous and foolish people; but, father, there are some among the white men worse than we are, and they have told us lies, and deceived us. Therefore we hope you will take pity on our women and children, and grant us peace." A band of Pottawattamies from St. Joseph's were also present, and, after excusing themselves for their past conduct by the stale plea of the uncontrollable temper of their young men, their orator proceeded as follows: —

"We are no more than wild creatures to you, fathers, in understanding; therefore we request you to forgive the past follies of our young people, and receive us for your children. Since you have thrown down our former father on his back, we have been wandering in the dark, like blind people. Now you have dispersed all this darkness, which hung over the heads of the several tribes, and have accepted them for your children, we hope you will let us partake with them the light, that our women and children may enjoy peace. We beg you to forget all that is past. By this belt we remove all evil thoughts from your hearts.

"Fathers, when we formerly came to visit our fathers the French, they always sent us home joyful; and we hope you, fathers, will have pity on our women and young men, who are in great want of necessaries, and not let us go home to our towns ashamed."

On the twenty-seventh of August, Croghan held a meeting with the Ottawas, and the other tribes of Detroit and Sandusky; when, adopting their own figurative language, he addressed them in the following speech, in which, as often happened when white men borrowed the tongue of the forest orator, he lavished a more unsparing profusion of imagery than the Indians themselves: —

"Children, we are very glad to see so many of you here present at your ancient council-fire, which has been neglected for some time past; since then, high winds have blown, and raised heavy clouds over your country. I now, by this belt, rekindle your ancient fire, and throw dry wood upon it, that the blaze may ascend to heaven, so that all nations may see it, and know that you live in peace and tranquillity with your fathers the English.

"By this belt I disperse all the black clouds from over your heads, that the sun may shine clear on your women and children, that those unborn may enjoy the blessings of this general peace, now so happily settled between your fathers the English and you, and all your younger brethren to the sunsetting.

"Children, by this belt I gather up all the bones of your deceased friends, and bury them deep in the ground, that the buds and sweet flowers of the earth may grow over them, that we may not see them any more.

"Children, with this belt I take the hatchet out of your hands, and pluck up a large tree, and bury it deep, so that it may never be found any more; and I plant the tree of peace, which all our children may sit under, and smoke in peace with their fathers.

"Children, we have made a road from the sun rising to the sunsetting. I desire that you will preserve that road good and pleasant to travel upon, that we may all share the blessings of this happy union."

On the following day, Pontiac spoke in behalf of the several nations assembled at the council.

"Father, we have all smoked out of this pipe of peace. It is your children's pipe; and as the war is all over, and the Great Spirit and Giver of Light, who has made the earth and every thing therein, has brought us all together this day for our mutual good, I declare to all nations that I have settled my peace with you before I came here, and now deliver my pipe to be sent to Sir William Johnson, that he may know I have made peace, and taken the King of England for my father, in presence of all the nations now assembled; and whenever any of those nations go to visit him, they may smoke out of it with him in peace. Fathers, we are obliged to you for lighting up our old council-fire for us, and desiring us to return to it; but we are now settled on the Miami River, not far from hence: whenever you want us, you will find us there."[1]

"Our people," he added, "love liquor, and if we dwelt near you in our old village of Detroit, our warriors would be always drunk, and quarrels would arise between us and you." Drunkenness was, in truth, the bane of the whole unhappy race; but Pontiac, too thoroughly an Indian in his virtues and his vices to be free from its destructive taint,

[1] *Journal of George Croghan, on his journey to the Illinois,* 1765. This journal has been twice published — in the appendix to Butler's *History of Kentucky,* and in the *Pioneer History* of Dr. Hildreth. A manuscript copy also may be found in the office of the secretary of state at Albany. Dr. Hildreth omits the speech of Croghan to the Indians, which is given above as affording a better example of the forms of speech appropriate to an Indian peace harangue, than the genuine productions of the Indians themselves, who are less apt to indulge in such a redundancy of metaphor.

A language extremely deficient in words of general and abstract signification renders the use of figures indispensable; and it is from this cause, above all others, that the flowers of Indian rhetoric derive their origin. In the work of Heckewelder will be found a list of numerous figurative expressions appropriate to the various occasions of public and private intercourse, — forms which are seldom departed from, and which are often found identical among tribes speaking languages radically distinct. Thus, among both Iroquois and Algonquins, the "whistling of evil birds" is the invariable expression to denote evil tidings or bad advice.

The Indians are much pleased when white men whom they respect adopt their peculiar symbolical language, — a circumstance of which the Jesuit missionaries did not fail to avail themselves. "These people," says Father Le Jeune, "being great orators, and often using allegories and metaphors, our fathers, in order to attract them to God, adapt themselves to their custom of speaking, which delights them very much, seeing we succeed as well as they."

concluded his speech with the common termination of an Indian harangue, and desired that the rum barrel might be opened, and his thirsty warriors allowed to drink.

At the end of September, having brought these protracted conferences to a close, Croghan left Detroit, and departed for Niagara, whence, after a short delay, he passed eastward, to report the results of his mission to the commander-in-chief. But before leaving the Indian country, he exacted from Pontiac a promise that in the spring he would descend to Oswego, and, in behalf of the tribes lately banded in his league, conclude a treaty of peace and amity with Sir William Johnson.[1]

Croghan's efforts had been attended with signal success. The tribes of the west, of late bristling in defiance, and hot for fight, had craved forgiveness, and proffered the calumet. The war was over; the last flickerings of that wide conflagration had died away; but the embers still glowed beneath the ashes, and fuel and a breath alone were wanting to rekindle those desolating fires.

In the mean time, a hundred Highlanders of the 42d Regiment, those veterans whose battle-cry had echoed over the bloodiest fields of America, had

[1] In a letter to Gage, without a date, but sent in the same enclosure as his journal, Croghan gives his impression of Pontiac in the following words: —

"Pondiac is a shrewd, sensible Indian, of few words, and commands more respect among his own nation than any Indian I ever saw could do among his own tribe. He, and all the principal men of those nations, seem at present to be convinced that the French had a view of interest in stirring up the late differences between his Majesty's subjects and them, and call it a beaver war."

left Fort Pitt under command of Captain Sterling, and, descending the Ohio, arrived at Fort Chartres just as the snows of early winter began to whiten the naked forests.[1] The flag of France descended from the rampart; and with the stern courtesies of war, St. Ange yielded up his post, the citadel of the Illinois, to its new masters. In that act was consummated the double triumph of British power in America. England had crushed her hereditary foe; and France, in her fall, had left to irretrievable ruin the savage tribes to whom her policy and self-interest had lent a transient support.

[1] MS. *Gage Papers.* M. Nicollet, in speaking of the arrival of the British troops, says, "At this news Pontiac raved." This is a mistake. Pontiac's reconciliation had already taken place, and he had abandoned all thoughts of resistance.

CHAPTER XXXI.

1766–1769.

DEATH OF PONTIAC.

THE winter passed quietly away. Already the Indians began to feel the blessings of returning peace in the partial reopening of the fur-trade; and the famine and nakedness, the misery and death, which through the previous season had been rife in their encampments, were exchanged for comparative comfort and abundance. With many precautions, and in meagre allowances, the traders had been permitted to throw their goods into the Indian markets; and the starving hunters were no longer left, as many of them had been, to gain precarious sustenance by the bow, the arrow, and the lance — the half-forgotten weapons of their fathers. Some troubles arose along the frontiers of Pennsylvania and Virginia. The reckless borderers, in contempt of common humanity and prudence, murdered several straggling Indians, and enraged others by abuse and insult; but these outrages could not obliterate the remembrance of recent chastisement, and, for the present at least, the injured warriors forbore to draw down the fresh vengeance of their destroyers.

Spring returned, and Pontiac remembered the promise he had made to visit Sir William Johnson at Oswego. He left his encampment on the Maumee, accompanied by his chiefs, and by an Englishman named Crawford, a man of vigor and resolution, who had been appointed, by the superintendent, to the troublesome office of attending the Indian deputation, and supplying their wants.[1]

We may well imagine with what bitterness of mood the defeated war-chief urged his canoe along the margin of Lake Erie, and gazed upon the horizon-bounded waters, and the lofty shores, green with primeval verdure. Little could he have dreamed, and little could the wisest of that day have imagined, that, within the space of a single human life, that lonely lake would be studded with the sails of commerce; that cities and villages would rise upon the ruins of the forest; and that the poor mementoes of his lost race — the wampum beads, the rusty tomahawk, and the arrowhead of stone, turned up by the ploughshare — would become the wonder of school-boys, and the prized relics of the antiquary's cabinet. Yet it needed no prophetic eye to foresee that, sooner or later, the doom must come. The star of his people's destiny was fading from the sky; and, to a mind like his, the black and withering future must have stood revealed in all its desolation.

The birchen flotilla gained the outlet of Lake Erie, and, shooting downwards with the stream, landed beneath the palisades of Fort Schlosser.

[1] MS. *Johnson Papers.*

The chiefs passed the portage, and, once more embarking, pushed out upon Lake Ontario. Soon their goal was reached, and the cannon boomed hollow salutation from the batteries of Oswego.

Here they found Sir William Johnson waiting to receive them, attended by the chief sachems of the Iroquois, whom he had invited to the spot, that their presence might give additional weight and solemnity to the meeting. As there was no building large enough to receive so numerous a con course, a canopy of green boughs was erected to shade the assembly from the sun; and thither, on the twenty-third of July, repaired the chiefs and warriors of the several nations. Here stood the tall figure of Sir William Johnson, surrounded by civil and military officers, clerks, and interpreters; while before him reclined the painted sachems of the Iroquois, and the great Ottawa war-chief, with his dejected followers.

Johnson opened the meeting with the usual foı malities, presenting his auditors with a belt of wampum to wipe the tears from their eyes, with another to cover the bones of their relatives, another to open their ears that they might hear, and another to clear their throats that they might speak with ease. Then, amid solemn silence, Pontiac's great peace-pipe was lighted and passed round the assembly, each man present inhaling a whiff of the sacred smoke. These tedious forms, together with a few speeches of compliment, consumed the whole morning; for this savage people, on whose supposed simplicity poets and rhetoricians have lavished their praises, may challenge the world to outmatch their bigoted adherence to usage and ceremonial.

On the following day, the council began in earnest, and Sir William Johnson addressed Pontiac and his attendant chiefs.

"Children, I bid you heartily welcome to this place; and I trust that the Great Spirit will permit us often to meet together in friendship, for I have now opened the door and cleared the road, that all nations may come hither from the sunsetting. This belt of wampum confirms my words.

"Children, it gave me much pleasure to find that you who are present behaved so well last year, and treated in so friendly a manner Mr. Croghan, one of my deputies; and that you expressed such concern for the bad behavior of those, who, in order to obstruct the good work of peace, assaulted and wounded him, and killed some of his party, both whites and Indians; a thing before unknown, and contrary to the laws and customs of all nations. This would have drawn down our strongest resentment upon those who were guilty of so heinous a crime, were it not for the great lenity and kindness of your English father, who does not delight in punishing those who repent sincerely of their faults.

"Children, I have now, with the approbation of General Gage (your father's chief warrior in this country), invited you here in order to confirm and strengthen your proceedings with Mr. Croghan last year. I hope that you will remember all that then passed, and I desire that you will often repeat it to your young people, and keep it fresh in your minds.

"Children, you begin already to see the fruits of peace, from the number of traders and plenty of goods at all the garrisoned posts; and our enjoying the peaceable possession of the Illinois will be found of great advantage to the Indians in that country. You likewise see that proper officers, men of honor and probity, are appointed to reside at the posts, to prevent abuses in trade, to hear your complaints, and to lay before me such of them as they cannot redress.[1] Interpreters are likewise sent for the assistance of each of them; and smiths are sent to the posts to repair your arms and implements. All this, which is attended with a great expense, is now done by the great King, your father, as a proof of his regard; so that, casting from you all jealousy and apprehension, you should now strive with each other who should show the most gratitude to this best of princes. I do now, therefore, confirm the assurances which I give you of his Majesty's good will, and do insist on your casting away all evil thoughts, and shutting your ears against all flying idle reports of bad people."

The rest of Johnson's speech was occupied in explaining to his hearers the new arrangements for the regulation of the fur-trade; in exhorting them

[1] The Lords of Trade had recently adopted a new plan for the management of Indian affairs, the principal feature of which was the confinement of the traders to the military posts, where they would conduct their traffic under the eye of proper officers, instead of ranging at will, without supervision or control, among the Indian villages. It was found extremely difficult to enforce this regulation

to forbear from retaliating the injuries they might receive from reckless white men, who would meet with due punishment from their own countrymen; and in urging them to deliver up to justice those of their people who might be guilty of crimes against the English. "Children," he concluded, "I now, by this belt, turn your eyes to the sunrising, where you will always find me your sincere friend. From me you will always hear what is true and good; and I charge you never more to listen to those evil birds, who come, with lying tongues, to lead you astray, and to make you break the solemn engagements which you have entered into, in presence of the Great Spirit, with the King your father and the English people. Be strong, then, and keep fast hold of the chain of friendship, that your children, following your example, may live happy and prosperous lives."

Pontiac made a brief reply, and promised to return on the morrow an answer in full. The meeting then broke up.

The council of the next day was opened by the Wyandot chief, Teata, in a short and formal address; at the conclusion of which Pontiac himself arose, and addressed the superintendent in words, of which the following is a translation:

"Father, we thank the Great Spirit for giving us so fine a day to meet upon such great affairs. I speak in the name of all the nations to the westward, of whom I am the master. It is the will of the Great Spirit that we should meet here to-day; and before him I now take you by the hand. I call him to witness that I speak from my heart; for since I took Colonel Croghan by the hand last year, I have never let go my hold, for I see that the Great Spirit will have us friends.

"Father, when our great father of France was in this country, I held him fast by the hand. Now that he is gone, I take you, my English father, by the hand, in the name of all the nations, and promise to keep this covenant as long as I shall live."

Here he delivered a large belt of wampum.

"Father, when you address me, it is the same as if you addressed all the nations of the west. Father, this belt is to cover and strengthen our chain of friendship, and to show you that, if any nation shall lift the hatchet against our English brethren, we shall be the first to feel it and resent it."

Pontiac next took up in succession the various points touched upon in the speech of the superintendent, expressing in all things a full compliance with his wishes. The succeeding days of the conference were occupied with matters of detail relating chiefly to the fur-trade, all of which were adjusted to the apparent satisfaction of the Indians, who, on their part, made reiterated professions of friendship. Pontiac promised to recall the war-belts which had been sent to the north and west, though, as he alleged, many of them had proceeded from the Senecas, and not from him; adding that, when all were gathered together, they would be more than a man could carry. The Iroquois sachems then addressed the western nations, exhorting them to stand true to their engagements, and hold fast the chain of friendship; and the councils closed on the thirty-first, with a bountiful distribution of presents to Pontiac and his followers.[1]

Thus ended this memorable meeting, in which Pontiac sealed his submission to the English, and renounced for ever the bold design by which he had trusted to avert or retard the ruin of his race. His hope of seeing the empire of France restored in America was scattered to the winds, and with it vanished every rational scheme of resistance to English encroachment. Nothing now remained but to stand an idle spectator, while, in the north and in the south, the tide of British power rolled westward in resistless might; while the fragments of the rival empire, which he would fain have set up as a barrier against the flood, lay scattered a miserable wreck; and while the remnant of his people melted away or fled for refuge to remoter deserts. For them the prospects of the future were as clear as they were calamitous. Destruction or civilization — between these lay their choice; and few who knew them could doubt which alternative they would embrace.

Pontiac, his canoe laden with the gifts of his enemy, steered homeward for the Maumee; and in this vicinity he spent the following winter, pitching his lodge in the forest with his wives and children,

[1] MS. *Minutes of Proceedings at a Congress with Pontiac and Chiefs of the Ottawas, Pottawattamies, Hurons, and Chippewais; begun at Oswego Tuesday*, July 23, 1766.

A copy of this document is preserved in the office of the secretary of state at Albany, among the papers procured in London by Mr. Brodhead.

and hunting like an ordinary warrior. With the succeeding spring, 1767, fresh murmurings of dis content arose among the Indian tribes, from the lakes to the Potomac, the first precursors of the disorders which, a few years later, ripened into a brief but bloody war along the borders of Virginia. These threatening symptoms might easily be traced to their source. The incorrigible frontiersmen had again let loose their murdering propensities; and a multitude of squatters had built their cabins on Indian lands beyond the limits of Pennsylvania, adding insult to aggression, and sparing neither oaths, curses, nor any form of abuse and maltreatment against the rightful owners of the soil.[1] The new regulations of the fur-trade could not prevent disorders among the reckless men engaged in it. This was particularly the case in the region of the Illinois, where the evil was aggravated by the renewed intrigues of the French, and especially of those who had fled from the English side of the Mississippi, and made their abode around the new settlement of St. Louis.[2] It is difficult to say how far Pontiac was involved in this agitation. It is certain that some of the English traders regarded him with jealousy and fear, as prime mover of the whole, and eagerly watched an opportunity to destroy him.

The discontent among the tribes did not diminish

[1] "It seems," writes Sir William Johnson to the lords of trade, "as if the people were determined to bring on a new war, though their own ruin may be the consequence."

[2] *Doc. Hist. N. Y.* II. 861–893, etc. MS. *Johnson Papers.* MS. *Gage Papers.*

with the lapse of time; yet for many months we can discern no trace of Pontiac. Records and traditions are silent concerning him. It is not until April, 1769, that he appears once more distinctly on the scene.[1] At about that time he came to the Illinois, with what design does not appear, though his movements excited much uneasiness among the few English in that quarter. Soon after his arrival, he repaired to St. Louis, to visit his former acquaintance, St. Ange, who was then in command at that post, having offered his services to the Spaniards after the cession of Louisiana. After leaving the fort, Pontiac proceeded to the house of which young Pierre Chouteau was an inmate; and to the last days of his protracted life, the latter could vividly recall the circumstances of the interview. The savage chief was arrayed in the full uniform of a French officer, which had been presented to him as a special mark of respect and favor by the Marquis of Montcalm, towards the close of the French war, and which Pontiac never had the bad taste to wear, except on occasions when he wished to appear with unusual dignity. St. Ange, Chouteau, and the other principal inhabitants of the infant settlement, whom he visited in turn, all received him cordially, and did their best to entertain him and his attend-

[1] Carver says that Pontiac was killed in 1767. This may possibly be a mere printer's error. In the *Maryland Gazette,* and also in the *Pennsylvania Gazette,* were published during the month of August, 1769, several letters from the Indian country, in which Pontiac is mentioned as having been killed during the preceding April. M. Chouteau states that, to the best of his recollection, the chief was killed in 1768; but oral testimony is of little weight in regard to dates. The evidence of the Gazettes appears conclusive.

ant chiefs. He remained at St. Louis for two or three days, when, hearing that a large number of Indians were assembled at Cahokia, on the opposite side of the river, and that some drinking bout or other social gathering was in progress, he told St Ange that he would cross over to see what was going forward. St. Ange tried to dissuade him, and urged the risk to which he would expose him self; but Pontiac persisted, boasting that he was a match for the English, and had no fear for his life. He entered a canoe with some of his followers, and Chouteau never saw him again.

He who, at the present day, crosses from the city of St. Louis to the opposite shore of the Missis sippi, and passes southward through a forest fes tooned with grape-vines, and fragrant with the scent of flowers, will soon emerge upon the ancient hamlet of Cahokia. To one fresh from the busy suburbs of the American city, the small French houses, scattered in picturesque disorder, the light-hearted, thriftless look of their inmates, and the woods which form the background of the picture, seem like the remnants of an earlier and simpler world. Strange changes have passed around that spot. Forests have fallen, cities have sprung up, and the lonely wilderness is thronged with human life. Nature herself has taken part in the general transformation; and the Mississippi has made a fearful inroad, robbing from the luckless Creoles a mile of rich meadow and woodland. Yet, in the midst of all, this relic of the lost empire of France has preserved its essential features through the lapse of a century, and offers at this day an aspect not widely different from that which met the eye of Pontiac, when he and his chiefs landed on its shore.

The place was full of Illinois Indians; such a scene as in our own time may often be met with in some squalid settlement of the border, where the vagabond guests, bedizened with dirty finery, tie their small horses in rows along the fences, and stroll idly among the houses, or lounge about the dramshops. A chief so renowned as Pontiac could not remain long among the friendly Creoles of Cahokia without being summoned to a feast; and at such primitive entertainment the whiskey-bottle would not fail to play its part. This was in truth the case. Pontiac drank deeply, and, when the carousal was over, strode down the village street to the adjacent woods, where he was heard to sing the medicine songs, in whose magic power he trusted as the warrant of success in all his undertakings.

An English trader, named Williamson, was then in the village. He had looked on the movements of Pontiac with a jealousy probably not diminished by the visit of the chief to the French at St. Louis; and he now resolved not to lose so favorable an opportunity to despatch him. With this view, he gained the ear of a strolling Indian, belonging to the Kaskaskia tribe of the Illinois, bribed him with a barrel of liquor, and promised him a farther reward if he would kill the chief. The bargain was quickly made. When Pontiac entered the forest, the assassin stole close upon his track; and, watching his moment, glided behind him, and buried a tomahawk in his brain.

The dead body was soon discovered, and startled cries and wild howlings announcd the event. The word was caught up from mouth to mouth, and the place resounded with infernal yells. The warriors snatched their weapons. The Illinois took part with their guilty countryman; and the few followers of Pontiac, driven from the village, fled to spread the tidings and call the nations to revenge. Meanwhile the murdered chief lay on the spot where he had fallen, until St. Ange, mindful of former friendship, sent to claim the body, and buried it with warlike honors, near his fort of St. Louis.[1]

[1] Carver, *Travels*, 166, says that Pontiac was stabbed at a public council in the Illinois, by "a faithful Indian who was either commissioned by one of the English governors, or instigated by the love he bore the English nation." This account is without sufficient confirmation. Carver, who did not visit the Illinois, must have drawn his information from hearsay. The open manner of dealing with his victim, which he ascribes to the assassin, is wholly repugnant to Indian character and principles; while the gross charge, thrown out at random against an English governor, might of itself cast discredit on the story.

I have followed the account which I received from M. Pierre Chouteau, and from M. P. L. Cerré, another old inhabitant of the Illinois, whose father was well acquainted with Pontiac. The same account may be found, concisely stated, in Nicollet, p. 81. M. Nicollet states that he derived his information both from M. Chouteau and from the no less respectable authority of the aged Pierre Menard of Kaskaskia. The notices of Pontiac's death in the provincial journals of the day, to a certain extent, confirm this story. We gather from them, that he was killed at the Illinois, by one or more Kaskaskia Indians, during a drunken frolic, and in consequence of his hostility to the English. One letter, however, states on hearsay that he was killed near Fort Chartres; and Gouin's traditional account seems to support the statement. On this point, I have followed the distinct and circumstantial narrative of Chouteau, supported as it is by Cerré. An Ottawa tradition declares that Pontiac took a Kas

Thus basely perished this champion of a ruined race. But could his shade have revisited the scene of murder, his savage spirit would have exulted in the vengeance which overwhelmed the abettors of the crime. Whole tribes were rooted out to expiate it. Chiefs and sachems, whose veins had thrilled with his eloquence; young warriors, whose aspiring hearts had caught the inspiration of his greatness, mustered to revenge his fate; and, from the north and the east, their united bands descended on the villages of the Illinois. Tradition has but faintly preserved the memory of the event; and its only annalists, men who held the intestine feuds of the savage tribes in no more account than the quarrels of panthers or wildcats, have left but a meagre record. Yet enough remains to tell us that over the grave of Pontiac more blood was poured out in atonement, than flowed from the veins of the slaughtered heroes on the corpse of Patroclus; and the remnant of the Illinois who survived the carnage remained for ever after sunk in utter insignificance.[1]

kaskia wife, with whom he had a quarrel, and she persuaded her two brothers to kill him.

I am indebted to the kindness of my friend Mr. Lyman C. Draper for valuable assistance in my inquiries in relation to Pontiac's death.

[1] "This murder, which roused the vengeance of all the Indian tribes friendly to Pontiac, brought about the successive wars, and almost total extermination, of the Illinois nation." — Nicollet, 82.

"The Kaskaskias, Peorias, Cahokias, and Illonese are nearly all destroyed by the Sacs and Foxes, for killing in cool blood, and in time of peace, the Sac's chief, Pontiac." — *Mass. Hist. Coll. Second Series*, II. 8.

The above extract exhibits the usual confusion of Indian names, the Kaskaskias, Peorias, and Cahokias being component tribes of the Illonese or Illinois nation. Pontiac is called a chief of the Sacs. This with

Neither mound nor tablet marked the burial-place of Pontiac. For a mausoleum, a city has risen above the forest hero; and the race whom he hated with such burning rancor trample with unceasing footsteps over his forgotten grave.

similar mistakes, may easily have arisen from the fact that he was accustomed to assume authority over the warriors of any tribe with whom he chanced to be in contact.

Morse says, in his *Report*, 1822: "In the war kindled against these tribes, [Peorias, Kaskaskias, and Cahokias,] by the Sauks and Foxes, in revenge for the death of their chief, Pontiac, these 3 tribes were nearly exterminated. Few of them now remain. About one hundred of the Peorias are settled on Current River, W. of the Mississippi; of the Kaskaskias 36 only remain in Illinois." — Morse, 363.

General Gage, in his letter to Sir William Johnson, dated July 10, 176–, says: "The death of Pontiac, committed by an Indian of the Illinois, believed to have been excited by the English to that action, had drawn many of the Ottawas and other northern nations towards their country to revenge his death."

"From Miami, Pontiac went to Fort Chartres on the Illinois. In a few years, the English, who had possession of the fort, procured an Indian of the Peoria [Kaskaskia] nation to kill him. The news spread like lightning through the country. The Indians assembled in great numbers, attacked and destroyed all the Peorias, except about thirty families, which were received into the fort. These soon began to increase. They removed to the Wabash, and were about to settle, when the Indians collected in the winter, surrounded their village, and killed the whole, excepting a few children, who were saved as prisoners. Old Mr. Gouin was there at the time. He was a trader; and, when the attack commenced, was ordered by the Indians to shut his house and not suffer a Peoria to enter." — *Gouin's Account*, MS.

Pontiac left several children. A speech of his son Shegenaba, in 1775, is preserved in Force's *American Archives, 4th Series*, III. 1542. There was another son, named Otussa, whose grave is on the Maumee. In a letter to the writer, Mr. H. R. Schoolcraft says, "I knew *Atóka*, a descendant of Pontiac He was the chief of an Ottawa village on the Maumee. A few years ago, he agreed to remove, with his people, to the west of the Mississippi"

APPENDIX A.

THE IROQUOIS.—EXTENT OF THEIR CONQUESTS.—POLICY PURSUED TOWARDS THEM BY THE FRENCH AND THE ENGLISH.—MEASURES OF SIR WILLIAM JOHNSON.

1. Territory of the Iroquois. (Vol. I. p. 7.)

Extract from a Letter—Sir W. Johnson to the Board of Trade, November 13, 1763:—

My Lords:

In obedience to your Lordships' commands of the 5th of August last, I am now to lay before you the claims of the Nations mentioned in the State of the Confederacies. The Five Nations have in the last century subdued the Shawanese, Delawares, Twighties, and Western Indians, so far as Lakes Michigan and Superior, received them into an alliance, allowed them the possession of the lands they occupied, and have ever since been in peace with the greatest part of them; and such was the prowess of the Five Nations' Confederacy, that had they been properly supported by us, they would have long since put a period to the Colony of Canada, which alone they were near effecting in the year 1688. Since that time, they have admitted the Tuscaroras from the Southward, beyond Oneida, and they have ever since formed a part of that Confederacy.

As original proprietors, this Confederacy claim the country of their residence, south of Lake Ontario to the great Ridge of the Blue Mountains, with all the Western Part of the Province of New York towards Hudson River, west of the Catskill, thence to Lake Champlain, and from Regioghne, a Rock at the East side of said Lake, to Oswegatche or La Gallette, on the River St. Lawrence, (having long since ceded their claim north of said line in favor of the Canada Indians, as Hunting-ground,) thence up the River St. Lawrence, and along the South side of Lake Ontario to Niagara.

In right of conquest, they claim all the country (comprehending the Ohio) along the great Ridge of Blue Mountains at the back of Virginia, thence to the head of Kentucky River, and down the same to the Ohio above the Rifts, thence Northerly to the South end of Lake Michigan, then along the Eastern shore of said lake to Michillimackinac, thence Easterly across the North end of Lake Huron to the great Ottawa River, (including the Chippewa or Mississagey County,) and down the said River to the Island of Montreal. However, these more distant claims being possessed by many powerful nations, the Inhabitants have long begun to render themselves independent, by the assistance of the French, and the great decrease of the Six Nations; but their claim to the Ohio and thence to the Lakes, is not in the least disputed by the Shawanese, Delawares, &c., who never transacted any sales of land or other matters without their consent, and who sent Deputies to the grand Council at Onondaga on all important occasions.

---

2. French and English Policy towards the Iroquois. — Measures of Sir William Johnson. (Vol. I. pp. 88–93.)

Extract from a Letter — Sir W. Johnson to the Board of Trade, May 24, 1765: —

The Indians of the Six Nations, after the arrival of the English, having conceived a desire for many articles they introduced among them, and thereby finding them of use to their necessities, or rather superfluities, cultivated an acquaintance with them, and lived in tolerable friendship with their Province for some time, to which they were rather inclined, for they were strangers to bribery, and at enmity with the French, who had espoused the cause of their enemies, supplied them with arms, and openly acted against them. This enmity increased in proportion as the desire of the French for subduing those people, who were a bar to their first projected schemes. However, we find the Indians, as far back as the very confused manuscript records in my possession, repeatedly upbraiding this province for their negligence, their avarice, and their want of assisting them at a time when it was certainly in their power to destroy the infant colony of Canada, although supported bv many nations; and this is likewise confessed by the writings of the managers of these times. The French, after repeated losses discovering that the Six Nations were not to be subdued, but that they could without much difficulty effect their purpose (which I have good authority to show were . . . . standing) by favors and kindness, on a sudden, changed their conduct in the reign of Queen Anne, having first brought over many of their people to settle in Canada; and ever since, by the most endearing kindnesses, and by a vast profusion of favors, have secured them to their interest; and, whilst they aggravated our frauds and designs, they covered those committed by themselves under a load of gifts, which oblit erated the malpractices of . . . . among them, and enabled them to establish themselves wherever they pleased, without fomenting the Indians' jealousy. The able agents were made use of, and their unanimous indefatigable zeal for securing the Indian interest, were so much superior to any thing we had ever attempted, and to the futile transactions of the . . . . and trading Commissioners of Albany, that the latter became universally despised by the Indians, who daily withdrew from our interest, and conceived the most disadvantageous sentiments of our integrity and abilities. In this state of Indian affairs I was called to the management of these people, as my situation and opinion that it might become one day of service to the public, had induced me to cultivate a particular intimacy with these people, to accommodate myself to their manners, and even to their dress on many occasions. How I discharged this trust will best appear from the transactions of the war commenced in 1744, in which I was busily concerned. The steps I had then taken alarmed the jealousy of the French; rewards were offered for me, and I narrowly escaped assassination on more than one occasion. The French increased their munificence to the Indians, whose example not being at all followed at New York, I resigned the management of affairs on the ensuing peace, as I did not choose to continue in the name of an office which I was not empowered to discharge as its nature required. The Albany Commissioners (the men concerned in the clandestine trade to Canada, and frequently upbraided for it by the Indians) did then reassume their seats at that Board, and by their conduct so exasperated the Indians that several chiefs went to New York, 1753, when, after a severe speech to the Governor, Council, and Assembly, they broke the covenant chain of friendship, and withdrew in a rage. The consequences of which were then so much dreaded, that I was, by Governor, Council, and House of Assembly, the two latter then my enemies, earnestly entreated to effect a reconciliation with the Indians, as the only person equal to that task, as will appear by the Minutes of Council and resolves of the House. A commission being made out for me, I proceeded to Onondaga, and brought about the much wished for reconciliation, but declined having any further to say of Indian affairs, although the Indians afterwards refused to meet the Governor and Commissioners till I was sent for. At the arrival of General Braddock, I received his Commission with reluctance, at the same time assuring him that affairs had been so ill conducted, and the Indians so estranged from our interest, that I could not take upon me to hope for success. However, indefatigable labor, and (I hope I may say without vanity) personal interest, enabled me to exceed my own expectations; and my conduct since, if fully and truly known, would, I believe, testify that I have not been an unprofitable servant. 'Twas then that the Indians began to give public sign of their avaricious dispositions. The French had long taught them it; and the desire of some persons to carry a greater number of Indians into the field in 1755 than those who accompanied me, induced them to employ any agent at a high salary, who had the least interest with the Indians; and to grant the latter Cap tains' and Lieutenants' Commissions, (of which I have a number now by me,) with sterling pay, to induce them to desert me, but to little purpose, for tho' many of them received the Commissions, accompanied with large sums of money, they did not comply with the end proposed, but served with me; and this had not only served them with severe complaints against the English, as they were not afterwards all paid what had been promised, but has established a spirit of pride and avarice, which I have found it ever since impossible to subdue; whilst our extensive connections since the reduction of Canada, with so many powerful nations so long accustomed to partake largely of French bounty, has of course increased the expense, and rendered it in no small degree necessary for the preservation of our frontiers, outposts, and trade. . . .

Extract from a Letter — Cadwallader Colden to the Earl of Halifax, December 22, 1763: —

Before I proceed further, I think it proper to inform your Lordship of the different state of the Policy of the Five Nations in different periods of time. Before the peace of Utrecht, the Five Nations were at war with the French in Canada, and with all the Indian Nations who were in friendship with the French. This put the Five Nations under a necessity of depending on this province for a supply of every thing by which they could carry on the war or defend themselves, and their behavior towards us was accordingly.

After the peace of Utrecht, the French changed their measures. They took every method in their power to gain the friendship of the Five Nations, and succeeded so far with the Senecas, who are by far the most numerous, and at the greatest distance from us, that they were entirely brought over to the French interest. The French obtained the consent of the Senecas to the building of the Fort at Niagara, situated in their country.

When the French had too evidently, before the last war, got the ascendant among all the Indian Nations, we endeavored to make the Indians jealous of the French power, that they were thereby in danger of becoming slaves to the French, unless they were protected by the English. . .

APPENDIX B.

CAUSES OF THE INDIAN WAR.

Extract from a Letter — Sir W. Johnson to the Board of Trade, November 13, 1763. (Chap. VII. Vol. I. p. 171.)

. . . The French, in order to reconcile them [the Indians] to their encroachments, loaded them with favors, and employed the most intelligent Agents of good influence, as well as artful Jesuits among the several Western and other Nations, who, by degrees, prevailed on them to admit of Forts, under the Notion of Trading houses, in their Country; and knowing that these posts could never be maintained contrary to the inclinations of the Indians, they supplied them thereat with ammunition and other necessaries in abundance, as also called them to frequent congresses, and dismissed them with handsome presents, by which they enjoyed an extensive commerce, obtained the assistance of these Indians, and possessed their frontiers in safety; and as without these measures the Indians would never have suffered them in their Country, so they expect that whatever European power possesses the same, they shall in some measure reap the like advantages. Now, as these advantages ceased on the Posts being possessed by the English, and especially as it was not thought prudent to indulge them with ammunition, they immediately concluded that we had designs against their liberties, which opinion had been first instilled into them by the French, and since promoted by Traders of that nation and others who retired among them on the surrender of Canada and are still there, as well as by Belts of Wampum and other exhortations, which I am confidently assured have been sent among them from the Illinois, Louisiana, and even Canada for that purpose. The Shawanese and Delawares about the Ohio, who were never warmly attached to us since our neglects to defend them against the encroachments of the French, and refusing to erect a post at the Ohio, or assist them and the Six Nations with men or ammunition, when they requested both of us, as well as irritated at the loss of several of their people killed upon the communication of Fort Pitt, in the years 1759 and 1761, were easily induced to join with the Western Nations, and the Senecas, dissatisfied at many of our posts, jealous of our designs, and displeased at our neglect and contempt of them, soon followed their example.

These are the causes the Indians themselves assign, and which certainly occasioned the rupture between us, the consequence of which, in my opinion, will be that the Indians (who do not regard the distance) will be supplied with necessaries by the Wabache and several Rivers, which empty into the Mississippi, which it is by no means in our power to prevent, and in return the French will draw the valuable furs down that river to the advantage of their Colony and the destruction of our Trade; this will always induce the French to foment differences between us and the Indians, and the prospects many of them entertain, that they may hereafter become possessed of Canada, will incline them still more to cultivate a good understanding with the Indians, which, if ever attempted by the French, would, I am very apprehensive, be attended with a general defection of them from our interest, unless we are at great pains and expense to regain their friendship, and thereby satisfy them that we have no designs to their prejudice. . . .

The grand matter of concern to all the Six Nations (Mohawks excepted) is the occupying a chain of small Posts on the communication thro' their country to Lake Ontario, not to mention Fort Stanwix, exclusive of which there were erected in 1759 Fort Schuyler on the Mohawk River, and the Royal Blockhouse at the East end of Oneida Lake, in the Country of the Oneidas Fort Brewerton and a Post at Oswego Falls in the Onondagas Country; in order to obtain permission for erecting these posts, they were promised they should be demolished at the end of the war. General Shirley also made them a like promise for the posts he erected; and as about these posts are their fishing and hunting places, where they complain, that they are often obstructed by the troops and insulted, they request that they may not be kept up, the war with the French being now over.

In 1760, Sir Jeffrey Amherst sent a speech to the Indians in writing, which was to be communicated to the Nations about Fort Pitt, &c., by General Monkton, then commanding there, signifying his intentions to satisfy and content all Indians for the ground occupied by the posts, as also for any land about them, which might be found necessary for the use of the garrisons; but the same has not been performed, neither are the Indians in the several countries at all pleased at our occupying them, which they look upon as the first steps to enslave them and invade their properties.

And I beg leave to represent to your Lordships, that one very material advantage resulting from a continuance of good treatment and some favors to the Indians, will be the security and toleration thereby given to the Troops for cultivating lands about the garrisons, which the reduction of their Rations renders absolutely necessary. . . .

Ponteach: or the Savages of America. A Tragedy. London. Printed for the Author; and Sold by J. Millan, opposite the Admiralty, Whitehall. MDCCLXVI.

The author of this tragedy was evidently a person well acquainted with Indian affairs and Indian character. Various allusions contained in it, as well as several peculiar forms of expression, indicate that Major Rogers had a share in its composition. The first act exhibits in detail the causes which led to the Indian war. The rest of the play is of a different character. The plot is sufficiently extravagant, and has little or no historical foundation. Chekitan, the son of Ponteach, is in love with Monelia, the daughter of Hendrick, Emperor of the Mohawks. Monelia is murdered by Chekitan's brother Philip, partly out of revenge and jealousy, and partly in furtherance of a scheme of policy. Chekitan kills Philip, and then dies by his own hand; and Ponteach, whose warriors meanwhile have been defeated by the English, overwhelmed by this accumulation of public and private calamities, retires to the forests of the west to escape the memory of his griefs. The style of the drama is superior to the plot, and the writer displays at times no small insight into the workings of human nature.

The account of Indian wrongs and sufferings given in the first act accords so nearly with that conveyed in contemporary letters and documents, that two scenes from this part of the play are here given, with a few omissions, which good taste demands.

ACT I.

Scene I.—An Indian Trading House.

Enter M'Dole *and* Murphey, *Two Indian Traders, and their Servants*

M'Dole. So, Murphey, you are come to try your Fortune
Among the Savages in this wild Desart?
Murphey. Ay, any thing to get an honest Living,
Which, faith, I find it hard enough to do;
Times are so dull, and Traders are so plenty,
That Gains are small, and Profits come but slow.
M'Dole. Are you experienced in this kind of Trade?
Know you the Principles by which it prospers,
And how to make it lucrative and safe?
If not, you're like a Ship without a Rudder,
That drives at random, and must surely sink.
Murphey. I'm unacquainted with your Indian Commerce
And gladly would I learn the arts from you,
Who're old, and practis'd in them many Years.

M'Dole. That is the curst Misfortune of our Traders;
A thousand Fools attempt to live this Way,
Who might as well turn Ministers of State.
But, as you are a Friend, I will inform you
Of all the secret Arts by which we thrive,
Which if all practis'd, we might all grow rich,
Nor circumvent each other in our Gains.
What have you got to part with to the Indians?

Murphey. I've Rum and Blankets, Wampum, Powder, Bells,
And such like Trifles as they're wont to prize.

M'Dole. 'Tis very well: your Articles are good:
But now the Thing's to make a Profit from them,
Worth all your Toil and Pains of coming hither.
Our fundamental Maxim then is this,
That it's no Crime to cheat and gull an Indian.

Murphey. How! Not a Sin to cheat an Indian, say you?
Are they not Men? hav'nt they a Right to Justice
As well as we, though savage in their Manners?

M'Dole. Ah! If you boggle here, I say no more;
This is the very Quintessence of Trade,
And ev'ry Hope of Gain depends upon it;
None who neglect it ever did grow rich,
Or ever will, or can by Indian Commerce.
By this old Ogden built his stately House,
Purchased Estates, and grew a little King.
He, like an honest Man, bought all by weight,
And made the ign'rant Savages believe
That his Right Foot exactly weighed a Pound.
By this for many years he bought their Furs,
And died in Quiet like an honest Dealer.

Murphey. Well, I'll not stick at what is necessary;
But his Devise is now grown old and stale,
Nor could I manage such a barefac'd Fraud.

M'Dole. A thousand Opportunities present
To take Advantage of their Ignorance;
But the great Engine I employ is Rum,
More pow'rful made by certain strength'ning Drugs.
This I distribute with a lib'ral Hand,
Urge them to drink till they grow mad and valiant;
Which makes them think me generous and just,
And gives full Scope to practise all my Art.
I then begin my Trade with water'd Rum;
The cooling Draught well suits their scorching Throats.
Their Fur and Peltry come in quick Return:
My Scales are honest, but so well contriv'd,
That one small Slip will turn Three Pounds to One;
Which they, poor silly Souls! ignorant of Weights

And Rules of Balancing, do not perceive.
But here they come; you'll see how I proceed.
Jack, is the Rum prepar'd as I commanded?

Jack. Yes, Sir, all's ready when you please to call.

M'Dole. Bring here the Scales and Weights immediately;
You see the Trick is easy and conceal'd. [*Showing how to slip the Scale*

Murphey. By Jupiter, it's artfully contriv'd;
And was I King, I swear I'd knight th' Inventor.
Tom, mind the Part that you will have to act.

Tom. Ah, never fear; I'll do as well as Jack.
But then, you know, an honest Servant's Pain Deserves Reward.

Murphey. O! I'll take care of that.

[*Enter a Number of Indians with Packs of Fur*

1st Indian. So, what you trade with Indians here to-day?

M'Dole. Yes, if my Goods will suit, and we agree.

2d Indian. 'Tis Rum we want; we're tired, hot, and thirsty.

3d Indian. You, Mr. Englishman, have you got Rum?

M'Dole. Jack, bring a Bottle, pour them each a Gill.
You know which Cask contains the Rum. The Rum?

1st Indian. It's good strong Rum; I feel it very soon.

M'Dole. Give me a Glass. Here's Honesty in Trade;
We English always drink before we deal.

2d Indian. Good way enough; it makes one sharp and cunning.

M'Dole. Hand round another Gill. You're very welcome.

3d Indian. Some say you Englishmen are sometimes Rogues;
You make poor Indians drunk, and then you cheat.

1st Indian. No, English good. The Frenchmen give no Rum.

2d Indian. I think it's best to trade with Englishmen.

M'Dole. What is your Price for Beaver Skins per Pound?

1st Indian. How much you ask per Quart for this strong Rum?

M'Dole. Five Pounds of Beaver for One Quart of Rum.

1st Indian. Five Pounds? Too much. Which is't you call Five Pound?

M'Dole. This little Weight. I cannot give you more.

1st Indian. Well, take 'em; weigh 'em. Don't you cheat us now.

M'Dole. No; He that cheats an Indian should be hanged.

[*Weighing the Packs.*

There's Thirty Pounds precisely of the Whole;
Five times Six is Thirty. Six Quarts of Rum.
Jack, measure it to them; you know the Cask.
This Rum is sold. You draw it off the best.

[*Exeunt Indians to receive their Rum*

Murphey. By Jove, you've gained more in a single Hour
Than ever I have done in Half a Year:
Curse on my Honesty! I might have been
A *little King*, and lived without Concern,
Had I but known the proper Arts to thrive.

M'Dole. Ay, there's the Way, my honest Friend, to live.
[*Clapping his shoulder*
There's Ninety Weight of Sterling Beaver for you,
Worth all the Rum and Trinkets in my Store;
And, would my Conscience let me do the Thing,
I might enhance my Price, and lessen theirs,
And raise my Profits to a higher Pitch.

Murphey. I can't but thank you for your kind Instructions,
As from them I expect to reap Advantage.
But should the Dogs detect me in the Fraud,
They are malicious, and would have Revenge.

M'Dole. Can't you avoid them? Let their Vengeance light
On others Heads, no matter whose, if you
Are but Secure, and have the Gain in Hand;
For they're indiff'rent where they take Revenge,
Whether on him that cheated, or his Friend,
Or on a Stranger whom they never saw,
Perhaps an honest Peasant, who ne'er dreamt
Of Fraud or Villainy in all his Life;
Such let them murder, if they will, a Score,
The Guilt is theirs, while we secure the Gain,
Nor shall we feel the bleeding Victim's Pain. [*Exeunt*

SCENE II. — A DESART.

Enter ORSBOURN *and* HONNYMAN, *Two English Hunters.*

Orsbourn. Long have we toil'd, and rang'd the woods in vain;
No Game, nor Track, nor Sign of any Kind
Is to be seen; I swear I am discourag'd
And weary'd out with this long fruitless Hunt.
No Life on Earth besides is half so hard,
So full of Disappointments, as a Hunter's:
Each Morn he wakes he views the destin'd Prey,
And counts the Profits of th' ensuing Day;
Each Ev'ning at his curs'd ill Fortune pines,
And till next Day his Hope of Gain resigns.
By Jove, I'll from these Desarts hasten home,
And swear that never more I'll touch a Gun.

Honnyman. These hateful Indians kidnap all the Game.
Curse their black Heads! they fright the Deer and Bear,
And ev'ry Animal that haunts the Wood,
Or by their Witchcraft conjure them away
No Englishman can get a single Shot,

While they go loaded home with Skins and Furs.
'Twere to be wish'd not one of them survived,
Thus to infest the World, and plague Mankind.
Curs'd Heathen Infidels! mere savage Beasts!
They don't deserve to breathe in Christian Air,
And should be hunted down like other Brutes.

Orsbourn. I only wish the Laws permitted us
To hunt the savage Herd where-e'er they're found;
I'd never leave the Trade of Hunting then,
While one remain'd to tread and range the Wood.

Honnyman. Curse on the Law, I say, that makes it Death
To kill an Indian, more than to kill a Snake.
What if 'tis Peace? these Dogs deserve no Mercy;
They kill'd my Father and my eldest Brother,
Since which I hate their very Looks and Name.

Orsbourn. And I, since they betray'd and kill'd my Uncle,
Tho' these are not the same, 'twould ease my Heart
To cleave their painted Heads, and spill their Blood.
I do abhor, detest, and hate them all,
And now cou'd eat an Indian's Heart with Pleasure.

Honnyman. I'd join you, and soop his savage Brains for Sauce
I lose all Patience when I think of them,
And, if you will, we'll quickly have amends
For our long Travel and successless Hunt,
And the sweet Pleasure of Revenge to boot.

Orsbourn. What will you do? Present, and pop one down?

Honnyman. Yes, faith, the first we meet well fraught with Furs
Or if there's Two, and we can make sure Work,
By Jove, we'll ease the Rascals of their Packs,
And send them empty home to their own Country.
But then observe, that what we do is secret,
Or the Hangman will come in for Snacks.

Orsbourn. Trust me for that; I'll join with all my Heart,
Nor with a nicer Aim, or steadier Hand
Would shoot a Tyger than I would an Indian.
There is a Couple stalking now this way
With lusty Packs; Heav'n favor our Design.
Are you well charged?

Honnyman. I am. Take you the nearest,
And mind to fire exactly when I do.

Orsbourn. A charming Chance!

Honnyman. Hush, let them still come nearer.

[*They shoot, and run to rifle the Indians*

They're down, old Boy, a Brace of noble Bucks!

Orsbourn. Well tallow'd faith, and noble Hides upon 'em.

[*Taking up a Pack*

We might have hunted all the Season thro'
For Half this Game, and thought ourselves well paid.

Honnyman. By Jove, we might, and been at great Expense
For Lead and Powder; here's a single Shot.

Orsbourn. I swear, I have got as much as I can carry.

Honnyman. And faith, I'm not behind; this Pack is heavy.
But stop; we must conceal the tawny Dogs,
Or their bloodthirsty Countrymen will find them,
And then we're bit. There'll be the Devil to pay;
They'll murder us, and cheat the Hangman too.

Orsbourn. Right. We'll prevent all Mischief of this Kind.
Where shall we hide their savage Carcases?

Honnyman. There they will lie conceal'd and snug enough.
[*They cover them.*

But stay — perhaps ere long there'll be a War,
And then their Scalps will sell for ready Cash,
Two Hundred Crowns at least, and that's worth saving.

Orsbourn. Well! that is true; no sooner said than done —
[*Drawing his Knife*

I'll strip this Fellow's painted greasy Skull. [*Strips off the Scalp*

Honnyman. Now let them sleep to Night without their Caps,
[*Takes the other Scalp*

And pleasant Dreams attend their long Repose.

Orsbourn. Their Guns and Hatchets now are lawful Prize,
For they'll not need them on their present Journey.

Honnyman. The Devil hates Arms, and dreads the Smell of Powder;
He'll not allow such Instruments about him;
They're free from training now, they're in his Clutches.

Orsbourn. But, Honnyman, d'ye think this is not Murder?
I vow I'm shocked a little to see them scalp'd,
And fear their Ghosts will haunt us in the Dark.

Honnyman. It's no more Murder than to crack a Louse,
That is, if you've the Wit to keep it private.
And as to Haunting, Indians have no Ghosts,
But as they live like Beasts, like Beasts they die.
I've killed a Dozen in this selfsame Way,
And never yet was troubled with their Spirits.

Orsbourn. Then I'm content; my Scruples are removed.
And what I've done, my Conscience justifies.
But we must have these Guns and Hatchets alter'd,
Or they'll detect th' Affair, and hang us both.

Honnyman. That's quickly done — Let us with Speed return,
And think no more of being hang'd or haunted;
But turn our Fur to Gold, our Gold to Wine,
Thus gaily spend what we've so slily won,
And Bless the first Inventor of a Gun. [*Exeunt.*

The remaining scenes of this act exhibit the rudeness and insolence of British officers and soldiers in their dealings with the Indians, and the corruption of British government agents. Pontiac himself is introduced and represented as indignantly complaining of the reception which he and his warriors meet with. These scenes are overcharged with blasphemy and ribaldry, and it is needless to preserve them here. The rest of the play is written in better taste, and contains several vigorous passages.

APPENDIX C.

DETROIT AND MICHILLIMACKINAC.

1. The Siege of Detroit. (Chap. IX.–XV.)

The authorities consulted respecting the siege of Detroit consist of numerous manuscript letters of officers in the fort, including the official correspondence of the commanding officer; of several journals and fragments of journals; of extracts from contemporary newspapers; and of traditions and recollections received from Indians or aged Canadians of Detroit.

The Pontiac Manuscript.

This curious diary was preserved in a Canadian family at Detroit, and afterwards deposited with the Historical Society of Michigan. It is conjectured to have been the work of a French priest. The original is written in bad French, and several important parts are defaced or torn away. As a literary composition, it is quite worthless, being very diffuse and encumbered with dull and trivial details; yet this very minuteness affords strong internal evidence of its authenticity. Its general exactness with respect to facts is fully proved by comparing it with contemporary documents. I am indebted to General Cass for the copy in my possession, as well as for other papers respecting the war in the neighborhood of Detroit.

The manuscript appears to have been elaborately written out from a rough journal kept during the progress of the events which it describes It commences somewhat ambitiously, as follows: —

" Pondiac, great chief of all the Ottawas, Chippewas, and Pottawattamies, and of all the nations of the lakes and rivers of the North, a man proud, vindictive, warlike, and easily offended, under pretence of some insult which he thought he had received from Maj. Gladwin, Commander of the Fort, conceived that, being great chief of all the Northern nations, only himself and those of his nations were entitled to inhabit this portion of the earth, where for sixty and odd years the French had domiciliated for the purpose of trading, and where the English had governed during three years by right of the conquest of Canada. The Chief and all his nation, whose bravery consists in treachery, resolved within himself the entire destruction of the English nation, and perhaps the Canadians. In order to succeed in his undertaking, which he had not mentioned to any of his nation the Ottawas, he engaged their aid by a speech, and they, naturally inclined to evil, did not hesitate to obey him. But, as they found themselves too weak to undertake the enterprise alone, their chief endeavored to draw to his party the Chippewa nation by means of a council. This nation was governed by a chief named Ninevois. This man, who acknowledged Pondiac as his chief, whose mind was weak, and whose disposition cruel, listened to his advances, and joined him with all his band. These two nations consisted together of about four hundred men. This number did not appear to him sufficient. It became necessary to bring into their interests the Hurons. This nation, divided into two bands, was governed by two different chiefs of dissimilar character, and nevertheless both led by their spiritual father, a Jesuit. The two chiefs of this last nation were named, one Takee, of a temper similar to Pondiac's, and the other Teata, a man of cautious disposition and of perfect prudence. This last was not easily won, and having no disposition to do evil, he refused to listen to the deputies sent by Pondiac, and sent them back. They therefore addressed themselves to the first-mentioned of this nation, by whom they were listened to, and from whom they received the war-belt, with promise to join themselves to Pondiac and Ninevois, the Ottawas and Chippewas chiefs. It was settled by means of wampum belts, (a manner of making themselves understood amongst distant savages,) that they should hold a council on the 27th of April, when should be decided the day and hour of the attack, and the precautions necessary to take in order that their perfidy should not be discovered. The manner of counting used by the Indians is by the moon; and it was resolved in the way I have mentioned, that this council should be held on the 15th day of the moon, which corresponded with Wednesday the 27th of the month of April."

The writer next describes the council at the River Ecorces, and recounts at full length the story of the Delaware Indian who visited the Great Spirit. "The Chiefs," he says, "listened to Pondiac as to an oracle, and told him they were ready to do any thing he should require."

He relates with great minuteness how Pontiac, with his chosen warriors, came to the fort on the 1st of May, to dance the calumet dance, and observe the strength and disposition of the garrison, and describes the council subsequently held at the Pottawattamie village, in order to adjust the plan of attack.

"The day fixed upon having arrived, all the Ottawas, Pondiac at their head, and the bad band of the Hurons, Takee at their head, met at the Pottawattamie village, where the premeditated council was to be held. Care was taken to send all the women out of the village, that they might not discover what was decided upon. Pondiac then ordered sentinels to be placed around the village, to prevent any interruption to their council. These precautions taken, each seated himself in the circle, according to his rank, and Pondiac, as great chief of the league, thus addressed them: —

"It is important, my brothers, that we should exterminate from our land this nation, whose only object is our death. You must be all sensible, as well as myself, that we can no longer supply our wants in the way we were accustomed to do with our Fathers the French. They sell us their goods at double the price that the French made us pay, and yet their merchandise is good for nothing; for no sooner have we bought a blanket or other thing to cover us than it is necessary to procure others against the time of departing for our wintering ground. Neither will they let us have them on credit, as our brothers the French used to do. When I visit the English chief, and inform him of the death of any of our comrades, instead of lamenting, as our brothers the French used to do, they make game of us. If I ask him for any thing for our sick, he refuses, and tells us he does not want us, from which it is apparent he seeks our death. We must therefore, in return, destroy them without delay; there is nothing to prevent us: there are but few of them, and we shall easily overcome them, — why should we not attack them? Are we not men? Have I not shown you the belts I received from our Great Father the King of France? He tells us to strike, — why should we not listen to his words? What do you fear? The time has arrived. Do you fear that our brothers the French, who are now among us, will hinder us? They are not acquainted with our designs, and if they did know them, could they prevent them? You know, as well as myself, that when the English came upon our lands, to drive from them our father Bellestre, they took from the French all the guns that they have, so that they have now no guns to defend themselves with. Therefore now is the time: let us strike. Should there be any French to take their part, let us strike them as we do the English. Remember what the Giver of Life desired our brother the Delaware to do: this regards us as much as it does them. I have sent belts and speeches to our friends the Chippeways of Saginaw, and our brothers the Ottawas of Michillimacinac, and to those of the Rivière à la Tranche, (Thames River,) inviting them to join us, and they will not delay. In the mean time, let us strike. There is no longer any time to lose, and when the English shall be defeated, we will stop the way, so that no more shall return upon our lands.

"This discourse, which Pondiac delivered in a tone of much energy, had upon the whole council all the effect which he could have expected, and they all, with common accord, swore the entire destruction of the English nation.

"At the breaking up of the council, it was decided that Pondiac, with sixty chosen men, should go to the Fort to ask for a grand council from the English commander, and that they should have arms concealed under their blankets. That the remainder of the village should follow them armed with tomahawks, daggers, and knives, concealed under their blankets, and should enter the Fort, and walk about in such a manner as not to excite suspicion, whilst the others held council with the Commander. The Ottawa women were also to be furnished with short guns and other offensive weapons concealed under their blankets. They were to go into the back streets in the Fort. They were then to wait for the signal agreed upon, which was the cry of death, which the Grand Chief was to give, on which they should altogether strike upon the English, taking care not to hurt any of the French inhabiting the Fort."

The author of the diary, unlike other contemporary writers, states that the plot was disclosed to Gladwyn by a man of the Ottawa tribe, and not by an Ojibwa girl. He says, however, that on the day after the failure of the design Pontiac sent to the Pottawattamie village in order to seize an Ojibwa girl whom he suspected of having betrayed him.

"Pondiac ordered four Indians to take her and bring her before him; these men, naturally inclined to disorder, were not long in obeying their chief; they crossed the river immediately in front of their village, and passed into the Fort naked, having nothing but their breech-clouts on and their knives in their hands, and crying all the way that their plan had been defeated, which induced the French people of the Fort, who knew nothing of the designs of the Indians, to suspect that some bad design was going forward, either against themselves or the English. They arrived at the Pottawattamie village, and in fact found the woman, who was far from thinking of them; nevertheless they seized her, and obliged her to march before them, uttering cries of joy in the manner they do when they hold a victim in their clutches on whom they are going to exercise their cruelty: they made her enter the Fort, and took her before the Commandant, as if to confront her with him, and asked him if it was not from her he had learnt their design; but they were no better satisfied than if they had kept themselves quiet. They obtained from that Officer bread and beer for themselves, and for her. They then led her to their chief in the village."

The diary leaves us in the dark as to the treatment which the girl received; but there is a tradition among the Canadians that Pontiac, with his own hand, gave her a severe beating with a species of racket, such as the Indians use in their ball-play. An old Indian told Henry Conner, formerly United States interpreter at Detroit, that she survived her punishment, and lived for many years; but at length, contracting intemperate habits, she fell, when intoxicated, into a kettle of boiling maple sap, and was so severely scalded that she died in consequence.

The outbreak of hostilities, the attack on the fort, and the detention of Campbell and McDougal are related at great length, and with all the minuteness of an eye-witness. The substance of the narrative is incorporated in the body of the work. The diary is very long, detailing the incidents of every passing day, from the 7th of May to the 31st of July Here it breaks off abruptly in the middle of a sentence, the remaining part having been lost or torn away. The following extracts, taken at random will serve to indicate the general style and character of the journal: —

"Saturday, June 4th. About 4 P. M. cries of death were heard from the Indians. The cause was not known, but it was supposed they had obtained some prize on the Lake.

"Sunday, June 5th. The Indians fired a few shots upon the Fort to-day. About 2 P. M. cries of death were again heard on the opposite side of the River. A number of Indians were descried, part on foot and part mounted. Others were taking up two trading boats, which they had taken on the lake. The vessel fired several shots at them, hoping they would abandon their prey, but they reached Pondiac's camp uninjured. . . .

"About 7 P. M. news came that a number of Indians had gone down as far as Turkey Island, opposite the small vessel which was anchored there, but that, on seeing them, she had dropped down into the open Lake, to wait for a fair wind to come up the river.

"Monday, June 20th. The Indians fired some shots upon the fort. About 4 P. M. news was brought that Presquisle and Beef River Forts, which had been established by the French, and were now occupied by the English, had been destroyed by the Indians. . . .

"Wednesday, June 22d. The Indians, whose whole attention was directed to the vessel, did not trouble the Fort. In the course of the day, the news of the taking of Presquisle was confirmed, as a great number of the Indians were seen coming along the shore with prisoners. The Commandant was among the number, and with him one woman: both were presented to the Hurons. In the afternoon, the Commandant received news of the lading of the vessel, and the number of men on board. The Indians again visited the French for provisions.

"Thursday, June 23d. Very early in the morning, a great number of Indians were seen passing behind the Fort: they joined those below, and all repaired to Turkey Island. The river at this place is very narrow. The Indians commenced making intrenchments of trees, &c., on the beach, where the vessel was to pass, whose arrival they awaited. About ten of the preceding night, the wind coming aft, the vessel weighed anchor, and came up the river. When opposite the Island the wind fell, and they were obliged to throw the anchor; as they knew they could not reach the Fort without being attacked by the Indians, they kept a strict watch. In order to deceive the Indians, the captain had hid in the hold sixty of his men, suspecting that the Indians, seeing only about a dozen men on deck, would try to take the vessel, which occurred as he expected. About 9 at night they got in their canoes, and made for the vessel, intending to board her. They were seen far off by one of the sentinels. The captain immediately ordered up all his men in the greatest silence, and placed them along the sides of the vessel, with their guns in their hands, loaded, with orders to wait the signal for firing, which was the rap of a hammer on the mast. The Indians were allowed to approach within less than gunshot, when the signal was given, and a discharge of cannon and small arms made upon them. They retreated to their intrenchment with the loss of fourteen killed and fourteen wounded; from which they fired during the night, and wounded two men. In the morning the vessel dropped down to the Lake for a more favorable wind.

"Friday, June 24th. The Indians were occupied with the vessel. Two Indians back of the Fort were pursued by twenty men, and escaped.

"Saturday, June 25th. Nothing occurred this day.

"Sunday, June 26th. Nothing of consequence.

"Monday, June 27th. Mr. Gamelin, who was in the practice of visiting Messrs. Campbell and McDougall, brought a letter to the Commandant from Mr. Campbell, dictated by Pondiac, in which he requested the Commandant to surrender the Fort, as in a few days he expected Kee-no-cha-meck, great chief of the Chippewas, with eight hundred men of his nation; that he (Pondiac) would not then be able to command them, and as soon as they arrived, they would scalp all the English in the Fort. The Commandant only answered that he cared as little for him as he did for them. . . .

"This evening, the Commandant was informed that the Ottawas and Chippewas had undertaken another raft, which might be more worthy of attention than the former ones: it was reported to be of pine boards, and intended to be long enough to go across the river. By setting fire to every part of it, it could not help, by its length, coming in contact with the vessel, which by this means they expected would certainly take fire. Some firing took place between the vessel and Indians, but without effect.

"Tuesday, July 19th. The Indians attempted to fire on the Fort, but being discovered, they were soon made to retreat by a few shot.

"Wednesday, July 20th. Confirmation came to the Fort of the report of the 18th, and that the Indians had been four days at work at their raft, and that it would take eight more to finish it. The Commandant ordered that two boats should be lined or clapboarded with oak plank, two inches thick, and the same defence to be raised above the gunnels of the boats of two feet high. A swivel was put on each of them, and placed in such a way that they could be pointed in three different directions.

"Thursday, July 21st. The Indians were too busily occupied to pay any attention to the Fort; so earnest were they in the work of the raft that they hardly allowed themselves time to eat. The Commandant farther availed himself of the time allowed him before the premeditated attack to put every thing in proper order to repulse it. He ordered that two strong graplins should be provided for each of the barges, a strong iron chain of fifteen feet was to be attached to the boat, and conducting a strong cable under water, fastened to the graplins, and the boats were intended to be so disposed as to cover the vessel, by mooring them, by the help of the above preparations, above her. The inhabitants of the S. W. ridge, or hill, again got a false alarm. It was said the Indians intended attacking them during the night: they kept on their guard till morning.

"Friday, July 22d. An Abenakee Indian arrived this day, saying that he came direct from Montreal, and gave out that a large fleet of French was on its way to Canada, full of troops, to dispossess the English of the country. However fallacious such a story might appear, it had the effect of rousing Pondiac from his inaction, and the Indians set about their raft with more energy than ever. They had left off working at it since yesterday." . . .

It is needless to continue these extracts farther. Those already given will convey a sufficient idea of the character of the diary.

REMINISCENCES OF AGED CANADIANS.

About the year 1824, General Cass, with the design of writing a narrative of the siege of Detroit by Pontiac, caused inquiry to be made among the aged Canadian inhabitants, many of whom could distinctly remember the events of 1763. The accounts received from them were committed to paper, and were placed by General Cass, with great liberality, in the writer's hands. They afford an interesting mass of evidence, as worthy of confidence as evidence of the kind can be. With but one exception, — the account of Maxwell, — they do not clash with the testimony of contemporary documents. Much caution has, however, been observed in their use; and no essential statement has been made on their unsupported authority. The most prominent of these accounts are those of Peltier, St. Aubin, Gouin, Meloche, Parent, and Maxwell

Peltier's Account.

M. Peltier was seventeen years old at the time of Pontiac's war. His narrative, though one of the longest of the collection, is imperfect, since, during a great part of the siege, he was absent from Detroit in search of runaway horses, belonging to his father. His recollection of the earlier part of the affair is, however, clear and minute. He relates, with apparent credulity, the story of the hand of the murdered Fisher protruding from the earth, as if in supplication for the neglected rites of burial. He remembers that, soon after the failure of Pontiac's attempt to surprise the garrison, he punished, by a severe flogging, a woman named Catharine, accused of having betrayed the plot. He was at Detroit during the several attacks on the armed vessels, and the attempts to set them on fire by means of blazing rafts.

St. Aubin's Account.

St. Aubin was fifteen years old at the time of the siege. It was his mother who crossed over to Pontiac's village shortly before the attempt on the garrison, and discovered the Indians in the act of sawing off the muzzles of their guns, as related in the narrative. He remembers Pontiac at his headquarters, at the house of Meloche; where his commissaries served out provision to the Indians. He himself was among those who conveyed cattle across the river to the English, at a time when they were threatened with starvation. One of his most vivid recollections is that of seeing the head of Captain Dalzell stuck on the picket of a garden fence, on the day after the battle of Bloody Bridge. His narrative is one of the most copious and authentic of the series

Gouin's Account.

M. Gouin was but eleven years old at the time of the war. His father was a prominent trader, and had great influence over the Indians. On several occasions, he acted as mediator between them and the English; and when Major Campbell was bent on visiting the camp of Pontiac, the elder Gouin strenuously endeavored to prevent the attempt. Pontiac often came to him for advice. His son bears emphatic testimony to the extraordinary control which the chief exercised over his followers, and to the address which he displayed in the management of his commissary department. This account contains many particulars not elsewhere mentioned, though bearing all the appearance of truth. It appears to have been composed partly from the recollections of the younger Gouin, and partly from information derived from his father.

Meloche's Account.

Mad. Meloche lived, when a child, on the borders of the Detroit, between the river and the camp of Pontiac. On one occasion, when the English were cannonading the camp from their armed schooner in the river, a shot struck her father's house, throwing down a part of the walls. After the death of Major Campbell, she picked up a pocket-book belonging to him, which the Indians had left on the ground. It was full of papers, and she carried it to the English in the fort.

Parent's Account.

M. Parent was twenty-two years old when the war broke out. His recollections of the siege are, however, less exact than those of some of the former witnesses, though his narrative preserves several interesting incidents.

Maxwell's Account.

Maxwell was an English provincial, and pretended to have been a soldier under Gladwyn. His story belies the statement. It has all the air of a narrative made up from hearsay, and largely embellished from imagination. It has been made use of only in a few instances, where it is amply supported by less questionable evidence. This account seems to have been committed to paper by Maxwell himself, as the style is very rude and illiterate.

The remaining manuscripts consulted with reference to the siege of Detroit have been obtained from the State Paper Office of London, and from a few private autograph collections. Some additional information has been derived from the columns of the New York Mercury, and the Pennsylvania Gazette for 1763, where various letters written by officers at Detroit are published.

---

2. The Massacre of Michillimackinac. (Chap. XVII.)

The following letter may be regarded with interest, as having been written by the commander of the unfortunate garrison a few days after the massacre. A copy of the original was procured from the State Paper Office of London.

Michillimackinac, 12 June, 1763.

Sir:

Notwithstanding that I wrote you in my last, that all the savages were arrived, and that every thing seemed in perfect tranquillity, yet, on the 2d instant, the Chippewas, who live in a plain near this fort, assembled to play ball, as they had done almost every day since their arrival. They played from morning till noon; then throwing their ball close to the gate, and observing Lieut. Lesley and me a few paces out of it, they came behind us, seized and carried us into the woods.

In the mean time the rest rushed into the Fort, where they found their squaws, whom they had previously planted there, with their hatchets hid under their blankets, which they took, and in an instant killed Lieut. Jamet and fifteen rank and file, and a trader named Tracy. They wounded two, and took the rest of the garrison prisoners, five [seven, Henry] of whom they have since killed.

They made prisoners all the English Traders, and robbed them of every thing they had; but they offered no violence to the persons or property of any of the Frenchmen.

When that massacre was over, Messrs. Langlade and Farli, the Interpreter, came down to the place where Lieut. Lesley and me were prisoners; and on their giving themselves as security to return us when demanded, they obtained leave for us to go to the Fort, under a guard of savages, which gave time, by the assistance of the gentlemen above-mentioned, to send for the Outaways, who came down on the first notice, and were very much displeased at what the Chippeways had done.

Since the arrival of the Outaways they have done every thing in their power to serve us, and with what prisoners the Chippeways had given them, and what they have bought, I have now with me Lieut. Lesley and eleven privates; and the other four of the Garrison, who are yet living, remain in the hands of the Chippeways.

The Chippeways, who are superior in number to the Ottaways, have declared in Council to them that if they do not remove us out of the Fort, they will cut off all communication to this Post, by which means all the Convoys of Merchants from Montreal, La Baye, St. Joseph, and the upper posts, would perish. But if the news of your posts being attacked (which they say was the reason why they took up the hatchet) be false, and you can send up a strong reinforcement, with provisions, &c., accompanied by some of your savages, I believe the post might be re-established again.

Since this affair happened, two canoes arrived from Montreal, which put in my power to make a present to the Ottaway nation, who very well deserve any thing that can be done for them.

I have been very much obliged to Messrs. Langlade and Farli, the Interpreter, as likewise to the Jesuit, for the many good offices they have done us on this occasion. The Priest seems inclinable to go down to your post for a day or two, which I am very glad of, as he is a very good man, and had a great deal to say with the savages, hereabout, who will believe every thing he tells them on his return, which I hope will be soon. The Outaways say they will take Lieut. Lesley, me, and the Eleven men which I mentioned before were in their hands, up to their village, and there keep us, till they hear what is doing at your Post. They have sent this canot for that purpose.

I refer you to the Priest for the particulars of this melancholy affair, and am, Dear Sir,

Yours very sincerely,

[Signed] GEO. ETHERINGTON

TO MAJOR GLADWYN.

P. S. The Indians that are to carry the Priest to Detroit will not undertake to land him at the Fort, but at some of the Indian villages near it; so you must not take it amiss that he does not pay you the first visit. And once more I beg that nothing may stop your sending of him back, the next day after his arrival, if possible, as we shall be at a great loss for the want of him, and I make no doubt that you will do all in your power to make peace, as you see the situation we are in, and send up provision as soon as possible, and Ammunition, as what we had was pillaged by the savages.

Adieu.

GEO. ETHERINGTON.

APPENDIX D.

THE WAR ON THE BORDERS.

The Battle of Bushy Run. (Chap. XX.)

The despatches written by Colonel Bouquet, immediately after the two battles near Bushy Run, contain so full and clear an account of those engagements, that the collateral authorities consulted have served rather to decorate and enliven the narrative than to add to it any important facts. The first of these letters was written by Bouquet under the apprehension that he should not survive the expected conflict of the next day. Both were forwarded to the commander-in-chief by the same express, within a few days after the victory. The letters as here given were copied from the originals in the London offices.

Camp at Edge Hill, 26 Miles from Fort Pitt, 5th August, 1763.

Sir:

The Second Instant the Troops and Convoy Arrived at Ligonier, whence I could obtain no Intelligence of the Enemy; The Expresses Sent since the beginning of July, having been Either killed, or Obliged to Return, all the Passes being Occupied by the Enemy: In this uncertainty I Determined to Leave all the Waggons with the Powder, and a Quantity of Stores and Provisions, at Ligonier; And on the 4th pro ceeded with the Troops, and about 350 Horses Loaded with Flour.

I Intended to have Halted to Day at Bushy Run, (a Mile beyond this Camp,) and after having Refreshed the Men and Horses, to have Marched in the Night over Turtle Creek, a very Dangerous Defile of Several Miles, Commanded by High and Craggy Hills: But at one o'clock this Afternoon, after a march of 17 Miles, the Savages suddenly Attacked our Advanced Guard, which was immediately Supported by the two Light Infantry Companies of the 42d Regiment, Who Drove the Enemy from their Ambuscade, and pursued them a good Way. The Savages Returned to the Attack, and the Fire being Obstinate on our Front, and Extending along our Flanks, We made a General Charge, with the whole Line, to Dislodge the Savages from the Heights, in which attempt We succeeded without Obtaining by it any Decisive Advantage; for as soon as they were driven from One Post, they Appeared on Another, 'till, by continual Reinforcements, they were at last able to Surround Us, and attacked the Convoy left in our Rear; This Obliged us to March Back to protect it; The Action then became General, and though we were attacked on Every Side, and the Savages Exerted themselves with Uncommon Resolution, they were constantly Repulsed with Loss. — We also Suffered Considerably: Capt. Lieut. Graham, and Lieut. James McIntosh of the 42d, are Killed, and Capt. Graham Wounded.

Of the Royal Amer'n Regt., Lieut. Dow, who acted as A. D. Q. M. G. is shot through the Body.

Of the 77th, Lieut. Donald Campbell, and Mr. Peebles, a Volunteer, are Wounded.

Our Loss in Men, Including Rangers, and Drivers, Exceeds Sixty, Killed or Wounded.

The Action has Lasted from One O'Clock 'till Night, And We Expect to Begin again at Day Break. Whatever Our Fate may be, I thought it necessary to Give Your Excellency this Early Information, that You may, at all Events, take such Measures as You will think proper with the Provinces, for their own Safety, and the Effectual Relief of Fort Pitt, as in Case of Another Engagement I Fear Insurmountable Difficulties in protecting and Transporting our Provisions, being already so much Weakened by the Losses of this Day, in Men and Horses; besides the Additional Necessity of Carrying the Wounded, Whose Situation is truly Deplorable.

I Cannot Sufficiently Acknowledge the Constant Assistance I have Received from Major Campbell, during this long Action; Nor Express my Admiration of the Cool and Steady Behavior of the Troops, Who Did not Fire a Shot, without Orders, and Drove the Enemy from their Posts with Fixed Bayonets. — The Conduct of the Officers is much above my Praises.

I Have the
Honor to be, with great Respect,
Sir,
&ca.
HENRY BOUQUET

His Excellency SIR JEFFREY AMHERST.

Camp at Bushy Run, 6th August, 1763.

Sir

I Had the Honor to Inform Your Excellency in my letter of Yesterday of our first Engagement with the Savages.

We Took Post last Night on the Hill, where Our Convoy Halted, when the Front was Attacked, (a commodious piece of Ground, and Just Spacious Enough for our Purpose.) There We Encircled the Whole, and Covered our Wounded with the Flour Bags.

In the Morning the Savages Surrounded our Camp, at the Distance of about 500 Yards, and by Shouting and Yelping, quite Round that Extensive Circumference, thought to have Terrified Us, with their Numbers

They Attacked Us Early, and, under Favour of an Incessant Fire, made Several Bold Efforts to Penetrate our Camp; And tho' they Failed in the Attempt, our Situation was not the Less Perplexing, having Experienced that Brisk Attacks had Little Effect upon an Enemy, who always gave Way when Pressed, & Appeared again Immediately; Our Troops were besides Extremely Fatigued with the Long March, and as long Action of the Preceding Day, and Distressed to the Last Degree, by a Total Want of Water, much more Intolerable than the Enemy's Fire.

Tied to our Convoy We could not Lose Sight of it, without Exposing it, and our Wounded, to Fall a prey to the Savages, who Pressed upon Us on Every Side; and to Move it was Impracticable, having lost many horses, and most of the Drivers, Stupified by Fear, hid themselves in the Bushes, or were Incapable of Hearing or Obeying Orders.

The Savages growing Every Moment more Audacious, it was thought proper still to increase their Confidence; by that means, if possible, to Entice them to Come Close upon Us, or to Stand their Ground when Attacked. With this View two Companies of Light Infantry were Ordered within the Circle, and the Troops on their Right and Left opened their Files, and Filled up the Space that it might seem they were intended to Cover the Retreat; The Third Light Infantry Company, and the Grenadiers of the 42d, were Ordered to Support the two First Companys. This Manœuvre Succeeded to Our Wish, for the Few Troops who Took possession of the Ground lately Occupied by the two Light Infantry Companys being Brought in Nearer to the Centre of the Circle, the Barbarians, mistaking these Motions for a Retreat, Hurried Headlong on, and Advancing upon Us, with the most Daring Intrepidity, Galled us Excessively with their Heavy Fire; But at the very moment that, Certain of Success, they thought themselves Masters of the Camp, Major Campbell, at the Head of the two First Companys, Sallied out from a part of the Hill they Could not Observe, and Fell upon their Right Flank; They Resolutely Returned the Fire, but could not Stand the Irresistible Shock of our Men, Who, Rushing in among them, Killed many of them, and Put the Rest to Flight. The Orders sent to the Other Two Companys were Delivered so timely by Captain Basset, and Executed with such Celerity and Spirit, that the Routed Savages, who happened to Run that Moment before their Front, Received their Full Fire, when Uncovered by the Trees: The Four Companys Did not give them time to Load a Second time, nor Even to Look behind them, but Pursued them 'till they were Totally Dispersed. The Left of the Savages, which had not been Attacked, were kept in Awe by the Remains of our Troops, Posted on the Brow of the Hill, for that Purpose; Nor Durst they Attempt to Support, or Assist their Right, but being Witness to their Defeat, followed their Example and Fled. Our Brave Men Disdained so much to Touch the Dead Body of a Vanquished Enemy, that Scarce a Scalp was taken, Except by the Rangers, and Pack Horse Drivers.

The Woods being now Cleared and the Pursuit over, the Four Companys took possession of a Hill in our Front; and as soon as Litters could be made for the Wounded, and the Flour and Every thing Destroyed, which, for want of Horses, could not be Carried, We Marched without Molestation to this Camp. After the Severe Correction We had given the Savages a few hours before, it was Natural to Suppose We should Enjoy some Rest; but We had hardly Fixed our Camp, when they fired upon Us again: This was very Provoking! However, the Light Infantry Dispersed them, before they could Receive Orders for that purpose. — I Hope We shall be no more Disturbed, for, if We have another Action, We shall hardly be able to Carry our Wounded.

The Behavior of the Troops, on this Occasion, Speaks for itself so Strongly, that for me to Attempt their Eulogium, would but Detract from their merit.

I Have the Honor to be, most Respectfully,

Sir,

&ca.

HENRY BOUQUET.

P. S. I Have the Honor to Enclose the Return of the Killed, Wounded, and Missing in the two Engagements.

H B.

His Excellency SIR JEFFREY AMHERST.

APPENDIX E.

THE PAXTON RIOTS.

1. Evidence against the Indians of Conestoga. (Chap. XXIV.)

Abraham Newcomer, a Mennonist, by trade a Gunsmith, upon his affirmation, declared that several times, within these few years, Bill Soc and Indian John, two of the Conestogue Indians, threatened to scalp him for refusing to mend their tomahawks, and swore they would as soon scalp him as they would a dog. A few days before Bill Soc was killed, he brought a tomahawk to be steeled. Bill said, "If you will not, I'll have it mended to your sorrow," from which expression I apprehended danger.

Mrs. Thompson, of the borough of Lancaster, personally appeared before the Chief Burgess, and upon her solemn oath, on the Holy Evangelists, said that in the summer of 1761, Bill Soc came to her apartment, and threatened her life, saying, "I kill you, all Lancaster can't catch me," which filled me with terror; and this lady further said, Bill Soc added, "Lancaster is mine, and I will have it yet."

Colonel John Hambright, gentleman, an eminent Brewer of the Borough of Lancaster, personally appeared before Robert Thompson, Esq., a justice for the county of Lancaster, and made oath on the Holy Evangelists, that, in August, 1757, he, an officer, was sent for provision from Fort Augusta to Fort Hunter, that on his way he rested at M'Kee's old place, a Sentinel was stationed behind a tree, to prevent surprise. The Sentry gave notice Indians were near; the deponent crawled up the bank and discovered two Indians; one was Bill Soc, lately killed at Lancaster. He called Bill Soc to come to him, but the Indians ran off. When the deponent came to Fort Hunter, he learnt that an old man had been killed the day before; Bill Soc and his companion were believed to be the perpetrators of the murder. He, the deponent, had frequently seen Bill Soc and some of the Conestogue Indians at Fort Augusta, trading with the Indians, but, after the murder of the old man, Bill Soc did not appear at that Garrison.

John Hambright.

Sworn and Subscribed the 28th of Feb., 1764, before me,

Robert Thompson, Justice

Charles Cunningham, of the county of Lancaster, personally appeared before me Thomas Foster, Esq., one of the Magistrates for said county, and being qualified according to law, doth depose and say, that he, the deponent, heard Joshua James, an Indian, say, that he never killed a white man in his life, but six dutchmen that he killed in the Minisinks.

CHARLES CUNNINGHAM.

Sworn to, and Subscribed before THOMAS FOSTER, Justice.

Alexander Stephen, of the county of Lancaster, personally appeared before Thomas Foster, Esq., one of the Magistrates, and being duly qualified according to law, doth say, that Connayak Sally, an Indian woman, told him that the Conestogue Indians had killed Jegrea, an Indian, because he would not join the Conestogue Indians in destroying the English. James Cotter told the deponent that he was one of the three that killed old William Hamilton, on Sherman's Creek, and also another man, with seven of his family. James Cotter demanded of the deponent a canoe, which the murderers had left, as Cotter told him when the murder was committed.

ALEXANDER STEPHEN

THOMAS FOSTER, Justice.

Note. — Jegrea was a Warrior Chief, friendly to the Whites, and he threatened the Conestogue Indians with his vengeance, if they harmed the English. Cotter was one of the Indians, killed in Lancaster county, in 1763.

Anne Mary Le Roy, of Lancaster, appeared before the Chief Burgess, and being sworn on the Holy Evangelists of Almighty God, did depose and say, that in the year 1755, when her Father, John Jacob Le Roy, and many others, were murdered by the Indians, at Mahoney, she, her brother, and some others were made prisoners, and taken to Kittanning; that stranger Indians visited them; the French told them they were Conestogue Indians, and that Isaac was the only Indian true to their interest and that the Conestogue Indians, with the exception of Isaac, were ready to lift the hatchet when ordered by the French. She asked Bill Soc's mother whether she had ever been at Kittanning? she said "no, but her son, Bill Soc, had been there often; that he was good for nothing."

MARY LE ROY

---

2. PROCEEDINGS OF THE RIOTERS. (Chap. XXIV., XXV.)

Deposition of Felix Donolly, keeper of Lancaster Jail.

This deposition is imperfect, a part of the manuscript having been defaced or torn away. The original, in the handwriting of Edward Shippen, the chief magistrate of Lancaster, was a few years since in the possession of Redmond Conyngham, Esq.

The breaking open the door alarmed me; armed men broke in; they demanded the strange Indian to be given up; they ran by me; the Indians guessed their intention; they seized billets of wood from the pile; but the three most active were shot; others came to their assistance; I was stupefied; before I could shake off my surprise, the Indians were killed and their murderers away.

Q. You say, "Indians armed themselves with wood;" did those Indians attack the rioters?

A. They did. If they had not been shot, they would have killed the men who entered, for they were the strongest.

Q. Could the murder have been prevented by you?

A. No: I nor no person here could have prevented it

Q. What number were the rioters?

A. I should say fifty.

Q. Did you know any of them?

A. No; they were strangers.

Q. Do you now know who was in command?

A. I have been told, Lazarus Stewart of Donegal.

Q. If the Indians had not attempted resistance, would the men have fled? (fired?)

A. I couldn't tell; I do not know.

Q. Do you think or believe that the rioters came with the intent to murder?

A. I heard them say, when they broke in, they wanted a strange Indian.

Q. Was their object to murder him?

A. From what I have heard since, I think they meant to carry him off; that is my belief.

Q. What was their purpose?

A. I do not know.

Q. Were the Indians killed all friends of this province?

A. I have been told they were not. I cannot tell of myself; I do not know.

Donolly was suspected of a secret inclination in favor of the rioters. In private conversation he endeavored to place their conduct in as favorable a light as possible, and indeed such an intention is apparent in the above deposition.

Letter from Edward Shippen to Governor Hamilton.

Lancaster, ——, 1764.

Honoured Sir:

I furnish you with a full detail of all the particulars that could be gathered of the unhappy transactions of the fourteenth and twenty-seventh of December last, as painful for you to read as me to write. The Depositions can only state the fact that the Indians were killed. Be assured the Borough Authorities, when they placed the Indians in the Workhouse, thought it a place of security. I am sorry the Indians were not removed to Philadelphia, as recommended by us. It is too late to remedy. It is much to be regretted that there are evil-minded persons among us, who are trying to corrupt the minds of the people by idle tales and horrible butcheries — are injuring the character of many of our most respectable people. That printers should have lent their aid astonishes me when they are employed by the Assembly to print their laws. I can see no good in meeting their falsehoods by counter statements.

The Rev. Mr. Elder and Mr. Harris are determined to rely upon the reputation they have so well established.

For myself, I can only say that, possessing your confidence, and that of the Proprietaries, with a quiet conscience, I regard not the malignant pens of secret assailants — men who had not the courage to affix their names. Is it not strange that a too ready belief was at first given to the slanderous epistles? Resting on the favor I have enjoyed of the Government; on the confidence reposed in me, by you and the Proprietaries; by the esteem of my fellow-men in Lancaster, I silently remain passive.

Yours affectionately,

EDWARD SHIPPEN

Extract from a letter of the Rev. Mr. Elder to Governor Penn, December 27, 1763.

The storm which had been so long gathering, has at length exploded. Had Government removed the Indians from Conestoga, which had frequently been urged, without success, this painful catastrophe might have been avoided. What could I do with men heated to madness? All that I could do, was done; I expostulated; but *life* and *reason* were set at defiance. And yet the men, in private life, are virtuous and respectable; not cruel, but mild and merciful.

The time will arrive when each palliating circumstance will be calmly weighed. This deed, magnified into the blackest of crimes, shall be considered one of those youthful ebullitions of wrath caused by momentary excitement, to which human infirmity is subjected.

Extract from "The Paxtoniade," a poem in imitation of Hudibras, published at Philadelphia, 1764, by a partisan of the Quaker faction:—

O'Hara mounted on his Steed,
(Descendant of that self-same Ass,
That bore his Grandsire Hudibras,)
And from that same exalted Station,
Pronounced an hortory Oration:
For he was cunning as a Fox,
Had read o'er Calvin and Dan Nox;
A man of most profound Discerning,
Well versed in P————n Learning.
So after hemming thrice to clear
His Throat, and banish thoughts of fear,
And of the mob obtaining Silence,
He thus went on— "Dear Sirs, a while since

Ye know as how the Indian Rabble,
With practices unwarrantable,
Did come upon our quiet Borders,
And there commit most desperate murders
Did tomahawk, butcher, wound and cripple
With cruel Rage, the Lord's own People;
Did war most implacable wage
With God's own chosen heritage;
Did from our Brethren take their lives,
And kill our Children, kine and wives.
Now, Sirs, I ween it is but right,
That we upon these Canaanites,
Without delay, should Vengeance take,
Both for our own, and the K—k's sake;
Should totally destroy the heathen,
And never till we've killed 'em leave 'em;—
Destroy them quite frae out the Land;
And for it we have God's Command.
We should do him a muckle Pleasure,
As ye in your Books may read at leisure.'
He paused, as Orators are used,
And from his pocket quick produced
A friendly Vase well stor'd and fill'd
With good old whiskey twice distill'd,
And having refresh'd his inward man,
Went on with his harangue again.
"Is't not, my Brethren, a pretty Story
That we who are the Land's chief Glory,
Who are i' the number of God's elected,
Should slighted thus be and neglected?
That we, who're the only Gospel Church,
Should thus be left here in the lurch;
Whilst our most antichristian foes,
Whose trade is war and hardy blows,
(At least while some of the same Colour,
With those who've caused us all this Dolor,)
In matchcoats warm and blankets drest,
Are by the Q——rs much caress'd,
And live in peace by good warm fires,
And have the extent of their desires?
Shall we put by such treatment base?
By Nox, we wont!"—And broke his Vase.
"Seeing then we've such good cause to hate em,
What I intend's to extirpate 'em;
To suffer them no more to thrive,
And leave nor Root nor Branch alive;
But would we madly leave our wives

And Children, and expose our lives
In search of these wh' infest our borders.
And perpetrate such cruel murders;
It is most likely, by King Harry,
That we should in the end miscarry.
I deem therefore the wisest course is,
That those who've beasts should mount their horses,
And those who've none should march on foot,
With as much quickness as will suit,
To where those heathen, nothing fearful,
That we will on their front and rear fall,
Enjoy Sweet Otium in their Cotts,
And dwell securely in their Hutts.
And as they've nothing to defend them,
We'll quickly to their own place send them!"

The following letter from Rev. John Elder to Colonel Shippen will serve to exhibit the state of feeling among the frontier inhabitants.

Paxton, Feb. 1, 1764.

Dear Sir:

Since I sealed the Governor's Letter, which you'll please to deliver to him, I suspect, from the frequent meetings I hear the people have had in divers parts of the Frontier Counties, that an Expedition is immediately designed against the Indians at Philadelphia. It's well known that I have always used my utmost endeavors to discourage these proceedings; but to little purpose: the minds of the Inhabitants are so exasperated against a particular set of men, deeply concerned in the government, for the singular regards they have always shown to savages, and the heavy burden by their means laid on the province in maintaining an expensive Trade and holding Treaties from time to time with the savages, without any prospect of advantage either to his Majesty or to the province, how beneficial soever it may have been to individuals, that it's in vain, nay even unsafe for any one to oppose their measures; for were Col. Shippen here, tho' a gentleman highly esteemed by the Frontier inhabitants, he would soon find it useless, if not dangerous, to act in opposition to an enraged multitude. At first there were but, as I think, few concerned in these riots, & nothing intended by some but to ease the province of part of its burden, and by others, who had suffered greatly in the late war the gratifying a spirit of Revenge, yet the manner of the Quakers resenting these things has been, I think, very injurious and impolitick. The Presbyterians, who are the most numerous, I imagine, of any denomination in the province, are enraged at their being charged in bulk with these facts, under the name of Scotch-Irish, and other ill-natured titles, and that the killing the Conestogoe Indians is compared to the Irish Massacres, and reckoned the most barbarous of either, so that things are grown to that pitch now that the country seems determined that no Indian Treaties shall be held, or savages maintained at the expense of the province, unless his Majesty's pleasure on these heads is well known, for I understood to my great satisfaction that amid our great confusions, there are none, even of the most warm and furious tempers, but what are warmly attached to his Majesty, and would cheerfully risk their lives to promote his service. What the numbers are of those going on the above-mentioned Expedition, I can't possibly learn, as I'm informed they are collecting in all parts of the province; however, this much may be depended on, that they have the good wishes of the country in general, and that there are few but what are now either one way or other embarked in the affair, tho' some particular persons, I'm informed, are grossly misrepresented in Philadelphia; even my neighbor, Mr. Harris, it's said, is looked on there as the chief promoter of these riots, yet it's entirely false; he had aided as much in opposition to these measures as he could with any safety in his situation. Reports, however groundless, are spread by designing men on purpose to inflame matters, and enrage the parties against each other, and various methods used to accomplish their pernicious ends. As I am deeply concerned for the welfare of my country, I would do every thing in my power to promote its interests. I thought proper to give you these few hints; you'll please to make what use you think proper of them. I would heartily wish that some effectual measures might be taken to heal these growing evils, and this I judge may be yet done, and Col. Armstrong, who is now in town, may be usefully employed for this purpose.

Sir,

I am, etc.,

JOHN ELDER

Extracts from a Quaker letter on the Paxton riots.

This letter is written with so much fidelity, and in so impartial a spirit, that it must always remain one of the best authorities in reference to these singular events. Although in general very accurate, its testimony has in a few instances been set aside in favor of the more direct evidence of eye-witnesses. It was published by Hazard in the twelfth volume of his Pennsylvania Register. I have, however, examined the original, which is still preserved by a family in Philadelphia. The extracts here given form but a small part of the entire letter.

Before I proceed further it may not be amiss to inform thee that a great number of the inhabitants here approved of killing the Indians, and declared that they would not offer to oppose the Paxtoneers, unless they attacked the citizens, that is to say, themselves — for, if any judgment was to be formed from countenances and behavior, those who depended upon them for defence and protection, would have found their confidence shockingly misplaced.

The number of persons in arms that morning was about six hundred, and as it was expected the insurgents would attempt to cross at the middle or upper ferry, orders were sent to bring the boats to this side, and to take away the ropes. Couriers were now seen continually coming in, their horses all of a foam, and people running with the greatest eagerness to ask them where the enemy were, and what were their numbers. The answers to these questions were various: sometimes they were at a distance, then near at hand — sometimes they were a thousand strong, then five hundred, then fifteen hundred; in short, all was doubt and uncertainty.

About eleven o'clock it was recollected the boat at the Sweed's ford was not secured, which, in the present case, was of the utmost consequence, for, as there was a considerable freshet in the Schuylkill, the securing that boat would oblige them to march some distance up the river, and thereby retard the execution of their scheme at least a day or two longer. Several persons therefore set off immediately to get it performed; but they had not been gone long, before there was a general uproar — They are coming! they are coming! Where? where? Down Second street! down Second street! Such of the company as had grounded their firelocks, flew to arms, and began to prime; the artillery-men threw themselves into order, and the people ran to get out of the way, for a troop of armed men, on horseback, appeared in reality coming down the street and one of the artillery-men was just going to apply the fatal match, when a person, perceiving the mistake, clapped his hat upon the touch-hole of the piece he was going to fire. Dreadful would have been the consequence, had the cannon discharged; for the men that appeared proved to be a company of German butchers and porters, under the command of Captain Hoffman. They had just collected themselves, and being unsuspicious of danger, had neglected to give notice of their coming; — a false alarm was now called out, and all became quiet again in a few minutes. . . .

The weather being now very wet, Capt. Francis, Capt. Wood, and Capt. Mifflin, drew up their men under the market-house, which, not affording shelter for any more, they occupied Friends' meeting-house, and Capt. Joseph Wharton marched his company up stairs, into the monthly meeting room, as I have been told — the rest were stationed below. It happened to be the day appointed for holding of Youths' meeting, but never did the Quaker youth assemble in such a military manner — never was the sound of the drum heard before within those walls, nor ever till now was the Banner of War displayed in that rostrum, from whence the art has been so zealously declaimed against. Strange reverse of times, James —. Nothing of any consequence passed during the remainder of the day, except that Captain Coultas came into town at the head of a troop, which he had just raised in his own neighborhood. The Captain was one of those who had been marked out as victims by these devout conquerors, and word was sent to him from Lancaster to make his peace with Heaven, for that he had but about ten days to live.

In the evening our Negotiators came in from Germantown. They had conferred with the Chiefs of this illustrious —, and have prevailed with them to suspend all hostility till such time as they should receive an answer to their petition or manifesto, which had been sent down the day before. . . .

The weather now clearing, the City forces drew up near the Court House where a speech was made to them, informing them that matters had been misrepresented, — that the Paxtoneers were a set of very worthy men (or something to that purpose) who labored under great distress, — that Messrs Smith, &c., were come (by their own authority) as representatives, from several counties, to lay their complaints before the Legislature, and that the reason for their arming themselves was for fear of being molested or abused. By whom? Why, by the peaceable citizens of Philadelphia! Ha! ha! ha! Who can help laughing? The harangue concluded with thanks for the trouble and expense they had been at (about nothing), and each retired to their several homes. The next day, when all was quiet, and nobody dreamed of any further disturbance, we were alarmed again. The report now was, that the Paxtoneers had broke the Treaty, and were just entering the city. It is incredible to think with what alacrity the people flew to arms; in one quarter of an hour near a thousand of them were assembled, with a determination to bring the affair to a conclusion immediately, and not to suffer themselves to be harassed as they had been several days past. If the whole body of the enemy had come in, as was expected, the engagement would have been a bloody one, for the citizens were exasperated almost to madness; but happily those that appeared did not exceed thirty, (the rest having gone homewards), and as they behaved with decency, they were suffered to pass without opposition. Thus the storm blew over, and the Inhabitants dispersed themselves. . . .

The Pennsylvania Gazette, usually a faithful chronicler of the events of the day, preserves a discreet silence on the subject of the Paxton riots, and contains no other notice of them than the following condensed statement: —

On Saturday last, the City was alarmed with the News of Great Numbers of armed Men, from the Frontiers, being on the several Roads, and moving towards Philadelphia. As their designs were unknown, and there were various Reports concerning them, it was thought prudent to put the City in some Posture of Defence against any Outrages that might possibly be intended. The Inhabitants being accordingly called upon by the Governor, great numbers of them entered into an Association, and took Arms for the Support of Government, and Maintenance of good Order.

Six Companies of Foot, one of Artillery, and two Troops of Horse, were formed, and paraded, to which, it is said, some Thousands, who did not appear, were prepared to join themselves, in case any attempt should be made against the Town. The Barracks also, where the Indians are lodged, under Protection of the regular Troops, were put into a good Posture of Defence; several Works being thrown up about them, and eight Pieces of Cannon planted there.

The Insurgents, it seems, intended to rendezvous at Germantown; but the Precautions taken at the several Ferries over Schuylkill impeded their Junction; and those who assembled there, being made acquainted with the Force raised to oppose them, listened to the reasonable Discourses and Advice of some prudent Persons, who voluntarily went out to meet and admonish them; and of some Gentlemen sent by the Governor, to know the Reasons of their Insurrection; and promised to return peaceably to their Habitations, leaving only two of their Number to present a Petition to the Governor and Assembly; on which the Companies raised in Town were thanked by the Governor on Tuesday Evening, and dismissed, and the City restored to its former Quiet.

But on Wednesday Morning there was a fresh Alarm, occasioned by a false Report, that Four Hundred of the same People were on their March to Attack the Town. Immediately, on Beat of Drum, a much greater number of the Inhabitants, with the utmost Alacrity, put themselves under Arms; but as the Truth was soon known, they were again thanked by the Governor, and dismissed; the Country People being really dispersed, and gone home according to their Promise.—*Pennsylvania Gazette, No.* 1833.

The following extract from a letter of Rev. John Ewing to Joseph Reed affords a striking example of the excitement among the Presbyterians (See Life and Correspondence of Joseph Reed, I. 34.)

Feb. —, 1764

As to public affairs, our Province is greatly involved in intestine feuds, at a time, when we should rather unite, one and all, to manage the affairs of our several Governments, with prudence and discretion. A few designing men, having engrossed too much power into their hands, are pushing matters beyond all bounds. There are twenty-two Quakers in our Assembly, at present, who, although they won't absolutely refuse to grant money for the King's use, yet never fail to contrive matters in such a manner as to afford little or no assistance to the poor, distressed Frontiers; while our public money is lavishly squandered away in supporting a number of savages, who have been murdering and scalping us for many years past. This has so enraged some desperate young men, who had lost their nearest relations, by these very Indians, to cut off about twenty Indians that lived near Lancaster, who had, during the war, carried on a constant intercourse with our other enemies; and they came down to Germantown to inquire why Indians, known to be enemies, were supported, even in luxury, with the best that our markets afforded, at the public expense, while they were left in the utmost distress on the Frontiers, in want of the necessaries of life. Ample promises were made to them that their grievances should be redressed, upon which they immediately dispersed and went home. These persons have been unjustly represented as endeavoring to overturn Government, when nothing was more distant from their minds. However this matter may be looked upon in Britain, where you know very little of the matter, you may be assured that ninety-nine in an hundred of the Province are firmly persuaded, that they are maintaining our enemies, while our friends back are suffering the greatest extremities, neglected; and that few, but Quakers, think that the Lancaster Indians have suffered any thing but their just deserts. 'Tis not a little surprising to us here, that orders should be sent from the Crown, to apprehend and bring to justice those persons who have cut off that nest of enemies that lived near Lancaster. They never were subjects to his Majesty; were a free, independent state, retaining all the powers of a free state; sat in all our Treaties with the Indians, as one of the tribes belonging to the Six Nations, in alliance with us; they entertained the French and Indian spies — gave intelligence to them of the defenceless state of our Province — furnished them with Gazette every week, or fortnight — gave them intelligence of all the dispositions of the Province army against them — were frequently with the French and Indians at their forts and towns - supplied them with warlike stores — joined with the strange Indians in their war-dances, and in the parties that made incursions on our Frontiers — were ready to take up the hatchet against the English openly, when the French requested it — actually murdered and scalped some of the Frontier inhabitants — insolently boasted of the murders they had committed, when they saw our blood was cooled, after the last Treaty at Lancaster — confessed that they had been at war with us, and would soon be at war with us again (which accordingly happened), and even went so far as to put one of their own warriors, Jegarie, to death, because he refused to go to war with them against the English. All these things were known through the Frontier inhabitants, and are since proved upon oath. This occasioned them to be cut off by about forty or fifty persons, collected from all the Frontier counties, though they are called by the name of the little Township of Paxton, where, possibly, the smallest part of them resided. And what surprises us more than all the accounts we have from England, is, that our Assembly, in a petition they have drawn up, to the King, for a change of Government, should represent this Province in a state of uproar and riot, and when not a man in it has once resisted a single officer of the Government, nor a single act of violence committed, unles you call the Lancaster affair such, although it was no more than going to war with that tribe, as they had done before with others, without a formal proclamation of war by the Government. I have not time, as you may guess by this scrawl, to write more at this time, but only that I am yours, &c.

JOHN EWING.

3. MEMORIALS OF THE PAXTON MEN. (Chap. XXV.)

5. To the Honorable John Penn, Esq., Governor of the Province of Pennsylvania, and of the Counties of New-Castle, Kent, and Sussex, upon Delaware; and to the Representatives of the Freemen of the said Province, in General Assembly met.

We, Matthew Smith and James Gibson, in Behalf of ourselves and his Majesty's faithful and loyal Subjects, the Inhabitants of the Frontier Counties of Lancaster, York, Cumberland, Berks, and Northampton, humbly beg Leave to remonstrate and lay before you the following Grievances, which we submit to your Wisdom for Redress

First. We apprehend that, as Freemen and English Subjects, we have an indisputable Title to the same Privileges and Immunities with his Majesty's other Subjects, who reside in the interior Counties of Philadelphia, Chester, and Bucks and therefore ought not to be excluded from an equal Share with them in the very important Privilege of Legislation; — nevertheless, contrary to the Proprietor's Charter, and the acknowledged Principles of common Justice and Equity, our five Counties are restrained from electing more than ten Representatives, *viz.*, four for Lancaster, two for York, two for Cumberland, one for Berks, and one for Northampton, while the three Counties and City of Philadelphia, Chester, and Bucks elect Twenty-six. This we humbly conceive is oppressive, unequal and unjust, the Cause of many of our Grievances, and an Infringement of our natural Privileges of Freedom and Equality; wherefore we humbly pray that we may be no longer deprived of an equal Number with the three aforesaid Counties to represent us in Assembly.

Secondly. We understand that a Bill is now before the House of Assembly, wherein it is provided, that such Persons as shall be charged with killing any Indians in Lancaster County, shall not be tried in the County where the Fact was committed, but in the Counties of Philadelphia, Chester, or Bucks. This is manifestly to deprive British Subjects of their known Privileges, to cast an eternal Reproach upon whole Counties, as if they were unfit to serve their Country in the Quality of Jury-men, and to contradict the well known Laws of the British Nation, in a Point whereon Life, Liberty, and Security essentially depend; namely, that of being tried by their Equals, in the Neighbourhood where their own, their Accusers, and the Witnesses Character and Credit, with the Circumstances of the Fact, are best known, and instead thereof putting their Lives in the Hands of Strangers, who may as justly be suspected of Partiality to, as the Frontier Counties can be of Prejudices against, Indians; and this too, in favour of Indians only, against his Majesty's faithful and loyal Subjects: Besides, it is well known, that the Design of it is to comprehend a Fact committed before such a Law was thought of. And if such Practices were tolerated, no Man could be secure in his most invaluable Interest. — We are also informed, to our great Surprise, that this Bill has actually received the Assent of a Majority of the House; which we are persuaded could not have been the Case, had our Frontier Counties been equally represented in Assembly. — However, we hope that the Legislature of this Province will never enact a Law of so dangerous a Tendency, or take away from his Majesty's good Subjects a Privilege so long esteemed sacred by Englishmen.

Thirdly. During the late and present Indian War, the Frontiers of this Province have been repeatedly attacked and ravaged by skulking Parties of the Indians, who have, with the most Savage Cruelty, murdered Men, Women, and Children, without Distinction, and have reduced near a Thousand Families to the most extreme Distress.—It grieves us to the very Heart to see such of our Frontier Inhabitants as have escaped Savage Fury, with the Loss of their Parents, their Children, their Wives or Relatives, left Destitute by the Public, and exposed to the most cruel Poverty and Wretchedness, while upwards of an Hundred and Twenty of these Savages, who are, with great Reason, suspected of being guilty of these horrid Barbarities, under the Mask of Friendship, have procured themselves to be taken under the Protection of the Government, with a View to elude the Fury of the brave Relatives of the Murdered, and are now maintained at the public Expense. — Some of these Indians, now in the Barracks of Philadelphia, are confessedly a Part of the Wyalusing Indians, which Tribe is now at War with us; and the others are the Moravian Indians, who, living with us, under the Cloak of Friendship, carried on a Correspondence with our known Enemies on the Great Island. — We cannot but observe, with Sorrow and Indignation, that some Persons in this Province are at Pains to extenuate the barbarous Cruelties practised by these Savages on our murdered Brethren and Relatives, which are shocking to human Nature, and must pierce every Heart, but that of the hardened Perpetrators or their Abettors. Nor is it less distressing to hear Others pleading, that although the Wyalusing Tribe is at War with us, yet that Part of it which is under the Protection of the Government, may be friendly to the English, and innocent: — In what Nation under the Sun was it ever the Custom, that when a neighbouring Nation took up Arms, not an Individual should be touched, but only the Persons that offered Hostilities? — Who ever proclaimed War with a Part of a Nation and not with the whole? — Had these Indians disapproved of the Perfidy of their Tribe, and been willing to cultivate and preserve Friendship with us, why did they not give Notice of the War before it happened, as it is known to be the Result of long Deliberations, and a preconcerted Combination among them? — Why did they not leave their Tribe immediately, and come among us, before there was Ground to suspect them, or War was actually waged with their Tribe? — No, they stayed amongst them, were privy to their Murders and Ravages, until we had destroyed their Provisions, and when they could no longer subsist at Home, they come not as Deserters, but as Friends, to be maintained through the Winter, that they may be able to scalp and butcher us in the Spring.

And as to the Moravian Indians, there are strong Grounds at least to suspect their Friendship, as it is known that they carried on a Correspondence with our Enemies on the Great Island. — We killed three Indians going from Bethlehem to the Great Island with Blankets, Ammunition, and Provisions, which is an undeniable Proof that the Moravian Indians were in Confederacy with our open Enemies. And we cannot but be filled with Indignation to hear this Action of ours painted in the most odious and detestable Colours, as if we had inhumanly murdered our Guides, who preserved us from perishing in the Woods; when we only killed three of our known Enemies, who attempted to shoot us when we surprised them. — And, besides all this, we understand that one of these very Indians is proved, by the Oath of Stinton's Widow, to be the very Person that murdered her Husband. — How then comes it to pass, that he alone, of all the Moravian Indians, should join the Enemy to murder that family? — Or can it be supposed that any Enemy Indians, contrary to their known Custom of making War, should penetrate into the Heart of a settled Country, to burn, plunder, and murder the Inhabitants, and not molest any Houses in their Return, or ever be seen or heard of? — Or how can we account for it, that no Ravages have been committed in Northampton County since the Removal of the Moravian Indians, when the Great Cove has been struck since? — These Things put it beyond Doubt with us that the Indians now at Philadelphia are his Majesty's perfidious Enemies, and therefore, to protect and maintain them at the public Expence, while our suffering Brethren on the Frontiers are almost destitute of the Necessaries of Life, and are neglected by the Public, is sufficient to make us mad with Rage, and tempt us to do what nothing but the most violent Necessity can vindicate. — We humbly and earnestly pray therefore, that those Enemies of his Majesty may be removed as soon as possible out of the Province.

Fourthly. We humbly conceive that it is contrary to the Maxims of good Policy and extremely dangerous to our Frontiers, to suffer any Indians, of what Tribe soever, to live within the inhabited Parts of this Province, while we are engaged in an Indian War, as Experience has taught us that they are all perfidious, and their Claim to Freedom and Independency, puts it in their Power to act as Spies, to entertain and give Intelligence to our Enemies, and to furnish them with Provisions and warlike Stores. — To this fatal Intercourse between our pretended Friends and open Enemies, we must ascribe the greatest Part of the Ravages and Murders that have been committed in the Course of this and the last Indian War. — We therefore pray that this Grievance be taken under Consideration, and remedied.

Fifthly. We cannot help lamenting that no Provision has been hitherto made, that such of our Frontier Inhabitants as have been wounded in Defence of the Province, their Lives and Liberties may be taken Care of, and cured of their Wounds, at the public Expence. We therefore pray that this Grievance may be redressed.

Sixthly. In the late Indian War this Province, with others of his Majesty's Colonies, gave Rewards for Indian Scalps, to encourage the seeking them in their own Country, as the most likely Means of destroying or reducing them to Reason; but no such Encouragement has been given in this War, which has damped the Spirits of many brave Men, who are willing to venture their Lives in Parties against the Enemy. — We therefore pray that public Rewards may be proposed for Indian Scalps, which may be adequate to the Dangers attending Enterprises of this Nature.

Seventhly. We daily lament that Numbers of our nearest and dearest Relatives are still in Captivity among the savage Heathen, to be trained up in all their Ignorance and Barbarity, or to be tortured to Death with all the Contrivances of Indian Cruelty, for attempting to make their Escape from Bondage. We see they pay no Regard to the many solemn Promises which they have made to restore our Friends who are in Bondage amongst them. — We therefore earnestly pray that no Trade may hereafter be permitted to be carried on with them until our Brethren and Relatives are brought Home to us.

Eighthly. We complain that a certain Society of People in this Province in the late Indian War, and at several Treaties held by the King's Representatives, openly loaded the Indians with Presents; and that F. P., a Leader of the said Society, in Defiance of all Government, not only abetted our Indian Enemies, but kept up a private Intelligence with them, and publickly received from them a Belt of Wampum, as if he had been our Governor, or authorized by the King to treat with his Enemies. — By this means the Indians have been taught to despise us as a weak and disunited People, and from this fatal Source have arose many of our Calamities under which we groan. — We humbly pray, therefore, that this Grievance may be redressed, and that no private Subject be hereafter permitted to treat with, or carry on a Correspondence with our Enemies.

Ninthly. We cannot but observe with Sorrow, that Fort Augusta, which has been very expensive to this Province, has afforded us but little Assistance during this or the last War. The Men that were stationed at that Place neither helped our distressed Inhabitants to save their Crops, nor did they attack our Enemies in their Towns, or patrol on our Frontiers. — We humbly request that proper Measures may be taken to make that Garrison more serviceable to us in our Distress, if it can be done.

N. B. We are far from intending any Reflection against the Commanding Officer stationed at Augusta, as we presume his Conduct was always directed by those from whom he received his Orders.

Signed on Behalf of ourselves, and by Appointment of a great Num ber of the Frontier Inhabitants,

MATTHEW SMITH
JAMES GIBSON.

THE DECLARATION of the injured Frontier Inhabitants, together with a brief Sketch of Grievances the good Inhabitants of the Province labor under.

Inasmuch as the Killing those Indians at Conestogoe Manor and Lancaster has been, and may be, the Subject of much Conversation, and by invidious Representations of it, which some, we doubt not, will industri ously spread, many, unacquainted with the true State of Affairs, may be led to pass a severe Censure on the Authors of those Facts, and any others of the like Nature which may hereafter happen, than we are persuaded they would, if Matters were duly understood and deliberated; we think it therefore proper thus openly to declare ourselves, and render some brief Hints of the Reasons of our Conduct, which we must, and frankly do, confess nothing but Necessity itself could induce us to, or justify us in, as it bears an Appearance of flying in the Face of Authority, and is attended with much Labour, Fatigue and Expence.

Ourselves then, to a Man, we profess to be loyal Subjects to the best of Kings, our rightful Sovereign George the Third, firmly attached to his Royal Person, Interest and Government, and of Consequence equally opposite to the Enemies of his Throne and Dignity, whether openly avowed, or more dangerously concealed under a Mask of falsely pretended Friendship, and chearfully willing to offer our Substance and Lives in his Cause.

These Indians, known to be firmly connected in Friendship with our openly avowed embittered Enemies, and some of whom have, by several Oaths, been proved to be Murderers, and who, by their better Acquaintance with the Situation and State of our Frontier, were more capable of doing us Mischief, we saw, with Indignation, cherished and caressed as dearest Friends; — But this, alas! is but a Part, a small Part, of that excessive Regard manifested to Indians, beyond his Majesty's loyal Subjects, whereof we complain, and which, together with various other Grievances, have not only inflamed with Resentment the Breasts of a Number, and urged them to the disagreeable Evidence of it, they have been constrained to give, but have heavily displeased, by far, the greatest Part of the good Inhabitants of this Province.

Should we here reflect to former Treaties, the exorbitant Presents, and great Servility therein paid to Indians, have long been oppressive Grievances we have groaned under; and when at the last Indian Treaty held at Lancaster, not only was the Blood of our many murdered Brethren tamely covered, but our poor unhappy captivated Friends abandoned to Slavery among the Savages, by concluding a Friendship with the Indians, and allowing them a plenteous trade of all kinds of Commodities, without those being restored, or any properly spirited Requisition made of them: — How general Dissatisfaction those Measures gave, the Murmurs of all good people (loud as they dare to utter them) to this Day declare. And had here infatuated Steps of Conduct, and a manifest Partiality in Favour of Indians, made a final Pause, happy had it been: — We perhaps had grieved in Silence for our abandoned enslaved Brethren among the Heathen, but Matters of a later Date are still more flagrant Reasons of Complaint. — When last Summer his Majesty's Forces, under the Command of Colonel Bouquet, marched through this Province, and a Demand was made by his Excellency, General Amherst, of Assistance, to escort Provisions, &c., to relieve that important Post, Fort Pitt, yet not one Man was granted, although never any Thing appeared more reasonable or necessary, as the Interest of the Province lay so much at Stake, and the Standing of the Frontier Settlements, in any Manner, evidently depended, under God, on the almost despaired of Success of his Majesty's little Army, whose Valour the whole Frontiers with Gratitude acknowledge, as the happy Means of having saved from Ruin great Part of the Province: — But when a Number of Indians, falsely pretended Friends and having among them some proved on Oath to have been guilty of

Murder, since this War begun; when they, together with others, known to be his Majesty's Enemies, and who had been in the Battle against Colonel Bouquet, reduced to Distress by the Destruction of their Corn at the Great Island, and up the East Branch of Susquehanna, pretend themselves Friends, and desire a Subsistence, they are openly caressed, and the Public, that could not be indulged the Liberty of contributing to his Majesty's Assistance, obliged, as Tributaries to Savages, to Support these Villains, these Enemies to our King and our Country; nor only so, but the Hands that were closely shut, nor would grant his Majesty's General a single Farthing against a savage Foe, have been liberally opened, and the public Money basely prostituted, to hire, at an exorbitant Rate, a mercenary Guard to protect his Majesty's worst of Enemies, those falsely pretended Indian Friends, while, at the same Time, Hundreds of poor, distressed Families of his Majesty's Subjects, obliged to abandon their Possessions, and fly for their Lives at least, are left, except a small Relief at first, in the most distressing Circumstances to starve neglected, save what the friendly Hand of private Donations has contributed to their Support, wherein they who are most profuse towards Savages have carefully avoided having any Part. — When last Summer the Troops raised for Defence of the Province were limited to certain Bounds, nor suffered to attempt annoying our Enemies in their Habitations, and a Number of brave Volunteers, equipped at their own Expence, marched in September up the Susquehanna, met and defeated their Enemy, with the Loss of some of their Number, and having others dangerously wounded, not the least Thanks or Acknowledgmont was made them from the Legislature for the confessed Service they had done, nor any the least Notice or Care taken of their Wounded; whereas, when a Seneca Indian, who, by the Information of many, as well as by his own Confession, had been, through the last War, our inveterate Enemy, had got a Cut in his Head last Summer in a Quarrel he had with his own Cousin, and it was reported in Philadelphia that his Wound was dangerous, a Doctor was immediately employed, and sent to Fort Augusta to take Care of him, and cure him, if possible. — To these may be added, that though it was impossible to obtain through the Summer, or even yet, any Premium for Indian Scalps, or Encouragement to excite Volunteers to go forth against them, yet when a few of them, known to be the Fast Friends of our Enemies, and some of them Murderers themselves, when these have been struck by a distressed, bereft, injured Frontier, a liberal Reward is offered for apprehending the Perpetrators of that horrible Crime of killing his Majesty's cloaked Enemies, and their Conduct painted in the most atrocious Colors; while the horrid Ravages, cruel Murders, and most shocking Barbarities, committed by Indians on his Majesty's Subjects, are covered over, and excused, under the charitable Term of this being their Method of making War.

But to recount the many repeated Grievances whereof we might justly complain, and Instances of a most violent Attachment to Indians, were tedious beyond the Patience of a Job to endure; nor can better be expected;

nor need we be surprised at Indians Insolence and Villainy, when it is considered, and which can be proved from the public Records of a certain County, that some Time before Conrad Weiser died, some Indians belonging to the Great Island or Wyalousing, assured him that Israel Pemberton, (an ancient Leader of that Faction which, for so long a Time, have found Means to enslave the Province to Indians,) together with others of the Friends, had given them a Rod to scourge the white People that were settled on the purchased Lands; for that Onas had cheated them out of a great Deal of Land, or had not given near sufficient Price for what he had bought; and that the Traders ought also to be scourged, for that they defrauded the Indians, by selling Goods to them at too dear a Rate; and that this Relation is Matter of Fact, can easily be proved in the County of Berks. — Such is our unhappy Situation, under the Villainy, Infatuation and Influence of a certain Faction, that have got the political Reins in their Hands, and tamely tyrannize over the other good Subjects of the Province! — And can it be thought strange, that a Scene of such Treatment as this, and the now adding, in this critical Juncture, to all our former Distresses, that disagreeable Burden of supporting, in the very Heart of the Province, at so great an Expence, between One and Two hundred Indians, to the great Disquietude of the Majority of the good Inhabitants of this Province, should awaken the Resentment of a People grossly abused, unrighteously burdened, and made Dupes and Slaves to Indians? — And must not all well-disposed People entertain a charitable Sentiment of those who, at their own great Expence and Trouble, have attempted, or shall attempt, rescuing a laboring Land from a Weight so oppressive, unreasonable, and unjust? — It is this we design, it is this we are resolved to prosecute, though it is with great Reluctance we are obliged to adopt a Measure not so agreeable as could be desired, and to which Extremity alone compels. — God save the King.

APPENDIX F.

CAMPAIGN OF 1764.

1. Bouquet's Expedition.

Letter — General Gage to Lord Halifax, December 13. 1764. (Chap XXVII.)

The Perfidy of the Shawanese and Delawares, and their having broken the ties, which even the Savage Nations hold sacred amongst each other, required vigorous measures to reduce them. We had experienced their treachery so often, that I determined to make no peace with them, but in the Heart of their Country, and upon such terms as should make it as secure as it was possible. This conduct has produced all the good effects which could be wished or expected from it. Those Indians have been humbled and reduced to accept of Peace upon the terms prescribed to them, in such a manner as will give reputation to His Majesty's Arms amongst the several Nations. The Regular and Provincial Troops under Colonel Bouquet, having been joined by a good body of Volunteers from Virginia, and others from Maryland and Pennsylvania, marched from Fort Pitt the Beginning of October, and got to Tuscaroras about the fifteenth. The March of the Troops into their Country threw the Savages into the greatest Consternation, as they had hoped their Woods would protect them, and had boasted of the Security of their Situation from our Attacks. The Indians hovered round the Troops during their March, but despairing of success in an Action, had recourse to Negotiations. They were told that they might have Peace, but every Prisoner in their possession must first be delivered up. They brought in near twenty, and promised to deliver the Rest; but as their promises were not regarded, they engaged to deliver the whole on the 1st of November, at the Forks of the Muskingham, about one hundred and fifty miles from Fort Pitt, the Centre of the Delaware Towns, and near to the most considerable settlement of the Shawanese. Colonel Bouquet kept them in sight, and moved his Camp to that Place. He soon obliged the Delawares and some broken tribes of Mohikons, Wiandots, and Mingoes, to bring in all their Prisoners, even to the Children born of White Women, and to tie those who were grown as Savage as themselves and unwilling to leave them, and bring them bound to the Camp. They were then told that they must appoint deputies to go to Sir William Johnson to receive such terms as should be imposed upon them, which the Nations should agree to ratify; and, for the security of their performance of this, and that no farther Hostilities should be committed, a number of their Chiefs must remain in our hands. The above Nations subscribed to these terms; but the Shawanese were more obstinate, and were particularly averse to the giving of Hostages. But finding their obstinacy had no effect, and would only tend to their destruction, the Troops having penetrated into the Heart of their Country, they at length became sensible that there was no safety but in Submission, and were obliged to stoop to the same Conditions as the other nations. They immediately gave up forty Prisoners, and promised the Rest should be sent to Fort Pitt in the Spring. This last not being admitted, the immediate Restitution of all the Prisoners being the *sine qua non* of peace, it was agreed, that parties should be sent from the Army into their towns, to collect the Prisoners, and conduct them to Fort Pitt. They delivered six of their principal Chiefs as hostages into our Hands, and appointed their deputies to go to Sir William Johnson, in the same manner as the Rest. The Number of Prisoners already delivered exceeds two hundred, and it was expected that our Parties would bring in near one hundred more from the Shawanese Towns. These Conditions seem sufficient Proofs of the Sincerity and Humiliation of those Nations, and in justice to Colonel Bouquet, I must testify the Obligations I have to him, and that nothing but the firm and steady conduct, which he observed in all his Transactions with those treacherous savages, would ever have brought them to a serious Peace.

I must flatter myself, that the Country is restored to its former Tranquillity, and that a general, and, it is hoped, lasting Peace is concluded with all the Indian Nations who have taken up Arms against his Majesty.

I remain,

etc.,

THOMAS GAGE.

IN ASSEMBLY, January 15, 1765, A. M.

To the Honourable Henry Bouquet, Esq., Commander in Chief of His Majesty's Forces in the Southern Department of America.

The Address of the Representatives of the Freemen of the Province of Pennsylvania, in General Assembly met

SIR:

The Representatives of the Freemen of the Province of Pennsylvania, in General Assembly met, being informed that you intend shortly to embark for England, and moved with a due Sense of the important Services you have rendered to his Majesty, his Northern Colonies in general, and to this Province in particular, during our late Wars with the French, and barbarous Indians, in the remarkable Victory over the savage Enemy, united to oppose you, near Bushy Run, in August, 1763, when on your March for the Relief of Pittsburg, owing, under God, to your Intrepidity and superior Skill in Command, together with the Bravery of your Officers and little Army; as also in your late March to the Country of the savage Nations, with the Troops under your Direction; thereby striking Terror through the numerous Indian Tribes around you; laying a Foundation for a lasting as well as honorable Peace, and rescuing, from savage Captivity, upwards of Two Hundred of our Christian Brethren, Prisoners among them. These eminent Services, and your constant Attention to the Civil Rights of his Majesty's Subjects in this Province, demand, Sir, the grateful Tribute of Thanks from all good Men; and therefore we, the Representatives of the Freemen of Pennsylvania, unanimously for ourselves, and in Behalf of all the People of this Province, do return you our most sincere and hearty Thanks for these your great Services, wishing you a safe and pleasant Voyage to England, with a kind and gracious Reception from his Majesty.

Signed, by Order of the House,

JOSEPH FOX, Speaker

---

2. CONDITION AND TEMPER OF THE WESTERN INDIANS.

Extract from a letter of Sir William Johnson to the Board of Trade, 1764, December 26: —

Your Lordships will please to observe that for many months before the march of Colonel Bradstreet's army, several of the Western Nations had expressed a desire for peace, and had ceased to commit hostilities, that even Pontiac inclined that way, but did not choose to venture his person by coming into any of the posts. This was the state of affairs when I treated with the Indians at Niagara, in which number were fifteen hundred of the Western Nations, a number infinitely more considerable than those who were twice treated with at Detroit, many of whom are the same people, particularly the Hurons and Chippewas. In the mean time it now appears, from the very best authorities, and can be proved by the oath of several respectable persons, prisoners at the Illinois and amongst the Indians, as also from the accounts of the Indians themselves, that not only many French traders, but also French officers came amongst the Indians, as they said, fully authorized to assure them that the French King was determined to support them to the utmost, and not only invited them to the Illinois, where they were plentifully supplied with ammunition and other necessaries, but also sent several canoes at different times up the Illinois river, to the Miamis, and others, as well as up the Ohio to the Shawanese and Delawares, as by Major Smallman's account, and several others, (then prisoners), transmitted me by Colonel Bouquet, and one of my officers who accompanied him, will appear. That in an especial manner the French promoted the interest of Pontiac, whose influence is now become so considerable, as General Gage observes in a late letter to me, that it extends even to the Mouth of the Mississippi, and has been the principal occasion of our not as yet gaining the Illinois, which the French as well as Indians are interested in preventing. This Pontiac is not included in the late Treaty at Detroit, and is at the head of a great number of Indians privately supported by the French, an officer of whom was about three months ago at the Miamis Castle, at the Scioto Plains, Muskingum, and several other places. The Western Indians, who it seems ridicule the whole expedition, will be influenced to such a pitch, by the interested French on the one side, and the influence of Pontiac on the other, that we have great reason to apprehend a renewal of hostilities, or at least that they and the Twightees (Miamis) will strenuously oppose our possessing the Illinois, which can never be accomplished without their consent. And indeed it is not to be wondered that they should be concerned at our occupying that country, when we consider that the French (be their motive what it will) loaded them with favors, and continue to do so, accompanied with all outward marks of esteem, and an address peculiarly adapted to their manners, which infallibly gains upon all Indians, who judge by extremes only, and with all their acquaintance with us upon the frontiers, have never found any thing like it, but on the contrary, harsh treatment, angry words, and in short any thing which can be thought of to inspire them with a dislike to our manners and a jealousy of our views. I have seen so much of these matters, and I am so well convinced of the utter aversion that our people have for them in general, and of the imprudence with which they constantly express it, that I absolutely despair of our seeing tranquillity established, until your Lordships' plan is fully settled, so as I may have proper persons to reside at the Posts, whose business it shall be to remove their prejudices, and whose interest it becomes to obtain their esteem and friendship.

The importance of speedily possessing the Illinois, and thereby securing a considerable branch of trade, as well as cutting off the channel by which our enemies have been and will always be supplied, is a matter I have very much at heart, and what I think may be effected this winter by land by Mr. Croghan, in case matters can be so far settled with the Twightees, Shawanoes, and Pontiac, as to engage the latter, with some chiefs of the before-mentioned nations, to accompany him with a garrison. The expense attending this will be large, but the end to be obtained is too considerable to be neglected. I have accordingly recommended it to the consideration of General Gage, and shall, on the arrival of the Shawanoes, Delawares, &c., here, do all in my power to pave the way for effecting it. I shall also make such a peace with them, as will be most for the credit and advantage of the crown, and the security of the trade and frontiers, and tie them down to such conditions as Indians will most probably observe.

NOTE.

Of the accompanying maps, the first two were constructed for the illustration of this work. The others are fac-similes from the surveys of the engineer Thomas Hutchins. The original of the larger of these fac-similes is prefixed to the *Account of Bouquet's Expedition.* That of the smaller will be found in Hutchins's *Topographical Description of Virginia,* etc. Both of these works are rare.

INDEX

INDEX.

D.

E.

F.

H.

I.

J.

K.

L.

M.

N.

O.

P.

Q.

R.

S.

T.

U.

V.

W.

University Press: John Wilson & Son, Cambridge.